Chocolate, Strawberry, and Vanilla

Chocolate, Strawberry, and Vanilla:

A History of American Ice Cream

Anne Cooper Funderburg

Bowling Green State University Popular Press
Bowling Green, OH 43403

Copyright © 1995 Bowling Green State University Press

Library of Congress Cataloging-in-Publication Data

Funderburg, Anne Cooper.
    Chocolate, strawberry, and vanilla : a history of American ice cream / Anne
Cooper Funderburg.
        p.   cm.
    Includes bibliographical references and index.
    ISBN 0-87972-691-1 (clothbound). -- ISBN 0-87972-692-X (pbk.)
    1. Ice cream, ices, etc.--United States--History. 2. Frozen desserts--United
States--History. I. Title.
    TX795.F86 1995
    641.3'74'0973--dc20   95-47434
                                                                                    CIP

Cover design by Laura Darnell-Dumm

WE SAT AT ONE OF THE TABLES and ice cream was brought. We could look out over a little pond while eating the ice cream and talking. Since then I have been to Monte Carlo, Nice, Bertolini's at Naples, Shepheard's at Cairo, and most of the other beauty spots where one sits and sips and looks out over the world; but the memory of none of them compares with the little ice-cream pavilion at Plainfield, New Jersey, where I used to go with my mother.

I suppose it was a very ordinary little place, with shabby tables, shabby awnings, shabby chairs, and a shabby little wooden building. I suppose the pond was a miserable little pond reeking with mosquitoes. But I saw it through the eyes of youth and inexperience, and it was transcendently beautiful.

The ice cream was the best in the world. Anyway, no ice cream in the world I have eaten since has compared with it. It had a flavor which no words could describe. . . .

—Hiram Percy Maxim, A Genius in the Family:
Sir Hiram Stevens Maxim through a Small Son's Eyes

Contents

Illustrations

Following page 84

1. Ice cream dreams

2. An early ice cream stand

3. Ice harvesting

4. Victorian ice cream parlor

5. Tufts fountain, 1876 Centennial Exhibition

6. Lightning hand-cranked freezer ad

7. White Mountain freezer trade card

8. White Mountain freezer trade card

9. Calendar art

10. Small town soda fountain

11. Movie stars' soda fountain

12. Crossroads, rural America

13. The Good Humor truck

14. Manufacturers' novelties

15. The "cream of the stars"

16. A 1934 ice cream plant

17. Dairy Queen stand

18. Soda fountain, Olmstead Falls, Ohio

19. Seattle's Igloo drive-in

20. Ben and Jerry's first shop

Acknowledgments

In researching the history of ice cream, I received assistance from many individuals and institutions. Numerous librarians patiently answered my questions and helped me locate sources. I was often amazed and cheered by the efforts they expended to help a stranger.

The list of libraries, museums, corporations, and historical societies that provided information is too long to publish here. Nevertheless, I am grateful for their aid and aware that they made this book possible. The staffs and resources of the libraries at the University of Delaware, Pennsylvania State University, and the Hagley Museum and Library were especially helpful.

In collecting photographs to illustrate this book, I again needed help from others. I owe a special debt of gratitude to Ed Marks and Wayne Smith of the Ice Screamers for their generous assistance. Michael Witzel was also kind enough to supply photographs and information about sources.

Most of all, I am grateful to Murry, Ellen, and Christopher. They indulged my strange obsession with ice cream and old books, even when they were inconvenienced by my work. They always supported and encouraged me.

Anne Cooper Funderburg
Lincoln University, Pennsylvania

Introduction

Traditionally, historians have focused on momentous subjects—wars, monarchs, presidents, revolutions, ideologies. Less historical attention has been given to the stuff of everyday living, such as foods and social customs. Not surprisingly, vast gaps exist in culinary and social history. Despite the acknowledged importance of such foods as hamburgers and ice cream in American society, few writers have approached the subject of cookery in a scholarly manner. Therefore, much of what has been published about American cuisine is more folklore than history. This book endeavors to separate fact from legend regarding one important food by providing a chronological, documented study of ice cream in the United States.

This study begins with ice cream in the American colonies, where frozen desserts were an aristocratic treat, just as they were in Europe. Wealthy families ate ice cream made by servants or purchased at pricey confectionaries. At lavish parties, the social and political elite feasted upon delicacies never seen in the average household. Then, with the advent of the pleasure gardens in American cities, the urban public was able to buy affordable, quality ice cream for the first time. Subsequent developments—including the growth of the ice industry and the invention of the hand-cranked freezer—accelerated the popularization of ice cream.

In the second half of the 19th century, the availability of ice cream expanded even further with the genesis of wholesale manufacturing. Nearly everyone ate ice cream during this period, but there was a noticeable gap between the classes. The urban poor bought cheap, often unsanitary ice cream from street vendors and consumed it on the spot. The more affluent classes ate fancy molded ice cream at home and frequented ornate ice cream parlors. During this era, ice cream became a staple at soda fountains due to the popularity of such new treats as ice cream sodas and sundaes. The temperance movement proved to be a blessing for both ice cream parlors and soda fountains because, as respectable society shunned strong drink, many men chose fountain treats as alternatives to intoxicating drink.

During the first half of the 20th century, technology began to play a more important role in the ice cream business. Industrial technology helped to make ice cream plants more efficient while automotive technology indirectly stimulated sales. With the advent of the car culture, roadside stands and chain restaurants enticed drivers to stop for an ice cream break. Ice cream cones and sandwiches proved to be enormously popular because they were both inexpensive and portable. Then Eskimo Pie and the Good Humor bar inspired a plethora of factory-packaged novelties that competed for the consumer's loose change. Meanwhile, grocery store sales escalated, even though the quality of supermarket brands declined as manufacturers vied to produce a cheap product for the mass market.

World Wars I and II demonstrated that, somewhere along the way, ice cream had become a potent American symbol. Wherever American soldiers were stationed, they longed for ice cream and savored it whenever it was available. After World War II, Dairy Queen, Carvel, and Tastee Freez prospered, selling a lowfat, soft product. Then Baskin-Robbins began to market a more traditional ice cream in an unprecedented variety of imaginative flavors. The chain's success proved that Americans still hungered for quality ice cream with high fat content and were willing to pay for it. The stage was set for the arrival of the superpremiums and the creation of a new market niche dominated by Häagen-Dazs and Ben and Jerry's.

In the following chapters, a number of trends and recurrent themes will become obvious to the reader, because the history of American ice cream reflects and reveals changes in social customs, diet and nutrition, class distinctions, leisure activities, gender stereotypes, and entrepreneurialism. In general, these themes remain an undercurrent because this is a straightforward, chronological account rather than an interpretation. Nevertheless, one theme emerges more strongly than all the others. Ice cream came to these shores from Europe, but it transcended its origins to become quintessentially American. As the new society evolved and defined itself, Americans rejected the idea of ice cream as an aristocratic treat and made it a democratic dish for all classes.

1

An Elite Treat:
The First Hundred Years

A Curious Rarity

Once upon a cold night, Martha Washington, for unknown reasons, placed a bowl of sweetened cream on her back doorstep. Surprisingly, no animal drank the cream, and it congealed as the temperature dropped. The next morning, the mistress of Mount Vernon tasted the frozen cream and loved the smooth, delicious custard. Ice cream had been invented![1]

This tale about Martha Washington has a certain charm to it, as do the stories attributing the discovery of ice cream to Thomas Jefferson or Dolley Madison. But none of them are true. Frozen desserts came to the New World from Europe, where the upper classes had long enjoyed icy desserts and iced drinks. However, Americans improved the texture and taste of ice cream, consumed it in quantities that amazed Europeans, and eventually made it as American as apple pie and Coca-Cola.

Although it is impossible to date the first spoonful of ice cream in America, the journal of William Black, written in 1744, is generally believed to contain the first description of an American meal where it was served. Black, a colonist from Scotland, was secretary to a commission appointed by the governor of Virginia to work with delegates from the Pennsylvania and Maryland colonies in negotiating with the Iroquois to buy lands west of the Allegheny Mountains.[2]

On Saturday, May 19, Black went with the Virginians to the home of Maryland's Governor Thomas Bladen in Annapolis, where they were lavishly entertained. Black describes the scene, as follows:

We were Received by his Excellency and his Lady in the Hall, where we were an hour Entertain'd by them, with some Glasses of Punch in the intervals of the Discourse; then the Scene was chang'd to a Dining Room, where you saw a plain proof of the Great Plenty of the Country, a Table in the most Splendent manner set out with Great Variety of Dishes, all serv'd up in the most Elegant way, after which came a Dessert no less Curious; Among the Rarities of which it was Compos'd, was some fine Ice Cream which, with the Strawberries and Milk, eat most Deliciously.[3]

Black called ice cream a rarity and so it must have been, even though there is scattered evidence that other dignitaries served ice cream—notably colonial Virginia's Governor Francis Fauquier and his successor, Baron de Botetourt. However, the average family was too busy surviving to indulge in a luxury that melted, consumed scarce ingredients, and required substantial preparation time. A household with several servants might make ice cream often, but the typical colonial housewife had more pressing chores.[4]

Before the hand-cranked freezer was invented, ice cream was made by the pot freezer method. This involved a number of steps, including removing ice from the icehouse and chipping it into small pieces, placing a container (such as a tin pot) inside a larger container (such as a wooden tub), packing the interstices with ice and salt, rotating the inner container by hand, and periodically using a long spoon or spatula to scrape the frozen particles off the inside wall of the tin pot. Scraping the frozen cream off the wall and mixing it evenly were very important because the finished product would contain icy lumps, like small hailstones, if it was not thoroughly blended.

Procuring the necessary ingredients for ice cream could be a problem. Until the ice-harvesting industry matured, a limited amount of the natural refrigerant was sold in cities. Many homeowners, in both rural and urban areas, conserved winter's bounty for summer use by storing it in a cellar or icehouse. Because removing ice from storage and breaking it into small pieces was a chore that required muscles, this task was often delegated to a man or strong boy. Some cooks made snow cream during the winter, but snow did not store well and efforts to preserve it for summer generally failed. In 1758, Fauquier, while serving as lieutenant governor, used ice from a hailstorm to freeze cream, but the occasional hailstorm was obviously not a reliable source of refrigerant.[5]

In early America, sugar was so expensive that housewives often kept it under lock and key. It could be purchased in several grades, from coarse to fine, with corresponding increases in the price. The coarsest sugar was the raw brown muscovado left after molasses was drained off in the first phase of sugar manufacture. Refineries produced single- and double-refined grades through several successive periods of boiling and evaporation. If a household could not afford refined sugar, the cook had to undertake a small-scale refining process at home—a tedious task outlined in early cookbooks.[6]

Refined sugar was sold in cones or loaves, which varied greatly in size but were always formidably hard. To cut off lumps of sugar, cooks wielded cleavers, hatchets, or mallets. Special sugar hammers, which looked somewhat like pickaxes, were available for the task, but any hammer would do. Sugar nippers, which resembled tongs, could also be used. To pulverize the lumps into granules, the cook utilized a rolling pin or a mortar and pestle.[7]

Although American society was largely agrarian, even cream was scarce at times. The destruction of cattle by British Red Dragoons under Lt. Gen. Banastre Tarleton caused a shortage of cream in Virginia immediately after the Revolutionary War, making ice cream a "prime luxury." Even Martha Washington found it difficult to obtain fresh cream while she and the President were residing in New York City, forcing her to serve an "unusually stale and rancid" trifle at one dinner party.[8]

For flavoring ice cream, city dwellers had the option of buying expensive spices or flavorings, but many housewives chose to make their own extracts or essences. Early cookbooks contained a variety of ice cream recipes using fresh fruit, which the cook had to pare and crush—adding to the preparation time.

Of course, not all ice cream was homemade in colonial America. In the larger cities, consumers had the option of buying it from a confectioner or caterer. One of the earliest advertisements for ice cream appeared in New York City in 1774 when Philip Lenzi, a confectioner who had recently immigrated from London, notified residents that he was selling jams, jellies, pastries, sugar plums, ice cream, and other luxuries. A subsequent ad for Lenzi enumerated a long list of expensive edibles, including "any sort of ice cream.'"[9]

In the New York *Gazette* on May 19, 1777, while the British army was occupying the city, Lenzi advertised that he had moved his shop from Dock Street to Hanover Square, where he would continue to sell sweetmeats, preserves, marmalade, jellies, fruits, and so forth "at very reasonable cost . . . for ready money only." Mindful of the British occupation, he promised that his dishes would "be executed to all perfection as in the first shops in London." Seemingly as an afterthought, he added, "May be had almost every day, ice cream."[10]

Lenzi's May 19 advertisement and variations appeared in the newspaper intermittently during the following months. In February 1778, he altered the wording, saying that he would provide customers with "ice cream of what sort they will please to order."[11]

Another early confectioner selling ice cream in New York City was J. Corree, whose shop was at 120 Hanover Square. In February 1779, he advertised in the New York *Gazette* that he would supply customers with pastries, cakes, sweetmeats, jellies, ice cream, and so forth. He also stated that he would deliver his products if orders were placed in advance.[12]

In 1781 Joseph Corre, a confectioner at 17 Hanover Square, advertised ice cream, sweetmeats, cakes, syrups, sugar candy, almonds, raisins, tamarinds, figs, and liqueurs. In this advertisement, ice cream was featured on a line by itself in large capital letters, making it stand out and implying that it was an important part of his business. (The similarity between "Corree" and "Corre" suggests that one of the two spellings may have been a misprint and that the confectioner had simply moved his shop from one location to another.)[13]

Other early confectioners advertising ice cream in New York City were Joseph Crowe in 1786 and A. Pryor in 1789. Pryor, who called himself "the federal confectioner," sold nuts, spices, candies, jellies, ice cream, and cakes. He promised "all kinds of desserts may be had at the shortest notice . . . and all sorts of cakes for tea may be had cheaper than at any place in the city."[14]

During the summer of 1794, New Yorkers could cool down by enjoying ice cream at confectionaries and tea gardens. Among New York confectioners at that time, Captain Collet had a reputation for making the best ices and sherbets. According to one of his compatriots, "It was the ladies, above all, who could not get enough of a pleasure so new to them as frozen food; nothing was more amusing than to watch the little grimaces they made while savoring it. It was especially difficult for them to understand how anything could stay so cold in the summer heat of 90 degrees."[15]

Emanuel Segur has been credited with teaching Philadelphians to make ice cream after the Revolutionary War,[15] and he may have been instrumental in popularizing the frozen dessert there. But it is unlikely that Philadelphia, a major port city with many European immigrants, lagged significantly behind Annapolis or New York in the introduction of ice cream.[16]

In July 1782, George Washington probably ate ice cream at a party in Philadelphia given by Monsieur de la Luzerne, the French minister, in honor of the birth of the Dauphin of France. An entry in Washington's ledger reveals that he bought "a cream machine for ice" two years later, while he was in Philadelphia, attending a meeting of the Society of Cincinnati. His Philadelphia household account book noted the purchase of an ice cream serving spoon in 1796. A room-by-room inventory at Mount Vernon, taken shortly after Washington's death, listed two pewter and eight tin ice cream pots among the kitchen equipment.[17]

Washington ate ice cream at a dinner given by Mrs. Alexander Hamilton, wife of the secretary of the treasury, in 1789. That same year, he attended a ball at the Count de Moustier's home, where the refreshment table was laden with apples, oranges, cakes, and ice creams.

While the federal government was temporarily headquartered in New York City, the Washingtons reportedly ordered more than $200 worth of ice cream from a local confectioner. They often served ice cream to their guests, which probably accounts for the large amount spent on it.[18]

The Washingtons borrowed the custom of the levee, a large afternoon assembly or reception, from the British court. At a typical Washington levee, the refreshments were simple: ice cream, cake, lemonade, tea, and coffee. Martha Washington's nephew described a reception at the President's home while the couple was residing in Philadelphia. "Refreshments were handed round by servants in livery; and about that period first appeared the luxury, not so universal, of ice cream," he recalled.[19]

Both the President and the First Lady held levees on a regular basis, but the chief executive's were much more formal than his wife's. The guest lists for Washington's levees were carefully screened, and, to discourage guests from shaking his hand, he always carried his hat in one hand while keeping his other hand on the hilt of his sword. The President addressed each guest briefly and then, one by one, each bowed and left the room. At his wife's receptions, Washington was considered to be a private citizen, permitting guests to approach him and converse in an informal manner.[20]

Senator William Maclay of Pennsylvania described a dinner party he attended at the Washingtons' home in August 1789. Among the guests were Vice President and Mrs. John Adams, Mr. and Mrs. John Jay, Governor and Mrs. George Clinton of New York, and the President's two secretaries. The menu included soup, roasted and boiled fish, meats, gammon (smoked ham), and fowl. For the dessert course, guests were offered apple pie, pudding, ice cream, jellies, watermelon, musk melon, apples, peaches, and nuts.

Maclay intimates that dinner with the Washingtons was dull, despite the impressive company. At the beginning of his description, he dutifully states, "It was a great dinner, and the best of the kind I was ever at." Later, he says, "It was the most solemn dinner ever I sat at." No toasts were made until dinner was finished and the cloth removed from the table. Then the President drank to the health of each individual at the table in a very formal manner, and the guests quickly reciprocated. After that, "there was a dead silence almost" even though "the bottles passed about."

Maclay was relieved when Mrs. Washington and the ladies withdrew, hoping that this would be the signal for lively conversation on affairs of state or another lofty subject. Instead, the President talked of mundane matters and tapped on the dinner table with his fork. When

Washington went upstairs for coffee, Maclay took his leave, seemingly grateful to escape.[21]

Maclay does not mention the flavor of the ice cream or how Mrs. Washington served it, but other sources reveal that hostesses often placed ice cream on the table in glaciers, iceries, or ice cellars (fancy china urns that held ice along with the dessert). For an individual serving, ice cream was spooned into a glass that had a handle, a two-handled china cup, or a saucer. (Due to the lack of refrigeration, ice cream tended to be slushy and some diners preferred to sip it.) The Washingtons' white-and-gold French china service, purchased during his presidency, included 2 iceries, 12 ice plates, and 36 ice pots (small, footed cups). For the dessert course, the ice plates and pots were placed at intervals along the table and filled from the icery. Molding ice cream into pyramids or towers was also fashionable at this time. The Washingtons' household account book reveals that they purchased an ice cream mold in 1795 but does not describe it.[22]

Always a Pleasure

In the late 1790s, the concept of the pleasure garden, which had been transported across the ocean from London to the American colonies before the Revolutionary War, came into full bloom. In New York City, the growing population craved entertainment and, in the summer, places to enjoy cold refreshments and escape the sweltering heat. Because ice cream was a staple of the pleasure gardens, they were immensely important in popularizing the frozen treat. The working class could not afford to buy ice cream from a fancy confectioner's shop, but a man did not have to be rich to escort a young lady to a pleasure garden.[23]

One of the first businessmen to see the potential for pleasure gardens was Joseph Corre, who was already in the confectionery business. He opened a large establishment, the Mount Vernon Garden, on the corner of Broadway and Leonard Street. Joseph Delacroix, another Frenchman, followed suit in 1798, launching the Vauxhall, named after the famous London garden.[24]

The two Frenchmen vied to offer the most popular entertainment, with something for every member of the family. Fireworks and music proved to be crowd-pleasers, as did balloon ascensions. Occasionally, an especially daring aeronaut parachuted from a balloon, to the astonishment of the spectators. At least one garden owner promoted ballooning as a cure for illness, advertising that "valetudinarians may experience a restoration of health."[25]

In 1800, Delacroix moved his garden away from the populated areas into a rural location where he could stage more grandiose fireworks displays. To compete, Corre offered the city's first summer stock theater in his garden. When fireworks lost their novelty, Delacroix built a large wooden shed for stage shows and advertised "no gentleman admitted unless accompanied by a lady." At a time when ladies never frequented taverns and were scarcely tolerated in the theater pit, Delacroix saw the potential for a place where the sexes could mingle. At Vauxhall, the booths were decorated "to represent mystic bowers . . . for the special accommodation of female visitors" while benches and chairs were scattered under the trees so male patrons could sip their brandy and smoke in the open air.[26]

Six years later, Delacroix opened an even grander Vauxhall with mazes of walkways, flowerbeds, rose arbors, trees, shrubs, fountains, and statuary. Musicians sat among the trees, playing for the guests as they enjoyed their ice cream and drinks. Since Vauxhall's refreshments were moderately priced and the rural location offered space for youngsters to play, it was crowded with women and children on holidays and warm afternoons. As the city grew, it became a favorite spot for holding large meetings and for orators seeking a ready-made audience.[27]

Pleasure gardens were a liberating influence for women, whose social life was largely confined to church and private homes. Ladies rarely ate in restaurants, which were a male domain where the air was usually thick with cigar smoke and men talked about business or other supposedly masculine topics. James Thompson, a confectioner, opened a shop on Broadway that he hoped would attract women who wanted some respite from shopping. Although his shop was situated in a very busy location and he gave it a feminine atmosphere by employing his sisters to run it, few women ventured inside because it was not considered ladylike to eat in public. Thompson eventually operated a very successful ice cream parlor, but it took years to change society's attitudes about women eating in restaurants. The pleasure gardens were instrumental in this change because they created a wholesome atmosphere that welcomed the entire family.[28]

In addition, pleasure gardens proved to be a democratizing influence because they were cheap entertainment for the masses yet genteel enough to appeal to more refined tastes. In a letter to a friend, Eliza Bowne, a proper young lady from New England visiting New York, wrote that she and her hosts frequented a garden at the Battery, where they would "sit half an hour, eat ice cream, drink lemonade, hear fine music, see a variety of people, and return home happy and refreshed." Mingling with the hoi polloi on a more or less equal footing was an unusual occurrence for sheltered young women like Bowne.[29]

Niblo's Suburban Pleasure Ground was a complex started by William Niblo, a well-known caterer. One corner of Niblo's property was occupied by a traditional saloon catering to older men, who "spun their yarns into the wee sma' hours, washing them down with frequent copious libations, in memory of their struggles in the battle of life."[30] Niblo's had a separate entrance "for the accommodation of those visitors whose tastes inclined them to seek umbrageous bowers for the full enjoyment of ice-cream, cooling port wine negus, or refreshing lemonade."

Under Mrs. Niblo's supervision, the garden walkways were kept neat and clean, the flowerbeds were colorful, and birds sang in cages hanging from the trees. Settees with little tables were situated around the grounds and in vine-clad gazebos. At night, this lovely scene was illuminated by "numberless lanterns of parti-colored glass of the glow-worm type," which flattered the complexion and eliminated the need for women to wear rouge or face powder.[31]

In the center of his property, Niblo erected an open-air saloon where he featured light entertainment, such as vaudeville, farce, and instrumental and vocal music. At first, women shunned the open-air saloon, but "after a brief space it became eminently proper for the fair sex, under the protection of a well assured escort" to sit in this area. In response to public demand, Niblo expanded the entertainment until his open-air saloon became a real theater. Eventually, the theater was enlarged until "though the name of Garden was retained, scarcely a vestige of a green plant was left as a witness to the original plan."[32]

Many New Yorkers applauded John Contoit for opening the New York Garden on Broadway because he did not serve alcoholic beverages. Dense shade made this garden a cool oasis even on the hottest days. At night, a multitude of small glass globes filled with whale oil hung from the lower branches of the trees, emitting light "about equal to the same number of June bugs." Situated on both sides of a long center aisle were green-and-white booths, each with a table that could accommodate four persons—"but if very intimate friends, six could in an emergency squeeze in and manage after a fashion." A young man with limited funds "could invite a fair friend to enter the enclosure, to be seated in a box and give her order without fear of discomfiture" because one saucer of Contoit's rich ice cream satisfied a healthy appetite. A large slice of pound cake cost sixpence, while a tumbler of spring water was free. "Eighteen pence, under these circumstances, was ample; the man with thousands at command could do no more."[33]

Contoit, who died a millionaire, emphasized the quality of his ice cream rather than the ambiance. While some pleasure gardens featured opulent surroundings and fancy tableware, he focused on his ice cream, which was served on earthenware saucers and eaten with black pewter spoons. As Contoit's reputation for producing superior ice cream spread, a tower of his vanilla became a must for society weddings. He also routinely supplied ice cream for many of the country's wealthiest households, including the Victor du Pont family.[34]

In the afternoons, Contoit's garden was populated almost exclusively by women and children. In the evenings, men brought their wives or sweethearts for vanilla or lemon ice cream, pound cake, and lemonade. Although the garden had no bar, a quarter surreptitiously dropped in the waiter's palm "would ensure a moderate supply of cognac to be poured over the lemon ice, which gentlemen almost always preferred to the more luscious vanilla, to the great surprise of their fair companions, who frequented this place by the consent of their watchful parents and guardians. The manoeuvres to elude detection were sometimes ludicrous in the extreme."[35]

Castle Garden, which was originally a fortress to protect the city against invaders, was converted into a pleasure garden. In an old white-washed barn, the proprietor served a menu limited to ice cream, lemonade, and sponge cake. At the garden entrance, the visitor paid one shilling for a ticket that could be redeemed inside for one serving of the customer's choice. Castle Garden did not offer entertainment of its own, but on summer evenings patrons could hear martial music played by a band on nearby Governor's Island.[36]

Because ice cream was a drawing card at the pleasure gardens, it is not surprising that Charles Barnard advertised that the ice cream at his United States Garden was prepared by Charles Collet, "well known as possessing ability in that line." Vanilla and lemon ice cream dominated the menus at the gardens until 1810, when Ensley's "new and elegant" Columbian Garden added pineapple, strawberry, and raspberry flavors.[37]

In Philadelphia, Gray's Gardens had opened at an earlier date than its better-known counterparts in New York. Gray's, which was located on the river, featured an illuminated ship, a waterfall, a temple, and a mill. The proprietor advertised vocal and instrumental music, fireworks, and "cold collations," but the ads did not specify whether the refreshments included ice cream. For its American independence celebration in 1790, Gray's went overboard with an illuminated artificial island complete with a farmhouse and gardens. In addition, young people dressed as shepherds and shepherdesses performed an "ode to liberty" at the temple.[38] (Exactly what shepherds and a temple had to do with Independence Day was probably a mystery to some visitors.)

Joseph Delacroix, a confectioner and perfumer, advertised ice cream in a Philadelphia newspaper in 1784. His ad stated that he sold ladies' millinery, scents, spices, nuts, sugar, lemonade, and liqueurs as well as ice cream. Over the next few years, Delacroix advertised frequently. Apparently, he believed in the wisdom of diversification and product mix because his stock ranged from food and ladies' clothing to patent medicines, artificial flowers, plumes, window glass, and "glass beads suitable for trading with the Indians." He also kept Mrs. Delacroix busy, advertising that she made gowns in the newest French fashions. In one ad, he informed Philadelphians that he could supply preserves, sweetmeats, ice cream, sugar plums, macaroons, cakes, and decorative desserts for "those who have splendid entertainments to give." He even offered a liberal return policy for uneaten desserts. In another paper, he advertised that he sold ice cream at noontime in molds and in glasses. This man was probably the Joseph Delacroix who later owned New York's Vauxhall, because there is evidence that he left Philadelphia.[39]

In June 1795, a Philadelphia newspaper printed an advertisement for ice cream "at the modest price of 11 pence per glass"—which was actually quite expensive—at Joseph Corre's shop at Eighth and Market streets. The city directory for that same year listed Joseph Carre as an ice cream seller on High Street. Market and High were actually the same street, and the similarity between the two names is striking. Given the vicissitudes of orthography at the time, Corre and Carre may have been alternate spellings of the same surname. Moreover, this Philadelphia confectioner may have been the Corre who advertised earlier in New York, but the scant information available about him is insufficient for drawing that conclusion. If it was the same man, he soon returned to New York to open a pleasure garden.[40]

Another French confectioner, Monsieur Collot, advertised in Philadelphia newspapers in 1795. Collot announced that he had moved his business into large quarters near the German Catholic Church and would continue to make ice cream "in all the perfection of the true Italian mode." To insure the quality of his product, he had arranged to have a fresh supply of cream daily, and his customers were invited to relax in the garden adjoining his shop.[41]

A French emigre reported that Collot was a creole from San Domingo (now Haiti) and the son of the former president of the High Council of Cap Francois (Cap Haitien, Haiti). Because Philadelphia had a reputation for being compassionate toward Frenchmen fleeing San Domingo, the city had a large colony of them. Many of these exiles had lost their wealth and had taken jobs or opened small shops, selling a variety of goods, including the first contraceptives in Philadelphia.

While Collot made a living by cooking, his avocation was playing violin in the Philadelphia Theater orchestra. One of his compatriots declared that Collot's ice cream compared favorably with that of the Palais Royal in Paris. (At least one source has identified this Collot as Collet of New York City, but it is likely that they merely had similar names.)[42]

Another Frenchman, named Mercier, sold ice cream at Philadelphia's comedy theater during this period. Even though his ice cream was only mediocre, it was the most expensive in the city because he had to pay the theater a large sum for the exclusive concession.[43]

Peter Bossee, or Bossu, moved to the City of Brotherly Love circa 1794, opened a wine shop on South Fifth Street, and soon was advertising Bossee's Gardens, complete with music and fireworks. When he began serving ice cream is unknown, but advertisements for Bossee's Ice Cream House, Germantown, appeared in *The Aurora Daily Advertiser* in July 1800:

Mr. Bossee takes the liberty of informing his friends and the public that he has established . . . for their accommodation, a house, which shall be constantly supplied with all kinds of Refreshments, as Ice Cream, Syrups, French Cordials, Cakes, Claret of the best kinds, Gellies [*sic*], etc., etc. He will spare no expense to render everything comfortable and agreeable to all those who will favor him with their company. . . . He continues to entertain as usual at his house in Philadelphia, No. 59 South Fifth Street.

Soon after Bossee advertised his ice cream houses, his name disappeared from the city directory, raising questions about the fate of his enterprise. However, other ice cream retailers flourished in Philadelphia. Of course, not all Philadelphians approved of ice cream or the places that served it. Some critics felt that frequenting ice cream houses was frivolous while others believed that ice cream was actually dangerous because cold foods were unhealthy. For example, Elizabeth Drinker, a member of a prominent Quaker family, wrote in her diary that she did not "admire or approve" of eating ice cream or going to the ice cream houses. She even objected when two of her middle-aged children, who surely were old enough to make their own decisions, patronized a local ice cream house one June evening.[44]

As in New York, the Philadelphia elite ate ice cream regularly. When Philadelphia experienced an early hot spell in March 1787, Abigail Adams, a temporary resident, ate ices to cool down. Molded ice cream was popular at Philadelphia social events, such as parties and weddings. In a letter describing one wedding feast, the mother of the bride wrote, "Vases of flowers were placed on different parts of the table, which when seen in contrast with the jellies, blanch mange [*sic*] and pyramid ice cream formed a very handsome variety."[45]

Ice cream became a staple at one of Philadelphia's most cherished institutions, the Wistar parties. In 1799, Dr. Caspar Wistar—physician, university professor, and author of the first American treatise on anatomy—moved into a home at Fourth and Prune streets, where he entertained guests informally on Sunday evenings. Because he was an eniment scholar and physician, his soirees attracted an impressive array of the intelligentsia. As the years passed, his parties became famous and invitations were treasured. Wistar, for whom the wisteria vine was named, served simple refreshments; one contemporary account stated that the menu customarily consisted of ice cream, cake, raisins, almonds, tea, coffee, and wine. This was relatively light fare for the time, indicating that the conversation was definitely more important than the food at Wistar's parties.[46]

In the late 1820s, Augustus Jackson, who had worked as a cook at the White House, moved to Philadelphia and started a catering business. Jackson became one of Philadelphia's wealthiest African Americans, making ice cream for his own clientele and also supplying two ice cream parlors owned by African Americans. (At least one source has erroneously credited Jackson with being the first American to make ice cream.)[47]

While ice cream was becoming a habit with the upper classes in New York and Philadelphia, it remained a rarity in many areas. In Boston in the 1790s, ice cream had not yet become a fashionable dessert at private parties. Shoppers and theatergoers were the major clientele of Boston's only confectioner who sold ice cream. It is uncertain how many flavors he carried, but he advertised that raspberry, strawberry, currant, and pineapple were available only in season.[48]

Early references to ice cream in the West and South are limited, but it appears that the treat was largely confined to the wealthy and that those regions lagged behind New York and Philadelphia in introducing it to the general public. One of the earliest records of ice cream on the western frontier came from General Anthony Wayne, hero of the Battle of Fallen Timbers in 1794, who wrote a letter describing a dinner he enjoyed with his officers at Greenville, Ohio, where he had gone to negotiate a treaty with the Indians: "Officers, waiting only long enough to wash away travel stains, sat at a table to dine sumptuously on roast venison, beef, boiled mutton, duck, raccoon, o'possum, mince and apple pies, plum cake, floating island, and to cap the jubilation, dishes of ice cream, a dainty which the Army had not seen since it left the East."[49]

Below the Mason-Dixon line, ice cream was eaten on plantations and advertised in urban newspapers. In 1798, confectioner John Stavely advertised ice cream in Alexandria, Virginia. Two years later, two more Alexandria shopkeepers listed ice cream in their newspaper ads. A letter written in August 1799 by Ann Blair Banister of Virginia's Shannon Hill stated that she and another guest had become sick after consuming too much ice cream, watermelon, and plums at a neighbor's house. "Alas! so much frigidity does not suit us old folks," she wrote. That same summer, hotel proprietor Jeremiah Jessop sold ice cream in Charleston, South Carolina.[50]

Martha Ogle Forman kept a diary with detailed descriptions of social events on her Maryland plantation. For the dessert course at one dinner party, Forman placed "a large silver goblet of ice cream ornamented with a half-blown moss rose" in the center of the table, flanked by silver bowls of floating island. Also on the table were color-coordinated glass bowls filled with fresh strawberries and preserved grapes and oranges. There were two plates with custards, two with pumpkin rice, and four plates with more ice cream. Finally, Forman filled three dishes with sweetmeats and decorated the table with roses for "a very pretty effect."[51]

In Baltimore, one of the first advertisements for ice cream appeared in the *Maryland Journal & Baltimore Advertiser* in June 1797, when Mr. DeLoubert notified the public that his new establishment offered games, including billiards, and refreshments, including ice cream of "the highest quality." In May 1798, an ad in Baltimore's *Federal Gazette* promoted another source of the dessert, Valette & Company, who promised to supply "ladies and gentlemen with the best ice cream in town."[52]

In April 1800, the services of Charles Collet were advertised in the *Federal Gazette*. The ad declared that he was "well known through all the continent, for his superiority in making ice creams" and would offer "his services to the curious, desirous of learning how to make them in the best manner and of the first quality." Presumably this was the Collet who was already well established in New York City, or perhaps his son. According to the ad, Collet was embarking from Havana, Cuba, on a tour of the United States and would stop in several cities to teach his method of making ice cream. It is not known if the Frenchman had already taught ice cream-making to the Cubans, but it is certain that he hoped to sell his technique in each American city that he visited.[53]

Another early ad in a Baltimore newspaper reveals that the pleasure garden craze had reached Maryland. In June 1803, the *Federal Gazette* printed an advertisement for "Chatsworthy Gardens, commonly called Gray's Gardens." The proprietor, C.L.D. Gunderman informed the public that he would offer his clientele a steady supply of ice cream in different flavors during the summer.[54]

William Wirt, U.S. attorney general and unsuccessful presidential candidate on the Anti-Masonic ticket, attended a society wedding in Williamsburg, Virginia, in 1806. Following the marriage ceremony, the guests adjourned to a supper room where the main table was decorated with cakes and "lofty pyramids of jellies, syllabubs, ice creams, etc."[55]

Founding Fathers Thomas Jefferson and James Madison were foremost among the wealthy Virginia planters who helped to popularize ice cream. An epicure as well as a great statesman, Jefferson relished good food, enjoyed sampling new dishes, and entertained with elegant simplicity. His love of fine food and wine matured during his years as ambassador to France, and he returned to the United States with sophisticated tastes that his political opponents criticized as extravagant and un-American. His frugal presidential predecessor, John Adams, complained, "I held levees once a week. Jefferson's whole eight years was a levee."[56]

During his service in Paris, Jefferson employed an excellent French chef, savored the intricacies of French cuisine, and meticulously copied some of his chef's best recipes to take home to Monticello. Among these recipes in Jefferson's own handwriting was one for vanilla ice cream, calling for two bottles of "good cream," six egg yolks, a half-pound of sugar, and a stick of vanilla. Jefferson was fond of vanilla, and some sources have credited him with introducing it to America. In 1791, while serving as U.S. secretary of state, he wrote to an American diplomat in Paris, complaining that he could find no vanilla in Philadelphia and requesting 50 pods from France. By the turn of the century, vanilla ice cream was commonly served in the pleasure gardens.[57]

During Jefferson's travels in Europe, he sampled the regional cuisines wherever he went and made notes about what he ate. During a visit to Rozzano, he tasted a frozen dessert and observed that "snow gives the most delicate flavor to creams, but ice is the most powerful congealer and lasts longer." Accordingly, his ice cream recipe included instructions for using alternating layers of ice and salt to freeze the mixture. His 1806 account book included an entry for wages for a kitchen helper to "turn ice cream."[58]

Jefferson's recipe called for freezing the cream mixture in a *sorbetière,* or covered pail with a handle attached to the lid. Some historians have speculated that Jefferson brought one with him when he returned from France, and there is evidence that *sorbetières* were known in the United States at an early date. In 1786, one of Jefferson's fellow Virginians, Theodorick Bland, asked his brother-in-law St. George Tucker to have a pewter "salbotiore" made for him in New York or

Philadelphia. He described it as "an obtuse cone with a top fitted to it" and suggested that Tucker consult a Frenchman for a pattern.[59]

For some of Jefferson's presidential dinner parties, ice cream was formed into small balls and enclosed in warm pastry shells, causing "great astonishment and murmurings" among the diners. One dinner guest, Catharine Mitchill, said that this unusual dish had "the appearance of having been just taken from the oven."[60]

Senator Samuel Latham Mitchell wrote the following description of a meal with Jefferson in February 1802:

Dined at the President's. . . . Rice soup, round of beef, turkey, mutton, ham, loin of veal, cutlets of mutton or veal, fried eggs, fried beef, a pie called macaroni . . . Ice cream very good, crust wholly dried, crumbled into thin flakes; a dish somewhat like a pudding—inside white as milk or curd, very porous and light, covered with cream-sauce—very fine. Many other jim cracks, a great variety of fruit, plenty of wines.[61]

Dolley Madison was one of Washington's most influential social leaders, entertaining in her own home and often serving as hostess for the widowed Jefferson before her husband became President. Descriptions of her parties indicate that, like Jefferson, she was partial to French cuisine and vintage wines. Contemporary writers also reported that she was a gracious, attractive, intelligent, and trend-setting First Lady who was noted for her sparkling conversation.

Shortly after moving to Washington from New York, Mitchill wrote an account of the first party she attended at the Madisons' home, while Madison was serving as Jefferson's secretary of state. After tea was served, several guests played chess while another group preferred cards, "picking each others pockets in this genteel manner." The remainder of the guests mingled and enjoyed the refreshments: ice cream, cake, cordials, punch, jellies, candied sugar, raisins, almonds, and fruit.[62]

After Madison was elected President, the First Family held evening drawing rooms in lieu of levees. These drawing rooms were announced in a Washington newspaper and, theoretically at least, were open to any citizen. While a military band played, the guests strolled through the executive mansion and were treated to simple refreshments, including tea, coffee, ice cream, and cake. Although there was no elaborate entertainment and neither dancing nor card playing was permitted, guests did not complain because they relished the honor of being with the President and First Lady.[63]

In November 1812, Josephine Seaton, the wife of a newspaper publisher, dined with the Madisons at the executive mansion. Although her account does not list the dishes served for the early courses, she goes into detail about the dessert course, which included ice cream, macaroons, preserves, and cakes. One of her comments reveals that the fashionable desserts in Washington were different from what she was accustomed to in her home state of North Carolina. "Pastry and puddings going out of date and wine and ice-creams coming in does not suit my taste, and I confess to preferring Raleigh hospitality," she declared.[64]

Seaton wrote a detailed account of "the most profuse ball ever given in Washington," which was hosted by Albert Gallatin, Madison's treasury secretary, and his wife in January 1813. The refreshments began with coffee, tea, warm cakes, ice cream, lemonade, punch, burgundy, claret, curacao, champagne, bonbons, apples, oranges, confectionery, nuts, almonds, and raisins. But all these were only the appetizers for a "set supper, composed of tempting solid dishes, meats, savory pasties [sic] garnished with lemon," and a variety of beverages, including hot chocolate.[65]

Seaton attended Madison's second inauguration in March 1813, when "every creature that could afford twenty-cents for hack-hire" came to see the President sworn in by the chief justice. She wrote, "The major part of the respectable citizens offered their congratulations, ate his ice creams and bonbons, drank his Madeira, made their bow and retired, leaving him fatigued beyond measure with the incessant bending to which his politeness urged him."[66]

On New Year's Day, 1814, Seaton joined a crush of people paying their respects to the Madisons. The reception rooms became so hot that women appeared grotesquely disfigured as their rouge and pearl-powder ran down their cheeks with perspiration. Seaton does not say how the ice cream fared in the heat, but she does mention that she ate some and drank a glass of Madeira. Perhaps she was learning to like the new custom of serving ice cream and wine.[67]

The letters of Mary Boardman Crowninshield, the wife of Madison's secretary of the navy, are another major source of information about Washington society during this era. Crowninshield described a drawing room hosted by the First Lady in December 1815, when the refreshments included tea, coffee, punch, wine, "ice cream, put in a silver dish, and a large cake—not good."[68]

Although Seaton and Crowninshield did not specify the flavor or flavors of ice cream served by Mrs. Madison, it is known that the First Lady was fond of strawberries and served them with ice cream at her husband's second inaugural. A contemporary account of a Madison dinner party noted, "Mrs. Madison always entertains with Grace and Charm, but last night there was a sparkle in her eye that set astir an Air of Expectancy among her Guests." When the visitors entered the dining room, they discovered "a table set with French china and English silver, laden with good things to eat, and in the centre high on a silver platter, a large, shining dome of pink ice cream."[69]

While the Madisons occupied the executive mansion, Harriott Pinckney Horry, a South Carolina woman, traveled north through the Middle Atlantic states all the way to New England. Her journal reveals that she ate ice cream on several occasions. In Richmond, Virginia, at the home of a Major Gibbons, the repast included green goose, ham, tongue, cauliflower, potatoes, salads, peas, French beans, sturgeon, chicken, veal, ice cream, strawberries, pudding, gooseberries, and white heart cherries. Horry also enjoyed ice cream and strawberries at two homes in Baltimore.[70]

In 1824, Henry Cogswell Knight, writing under the pseudonym of Arthur Singleton, published an account of his travels in the South and West. He gave an exhaustive description of the typical diet of a wealthy Virginian and stated that most plantations had an icehouse, but he did not mention ice cream in his long list of foods. When he traveled farther South to New Orleans, he was fascinated by the exotic people and the colorful cuisine. He wrote, as follows:

The crimson tomato, the dusky egg-plant, split and spiced, and the green fig, are common at table. . . . But the dish of dishes in New-Orleans is a French dish, called *gumbo*. It is a kind of save-all, salmagundi soup, made of the refuse ends of every variety of flesh, mingled with rice, and seasoned with chopped sassafras, or with okra, a vegetable esculent. . . . At a belle-assemblage, the sultry saloon of the nabobs is cooled by iced-creams.[71]

During the administration of John Quincy Adams, the traditional White House levees were held every other Wednesday while Congress was in session. Each levee was announced in a Washington newspaper and no invitation was necessary. Nevertheless, it was "very rare that any but the most distinguished and genteel people" went because "very few people would attempt to go to such a place, without making a genteel appearance, and believing themselves, more or less, entitled to mix in such society."[72]

At these levees, the customary menu was coffee, tea, cakes, jellies, ice cream, and red and white wines. In addition, liqueurs, cordials, and West India fruit were sometimes served. The author of a contemporary etiquette book advised the guests to take refreshments when the servants passed nearby with the trays because there were not many opportunities to do so, due to the large crowds. During the Adams administration, the food for a typical levee cost in the neighborhood of $50, a significant sum at that time.[73]

Mrs. Basil Hall, an Englishwoman, visited the United States in 1827–28. Her letters home provided excellent descriptions of American manners and social customs, although they were colored by her feeling that American entertaining generally fell short of British standards. For example, she attended one of President Adams's levees, where ices and "refreshments, smelling strong of gin, were handed round." Most of the food "was devoured by the most ordinary of the company, who pounced upon the trays like those not much accustomed to such fare."[74]

In one letter, Hall discussed the arrangement of the dishes and the number of courses at American dinners. She wrote that Americans "give prodigious feasts when they have company" and that a typical finale for company dinner was "a most profuse supply of puddings, pies, jellies, sweetmeats, and immense pillars of ice, after which there are pineapples and all manner of dessert."[75]

In two consecutive letters, Hall described social events hosted by Governor and Mrs. DeWitt Clinton of New York. On the first occasion, she joined Mrs. Clinton and a roomful of women for tea, cake, peaches, grapes, and "a magnificent pyramid of ice, supported on each side by preserved pineapple and other sweetmeats." Later, that same evening, the guests enjoyed wine and more ice cream. The following day, Hall ate a full-course dinner at the governor's home. She found the table setting and the arrangement of dishes so unusual that she asked her husband to draw a sketch to enclose with her letter. The primitive drawing of the second course included a triangle on a plate, labeled "a pyramid of ice, rivaling those of Egypt."[76]

In another missive, Hall reported that she had been invited to tea "at the very primitive hour of six," when the refreshments included ice cream, coffee, jellies, preserves, hot whisky punch, pickled oysters, collared port, and porter. On another occasion, she had "a dinner in much better taste than any I have before seen in New York." One of the reasons she liked this dinner was that there was "no mixing up of columns of ice along with pies and puddings."[77]

Hall wrote many accounts of dinner parties, teas, balls, and other social events. Although she ate ice cream with some regularity in the United States, she described many occasions when ices were not part of the menu. Overall, she seems to have eaten more meals without ice cream than with it.[78]

While Hall was dining on delicacies at upper-crust affairs, the common citizens of New York City could buy ice cream from street vendors. In 1828, *The National Advertiser* reported that noisy vendors, carrying kettles, had added "I scream, Ice cream!" to the cries heard on New York streets. (Strictly speaking, many of these street hawkers were selling ice milk due to the shortage of fresh cream in the city at that time.) More affluent New Yorkers could buy their treats at ice cream saloons, such as the upscale Taylor's and Thompson's across the street from A.T. Stewart's Broadway Emporium, an ancestor of the modern department store.[79]

Following John Quincy Adams's one-term presidency, Andrew Jackson, a hero with the common touch, assumed the highest office of the United States. His administration began somewhat dramatically, with a presidential levee that scandalized many Americans, who felt that it lacked dignity. When the Jacksons came to Washington, they brought servants from Tennessee, but none had the training or experience needed to take over the operation of the White House. Therefore, the Adams's steward, Antoine Giusta, agreed to supervise the preparations for the inaugural reception.[80]

Sensing that Jackson's inauguration would attract a larger and less genteel crowd than Adams's levees had accommodated, Guista set up long tables for food in the East Room as well as in the State Dining Room. He mixed large quantities of lemonade and orange punch, spiked with whiskey. Many pots of ice cream were prepared and carried down ladders into the cool depths of the ice cellar in the White House's west wing, where they were packed in ice and straw until needed. Bakers cooked staggering numbers of cakes, pies, and loaves of bread for the anticipated crowd.[81]

Following the swearing-in ceremony, Jackson was escorted to the White House, where he received guests. Within an hour of his arrival, so many people had poured into the mansion that the floors vibrated with the weight, and the crush was suffocating. The ice cream, cakes, and other refreshments piled high on the long tables rapidly disappeared and were replenished as quickly as the waiters could make their way through the mob. China was dropped and broken. People jostled for position, guests stood on tables and chairs to get a better view, and fistfights broke out.[82]

In the Oval Drawing Room, the President gasped for air as the press of the crowd crushed him against the wall. Rescued by aides who locked arms and cleared a path through the mob, Jackson escaped to a nearby hotel. But few guests realized that the President had gone, and masses of people continued to pour into the White House. Guista sent servants with ice cream, lemonade, and tubs of punch out to the lawn to lure the guests outside.[83]

During the Jackson and Van Buren administrations, ice cream remained a popular treat at Washington's elite social events. One account of a party during Van Buren's tenure reported an embarrassing *faux pas* when a guest mistook a pyramid of cake for one of ice cream, "cut away with a spoon," and "overthrew the whole structure." The most talked-about party during Van Buren's first term was given by the Russian minister De Bodisco, a handsome bachelor with a flair for lavish entertaining. Washington's social and political elite along with the top-ranking members of the foreign diplomatic corps eagerly awaited their invitations to the minister's first ball. The pre-supper refreshments, which were served on silver platters and eaten with gold spoons, included ice cream, iced chocolate, iced crab apple juice, iced punch, lemonade, and sangaree.[84]

In 1835, American hostesses vied for the honor of entertaining British author Harriet Martineau. Mrs. Samuel Harrison Smith, a Washington socialite, was delighted when she snared the famous Englishwoman for a dinner party. Anxiously, she sent for Harry Orr, "the most experienced and fashionable waiter in the city." He advised her that 30 meat dishes were "absolutely necessary" and that stewed celery, spinach, salsify, and cauliflower were the proper vegetables. He also told her that puddings and pies were old-fashioned. In his expert opinion, the dessert table should be decorated with forms of ice cream at the head and a pyramid of "grapes, oranges or anything handsome at the foot." Smith, who stubbornly insisted that eight meat dishes would be sufficient, seems to have ignored most of Orr's advice.[85]

When Martineau wrote her impressions of the United States, she noted the popularity of ice cream and reported that "towers" of it were available daily in Kentucky. She also mentioned the prevalence of ice cream in her sketch of New Orleans, where the Exchange Coffee-House had advertised the frozen dessert as early as 1808. "Except for the mixture of languages, and the ample provision of ices, fans, and ventilators," she wrote, "the drawing-room assemblages of New-Orleans bear a strong resemblance to the routs and dinner-parties of a country town in England."[86]

Despite the competition among fashionable hostesses who wanted to entertain Martineau, some of her American dining experiences were far from pleasant. While traveling through Virginia, she and her driver stopped at a farmhouse and asked for a snack. They were given sour bread and butter, which was probably the best the family had to offer. Since Martineau's driver ate the food with relish, she concluded that he was accustomed to spoiled food. She liked mutton but found that Americans rarely ate it. In Tennessee, she was served what passed for mutton and declared, "My own idea is that it was dog."[87]

When Martineau visited a plantation near Montgomery, Alabama, she was overwhelmed by the quantity of food on the table. A typical dinner there included turkey, ham, tongue, pork, hominy, pickles, squash, corn bread, apple pie, pumpkin pie, preserves, raisins, almonds, hickory nuts, "and to crown the whole, large blocks of ice cream."[88]

Domestic travelers, as well as foreign visitors, noted the popularity of ice cream in the 1830s. Yale graduate Henry Barnard, who traveled in the South, left a lengthy account of a memorable dinner at Virginia's Shirley Plantation in 1833. The feast began with soup, mutton, ham, beef, turkey, ducks, eggs, greens, potatoes, beets, and hominy. After a pause for champagne, the diners somehow found room for plum pudding, tarts, ice cream, West India preserves, brandied peaches, figs, raisins, almonds, Madeira, port, and "a sweet wine for the ladies."[89]

Barnard's experience at Shirley was typical of the bountiful tables set by the wealthy Southern landowners. John Grimball, a guest at Alston Plantation on the rice coast, was treated to a sumptuous repast of turtle soup, leg of boiled mutton, turtle steaks and fins, macaroni pie, oysters, a haunch of venison, roast turkey, bread pudding, jelly, ice cream, pie, bananas, oranges, apples, Madeira, sherry, and champagne.[90]

A new bride from Philadelphia who moved to her husband's Carolina plantation sent her father a letter detailing some of the Southern social customs. Like other Northerners, she was impressed by the variety, quantity, and quality of the regional food. "The ice cream and jelly here are the best I ever tasted," she wrote.[91]

Even at this early date, ice cream was already a tradition on the Fourth of July in some locations. Richard Henry Dana, Jr., whose chronicles of life at sea have become classics of American literature, described Independence Day in Boston in his journal entry for July 4, 1836. The celebration included the "firing of guns, ringing of bells, and rejoicing of all sorts." The ladies, shaded by their parasols, and the dandies, wearing white pantaloons and silk stockings, strolled along the city streets, consuming large quantities of ice cream and iced drinks to combat the heat.[92]

Two years later, a Philadelphia man wrote a series of newspaper articles about his trip to Boston. Among the sites he visited was Fresh Pond, a favorite resort where Bostonians went in the summer to "swing, promenade, bathe, sail, fish, eat ice creams, play at various athletic games, and enjoy all the other innocent pleasures that a cool, romantic spot can afford." Although his Boston hosts bragged about their ice cream, he proclaimed that Philadelphia's was definitely superior.[93]

In the 1830s ice cream became more readily available in frontier areas where settlers were creating new cities. By the middle of the decade, ice cream was being sold by commercial establishments in both Chicago and St. Louis, although it remained a rarity in less-populated areas. Capt. Frederick Marryat, an English traveler, stopped at an ice cream parlor in St. Louis where "about a dozen . . . fellows, employed at the iron-foundry close at hand, with their dirty shirt-sleeves tucked up, and without their coats and waistcoats, came in, and sitting down, called for ice creams."[94]

St. Louis had high standards when it came to ice cream, if a newspaper restaurant review is any indication. The critique of the Broadway Cottage, a pleasure garden owned by a Miss Renou, began diplomatically but soon plunged to the heart of the problem:

Since the opening of her Garden, it has been a general and fashionable place of resort, and we have witnessed with pleasure that eminent success which has rewarded her labors. As is the case with most matters in this world, however, there are faults at the cottage which might be easily remedied, and which are too glaring to be tolerated. . . . In the first place, then, her Ice Cream, or her cold flour and sugar, is decidedly unpalatable, to say the least of it, and we believe, unhealthy. It is our sincere belief that flour, eggs, and sugar form four-fifths of the mixture which is sold at the cottage for Ice Cream. . . .

Let her Ice Cream be made of cream, milk, and loaf-sugar, without the slightest mixture of flour, eggs, or rice, and we shall be most happy to inform the public of of the reformation.

The reviewer found the rest of Renou's food to be acceptable, although he complained about her musicians, urging her to dismiss them "or compel them to pay attention to their business."[95]

Another article published in a Missouri newspaper stated that many farm families considered ice cream to be a city treat. The reporter sought to remedy that situation by giving a detailed explanation of how to make it at home.[96]

Chicago's first large drugstore, established in 1835, sold ice cream. Five years later, a Frenchman named Lefort opened the French and American Confectionary, offering Chicagoans an assortment of ice creams, coffees, chocolates, candies, cakes, pastries, and so forth. During this same era, ice cream saloons began to appear to supply the Windy City's growing demand for ice cream and soda water.[97]

Memoirs of Washington's social leaders reveal that the political elite considered ice cream to be more or less essential for a successful party in the 1840s. In January 1842, Daniel Webster hosted a party "which was the crowning entertainment of the season." Although there was no music or dancing, the guests enjoyed "plenty of lively conversation, promenades, eating of ices, and sipping of rich wines, with the usual spice of flirtation."[98]

During this era, a New York newspaper described a new dining custom, borrowed from the French. "The company assembles at about one o'clock and partakes of coffee and chocolate, light dishes of meat, ice-cream and confectionery, with lemonade and French and German wines." Called "breakfast-dinner" by the newspaper, this innovation was an early indication that eating customs were changing and that a light, quick lunch would become standard in many households.[99]

In 1843, Mrs. Robert Tyler, serving as hostess for her widowed father-in-law, President John Tyler, invited 200 of Washington's upper crust to a party honoring the French Marshal Bertrand. In a letter to her sister, Tyler boasted that she had scored a major social coup and that everything was perfect, including the refreshments:

The prettiest things on the table were two pyramids composed of pomegranates with the skins peeled off, and Malaga grapes. They looked like rubies and emeralds. I had quantities of vases of natural flowers down the table, and festoons of grapes going from vase to vase the whole length of the table, which, of course, was covered with everything possible in the way of jellies, ices, creams, etc., etc., and quantities of the most beautiful French bonbons. Nothing was on the principal long table but things of the most aerial, glittering description.[100]

In contrast to Mrs. Tyler, who obviously placed a great deal of importance on lavish entertaining, Ralph Waldo Emerson worried that Americans were becoming too materialistic and were spending their money unwisely. "It is for cake that we run in debt; it is not the intellect, not the heart, not beauty, not worship, that costs so much," he observed. "We dare not trust our wit for making our house pleasant to our friend, and so we buy ice-creams."[101]

One of Emerson's fellow New Englanders, Catherine Beecher, advised against eating ice cream for health reasons. "Taking large quantities of cold drinks, or eating ice creams, after a meal, tend to reduce the temperature of the stomach, and thus to stop digestion," wrote Beecher. "This shows the folly of those refreshments in convivial meetings, where the guests are tempted to load the stomach with a variety, such as would require the stomach of a stout farmer to digest, and then to wind up with ice creams, thus destroying whatever ability might otherwise have existed to digest the heavy load."[102]

Beecher was not alone in her concern about eating cold foods. A newspaper warned that eating ice cream caused acidity and "unseemly belching." When one of Abigail Adams's servants was struck with severe stomach cramps and became very ill, she attributed it to the fact that he had eaten some of the ice cream he was making.[103] A popular patent medicine capitalized on the fears about cold foods and the tendency to overindulge at parties, in the following advertisement:

Whoever goes to parties eats too much trash of all kinds—oysters and ice cream—cold tongue and cream kisses—sugar plums and celery—drinks too much brandy, hock, sherry, madeira, and champagne. What is the cure? Leave off, if you will, and if you will not, then take a tablespoonful of Dr. Spolen's Elixir of Health before you go to bed.[104]

Sarah Mytton Maury, yet another English visitor, traveled around the United States in 1846. In a book about her trip, she described the menu in the Ladies' Ordinary at New York City's Astor House, where a guest could order turtle soup, oyster pies, ham, poultry, game in season, jellies, blancmange, and other sweets. Shad, sheep's head, partridge, canvassback ducks, and venison were also available, if ordered in advance. "To give a zest to these delicacies," Maury recommended iced champagne. A plate of ice cream and fruit capped off Maury's typical meal in the Ladies' Ordinary.[105]

Maury, who was intrigued by United States politics, spent time in Washington observing how the American political system worked. She was very favorably impressed with the oratory of Senator Edward Hannegan of Indiana, who became a close friend. "One of the most agreeable evenings I spent in Washington was at an ice-cream party given by Mr. Hannegan," she wrote.[106]

Catherine Elizabeth Havens, a young girl growing up in New York City, kept a diary that is still delightful reading because it captures the innocence and exuberance of youth in the mid-19th century. For a treat, Havens's mother would give her and a friend a shilling to go to the ice cream parlor, where a half-plate of ice cream cost sixpence. Once, the two girls ordered a half-plate with two spoons and did not mind that the clerk laughed at them, because they had money left over for another treat.[107]

On another occasion, Havens and her friend decided to hold a fair. They made bookmarks, cardboard thimble boxes, and bachelor's pin cushions to sell. They also sold apples and candy. Although ice cream was customary at such events, they had none. Instead, they sold bonny clabber (sour, thick milk) for five cents a saucer. Havens's older brother "paid for ever so many saucers and said it was delicious, just as good as ice cream, and we thought he was so kind to eat so much of it," wrote Havens. Later, she learned that he hated bonny clabber and had not eaten a drop but had bought it merely to please her. Moreover, he had placed a bucket on the grass underneath a window and, when she wasn't looking, had poured the clabber into the pail. Later it had been fed to a cow.[108]

Like most of the journals and letters that have survived to give the modern reader an impression of American society in the early 19th century, Havens's diary reflects the lifestyle of the elite. Obviously, the elegant, extensive menus served at upper-crust social events were not characteristic of the average American diet. To keep the eating habits of the elite in perspective, it is necessary to contrast them with the diet of the working class. As one historian has observed, "American cooking at this period was generally bad, and the diet worse." The daily cuisine of many Americans was dominated by salt pork, dried beans, dried corn or cornmeal, turnips, and potatoes.[109]

During this era, Americans generally suffered from a shortage of wholesome milk, fresh fruits, and vegetables. Ironically, many foods that are now known to be very nutritious were avoided. Eating fruit was blamed for more than one cholera outbreak, prompting a New York newspaper to advise its readers that fresh fruit "should be religiously forbidden to all classes, especially children." Dr. Martyn Payne, a leading physician, declared that both fruit and garden vegetables caused cholera and cautioned Americans to restrict their diet to lean meat, potatoes, and beverages. President Zachary Taylor was diagnosed with cholera after consuming cold milk and fresh cherries. Only five days later, he died—no doubt, reinforcing the fear of cold foods and fresh fruits. Due to the widespread paranoia about fruits, fashionable hostesses may have served them more for their colorful, ornamental value than for their nutritional worth.[110]

Members of the urban working class ate fresh meat perhaps once a week and rarely tasted other expensive perishables. They relied heavily on bread as a source of calories and commonly used molasses as a sweetener because it was cheaper than sugar. Blood pudding, a mixture of hog or beef blood and seasoned pork stuffed in a casing, was a staple for many working class families in Northern cities.[111]

In the 1850s, the everyday fare of many white Southerners was bacon (sometimes cooked with turnip greens), baked or fried corn bread, and coffee sweetened with molasses. Slaves on modest plantations survived on corn meal, salt pork, and sweet potatoes—sometimes augmented with vegetables grown in their own little gardens. In the backwoods, a family dinner might consist of only fried ham, corn cake, and coffee.[112]

In 1833, a writer recorded the following weekly shopping list for a family of three in Philadelphia: bread, meat, butter, potatoes, sugar or molasses, milk, tea, salt, pepper, and vinegar. In 1851, a newspaper reported that a typical family of five in Philadelphia spent approximately $4.27 per week on meat, flour, butter, potatoes, sugar, coffee, tea, milk, salt, pepper, vinegar, starch, soap, soda, yeast, cheese, and eggs.[113]

In general, the diets of working class families were dominated by plain, basic foods. The average worker would have been astonished to see the extravagant refreshments at a party hosted by a New York socialite or a Washington diplomat. Moreover, even the affluent did not always eat the fancy fare served at parties. One Washington hostess wrote to her sister that she normally prepared soup, one meat dish, and two vegetables for a family dinner at home.[114]

At the mid-point of the 19th century, William Black's rarity was familiar to the American elite and was being sold to city dwellers at pleasure gardens and confectionaries. However, it was too expensive for many working families and was still unknown in remote areas. American consumption of the frozen treat had only begun.

2

Homemade and Hand-cranked:
Making Ice Cream in the 18th and 19th Centuries

Housewives and Cookbooks

While the popularity and availability of ice cream increased, the method of making it remained basically unchanged until 1843. Whether ice cream was being produced by a professional cook or by a frontier homemaker, variations of the pot freezer method were used. The occasional ice cream maker probably used any tin pot that was handy, while the professional owned equipment especially for freezing cream. Undoubtedly, some immigrants who planned to open confectionaries in the New World brought *sorbetières* or other equipment with them. Others probably decided to travel light and acquire the tools of the trade after they settled in the colonies.

The following list compiled by a Philadelphia confectioner enumerates the equipment needed by a commercial ice cream maker using the pot freezer method:

1. Pewter pots of various sizes suitable to the quantity of mixture intended to be frozen. Tin or zinc will not answer the purpose, as it congeals the mixture too quickly without allowing it a sufficient time to become properly incorporated and forms it in lumps like hailstones.
2. Moulds.
3. Ice pails.
4. The spatula. This is an instrument somewhat resembling a gardener's spade; it should be made of stout copper and tinned, the blade being about four inches long by three in width, round at the end, and having a socket to receive a wooden handle; this is for scraping the ice cream, etc., from the sides of the pot as it freezes and for mixing it.
5. Either a large mortar and pestle, or a strong box and mallet for pounding the ice.
6. A spade wherewith to mix the ice and salt together . . .
7. A tin case or box for keeping the ices . . . after they are finished.[1]

America's first ice cream makers brought their recipes—in their own handwriting, in cookbooks, or in their memories—with them from their homelands. The best-known cookbooks in early America were published in English in Britain. Among the earliest British cookbooks with ice cream recipes were *Mrs. Eales Receipts* by Mary Eales, 1718, and *The Modern Cook* by Vincent La Chapelle, 1733. Both of these English manuals contained ice cream recipes derived from earlier French sources.[2]

Dictionarium Domesticum, Being a New and Compleat Household Dictionary by Nathaniel Bailey, published in London in 1736, gave directions for freezing ice cream in a tin icing pot, which could be purchased from a tinsmith. Bailey instructed the cook to use three pounds of ice, mixed with a pound of bay salt, for each pot of cream—plain, sweetened, or flavored with fruit. After closing the pot tightly, the cook was directed to place it inside a pail filled with the ice and salt, to cover the pail with straw, and to leave it in a dark cellar for four hours or longer.[3]

The first edition of *The Art of Cookery Made Plain and Easy*, a very popular work by Hannah Glasse, was published in England in 1747. Four years later, when a new edition was printed, Glasse added a recipe for a simple raspberry puree and cream mixture frozen in pewter basins.[4]

In 1769, Elizabeth Raffald published *The Experienced English Housekeeper* in Britain. Raffald's book was especially noteworthy because it contained an ice cream recipe that would be reprinted, without giving her credit, in several later cookbooks, including the 1805 American edition of Glasse's *The Art of Cookery Made Plain and Easy*. Since a great deal of borrowing (or downright plagiarism) was customary in early cookbooks, it is possible that this recipe did not actually originate with Raffald but came from an even earlier source.

Raffald told her reader to pare, stone, and scald 12 apricots; grind them into small pieces in a marble mortar; and add six ounces of double-refined sugar and a pint of scalding cream. She directed the cook to strain the mixture "through a hair sieve, then put it into a tin which has a close cover, set it in a tub of ice broken small, and a large quantity of salt put amongst it." After the cream thickened, the cook could remove it from the tin pot, place it in a decorative mold, and pack it in ice and salt for four or five hours.[5]

In 1788, Richard Briggs, a well-known London chef, published *The English Art of Cookery, According to the Present Practice, Being a Complete Guide to All Housekeepers, on a Plan Entirely New*. This tome included Raffald's apricot ice cream recipe, as did Briggs's *The New Art of Cookery, According to the Present Practice, Being a Complete Guide to All Housekeepers, on a Plan Entirely New*, which was published in Philadelphia in 1792 and was one of the first cookbooks with an American imprint to contain an ice cream recipe. However, this was not a truly American cookbook because it was a reprint, with minor revisions, of Briggs's earlier British opus.[6]

Frederic Nutt's *The Complete Confectioner, or, the Whole Art of Confectionery*, which was written especially for "genteel families," was published in London as early as 1789 and later reprinted in New York. Nutt, who catered to the highest of high society, set a record by offering recipes for 32 ice cream flavors, including barberry, chocolate, pistachio, brown bread, currant, ginger, lemon, millefruit, cedraty, parmesan cheese, damson, and prunello.[7]

American Cookery; or, the Art of Dressing Viands, Fish, Poultry and Vegetables, and the Best Modes of Making Pastes, Puffs, Pies, Tarts, Puddings, Custards and Preserves, and All Kinds of Cakes, from the Imperial Plumb to Plain Cake by Amelia Simmons, published in Connecticut in 1796, claimed the distinction of being the first truly American cookbook. Although Simmons borrowed a few recipes from British sources, she emphasized native American foods, such as buffalo steak, corn bread, wild turkey, pumpkin, cranberry sauce, pawpaws, and New England election cake. Simmons, who stated that her recipes were for American women of all classes, did not include an ice cream recipe.[8]

Subsequent American cookbooks would rectify Simmons's oversight by publishing a plethora of ice cream recipes. In 1814, *The Universal Receipt Book* by a Society of Gentlemen in New York offered a recipe for pineapple ice cream flavored with pineapple syrup and the juice of two lemons and two oranges. The cook was instructed to place the mixture in a pot, surrounded by ice and salt, inside a pail and to alternately turn the pot and scrape the ice off the sides until the cream was the consistency of new butter.[9]

A decade later, Mary Randolph's *The Virginia Housewife* told cooks how to freeze ice cream flavored with vanilla, raspberries, strawberries, coconut, chocolate, peaches, coffee, quince, apples, pears, citron melons, pineapple, almonds, walnuts, lemon, and oyster soup. She wrote that ice cream should always be served in glasses with handles unless it had been frozen in decorative molds, which were becoming both more popular and more intricate.

Randolph, an industrious woman who ran a Richmond boarding-house that attracted a genteel clientele, warned, "It is the practice with some indolent cooks to set the freezer, containing the cream, in a tub with ice and salt, and put it in the ice-house; it will certainly freeze there, but not until the watery particles have subsided, and by the separation destroyed the cream." She recommended placing a wide, deep pot inside a large tub that would permit the cook to pack four or five inches of ice and salt around the freezer, which "must be kept constantly in motion . . . and ought to be made of pewter, which is less liable than tin to be worn in holes."[10]

Eliza Leslie, who published her first book four years after Randolph's, was one of the 19th century's most influential women because millions of homemakers relied on her advice about cooking and household matters. Leslie, who was born in Pennsylvania but spent her childhood in England, returned to Philadelphia when she was an adolescent. When her father died a few years later, leaving his family impoverished, Leslie's mother opened a boardinghouse and sent her daughter to a local cooking school.[11]

Leslie, who longed for a literary career, combined her knowledge of American cookery with her writing skills to produce a series of immensely popular cookbooks. *Directions for Cookery; Being a System of the Art in Its Various Branches*, published in 1837, contained recipes for lemon, strawberry, raspberry, pineapple, vanilla, and almond ice cream. Leslie assumed that many of her readers owned pot freezers with lids and handles, which could be purchased from metalsmiths for a very reasonable price. She wrote, "Keep turning the freezer about by the handle till the cream is frozen, which it will generally be in two hours." She believed that snow was preferable to ice for freezing cream. When serving ice cream, she advised, "Send round sponge-cake with it, and wine or cordials immediately after."[12]

New Receipts for Cooking, one of Leslie's later books, offered an intriguing recipe for ice cream cakes. After preparing a batter of powdered sugar, butter, eggs, milk, flour, sweet wine, and grated nutmeg, the cook was instructed to bake it in cups or small, deep pans in a brisk oven. The cakes, or muffins, would be hollow in the middle "if very light, and properly baked"—a tricky proposition in the days before modern ovens. The final step directed the cook to make a small slit in each cake and fill the cavity with ice cream.[13]

Lettice Bryan may have been inspired by Randolph to write *The Kentucky Housewife*, or perhaps she was simply trying to exploit Randolph's popularity by using a similar title. Published in 1839, Bryan's cookbook contained recipes for 18 flavors of ice cream, including peach, orange, cherry, gooseberry, grape, sassafras, and tea. Like Randolph, Bryan recommended using a freezer with a large circumference. Explaining the process, she wrote, "Cream will generally freeze sufficiently hard for what is called the first freezing, in two hours; that is, to make the cream of the proper consistence to put into moulds, and then to make it smooth and firm, it will require from two to three hours longer . . . which is called the second freezing or congelation." Bryan directed her readers to cover the freezer with a piece of folded carpet when rotating it, which provided insulation while preventing spills.[14]

In keeping with the trend toward cookbooks written by homemakers rather than professional chefs, Elizabeth Ellicott Lea published *Domestic Cookery* in 1845. This Quaker widow's recipes, which reflected the simple eating habits of rural families before the Civil War, proved to be immensely popular, going through 19 editions in 34 years. She included only three recipes for ice cream, along with directions for tinting it with pokeberry juice or a mixture of powdered cochineal, tartar, and powdered alum.[15]

In 1847, *The Carolina Housewife, or House and Home* by A Lady of Charleston continued the trend started by Randolph. The lady, whose name was Sarah Rutledge, claimed that most of her recipes were original, although she acknowledged that she had borrowed a few, which she had translated from French or German. In fact, a number of her recipes were very similar to some of Lea's. However, culinary historians believe that Rutledge did not borrow directly from Lea and that both women relied on the recipes of Elizabeth Coane Goodfellow, who never wrote a cookbook but did operate a very successful cooking school. Rutledge's book contained several recipes for sherbets and ices made with a combination of milk and cream, two of which were credited to Madame de Genlis, a popular French author.[16]

Despite the proliferation of cookbooks with ice cream recipes, an article in the *Prairie Farmer* magazine reported that many farm families still viewed ice cream as an urban treat because they did not know how to make it or did not own the necessary equipment. The author declared:

There is a cool and pleasant refective exceedingly agreeable in social parties, large or small, at all seasons of the year, and especially so in the hot weather of our long dry summers. Though it is a preparation more especially kept in cities and towns . . . we cannot see why it cannot become a common dish upon the tables of those cultivators of large farms and keepers of large families who have the ability and disposition to attend upon the pleasures of taste.

To remedy the shortage of ice cream on the prairie, the author recommended the purchase of a freezer, "which consists of a cylindrical jar, made of block tin, and fitted with a close cover, which is so fastened as that the whole can be turned by a large strong handle, with which the cover is furnished. This can be had at the tin shop for one or two dollars."

After giving instructions for making a cream mixture flavored with either vanilla or lemon, the author provided detailed directions for placing ice and salt, along with the freezer, inside "a common nail keg, or any cask holding about twelve gallons, having only one head . . . Then taking the freezer by the handle, turn it back and forth horizontally right and left, a few times every few minutes until the cream is frozen."[17]

From the preceding sample of recipes, it is obvious that American homemakers as well as professional chefs made ice cream in a variety of flavors. Unless the ice cream maker was one of those indolent cooks whom Randolph deplored, the chore required time, attention, and strong arms. As one writer advised, "Bear in mind that the making of ice-cream, under any circumstances, is an operation requiring considerable dexterity and practice."[18]

Undoubtedly, many cooks wished for something to make the job easier.

The Hand-cranked Freezer

On September 9, 1843, the U.S. Patent Office issued Patent No. 3254 to Nancy M. Johnson for an "artificial freezer" with three major parts: a tall tub, a slender cylinder with a close-fitting lid, and a dasher with a removable crank. When the dasher was placed inside the cylinder, a hole in the cylinder lid permitted the dasher shaft to protrude so that the crank could be attached to it, enabling the cook to turn the dasher with ease.[19]

With the pot freezer method, the cook had to stop turning the freezer periodically and scrape the frozen particles off the inner wall with a spatula or long spoon. Johnson's freezer represented an advance because the crank turned the dasher, moving the frozen particles from the wall of the cylinder toward the center, causing the cream mixture to freeze more evenly and giving it a smooth, fluffy texture. Moreover, turning the dasher via the crank was less fatiguing than rotating the pot freezer by hand.

Although not much is known about Johnson, the patent application hints that she was a very practical woman. She recommended wrapping a thick blanket around the tub for insulation, in order to reduce the amount of ice that was needed. In addition, after the cream had been frozen, she advised the cook not to dump the brine but to allow the water to evaporate, leaving salt that could be reused.[20]

Various sources have described Johnson as the wife of a naval officer, a New Jersey woman, and a lifelong resident of Washington, D.C. However, her patent application had a Philadelphia address and her name appears in the Philadelphia city directory for 1842. Even though the directory includes designations for some women, such as seamstress or gentlewoman, Johnson's entry gives no hint about her status or occupation.[21]

Evidently the patent office was uncertain about Johnson's gender because in one letter to the commissioner she complained, "I had some difficulty in obtaining your letter of acknowledgment from the post office in consequence of its having been directed to Mr. N.M. Johnson." Subsequent patent documents indicated that she was married to Walter R. Johnson but gave no further information about him. (The only entry for Walter R. Johnson in Philadelphia's directory during this time frame was for a professor, but it is questionable whether this was her husband because the street address was different from hers.)[22]

Ice cream freezers had been patented in France as early as 1829, and a British patent for a freezer with a revolving dasher was issued only two months before Johnson received hers. However, it is not known if Johnson was familiar with the French or British freezers. According to some sources, Johnson sold her invention for $1,500 although it was potentially worth much more. In fact, patent files stated that Johnson and her husband assigned her rights to Isaac S. Williams and Samuel E. Riesseir, doing business as Williams and Company, for $200 and "other considerations" not specified in the indenture.[23]

Williams and Company, which manufactured and imported tin ware, advertised Johnson's patent ice cream freezer in O'Brien's 1845 wholesale business directory. The firm included the freezer as one of a long list of items in its ad, which featured a slogan that sounds quite relevant today: "Encourage American Manufactures." Five years later, a drawing of Johnson's freezer dominated the firm's ad in O'Brien's. That same edition of the wholesale directory promoted two other patent freezers, Reip's and Masser's.[24]

Johnson's ingenuity inspired other inventors to design freezers, and before long consumers could choose from a variety of models. In the 30 years after Johnson received her patent, at least 70 designs for hand-cranked ice cream freezers were patented in the United States, and more followed until electricity became commonplace. In general, the freezers were variations on her basic concept, with the crank on the top or the side. Most featured a metal cylinder inside a wooden tub, although a few all-metal models were marketed.

In 1848, William G. Young of Baltimore received the second U.S. patent for an ice cream freezer and assigned it to A.H. Reip. Young claimed that his design was an improvement over Johnson's because both the cylinder and the dasher revolved, agitating the cream more completely.[25]

That same year, H.B. Masser, who edited German and English newspapers in Sunbury, Pennsylvania, was issued a patent for an ice cream freezer where the ice was placed inside a narrow inner cylinder and the cream mixture revolved around it in a larger cylinder. But Masser soon decided that this design was inefficient and began to experiment with variations. As early as 1850, his box-shaped Self-Acting Patent Ice Cream Freezer and Beater was advertised in wholesale catalogs. Ads claimed that it was the only freezer based on scientific principles and that it could produce ice cream in less than ten minutes.[26]

In 1856, the bilingual editor was promoting a five-minute freezer with a revolving cylinder and a spring blade dasher, claiming that "the one hastens the freezing of the cream; the other removes it as fast as frozen." Thousands of circulars promised the following:

This new and popular invention, by its peculiar construction, will freeze ice cream and water ices more perfectly and in much less time than any other freezer known. At numerous trials and public exhibitions of Masser's freezers before large audiences, the operation has been most satisfactorily accomplished within five minutes, and on several occasions the cream was actually frozen in three and a half minutes by the watch.

Nevertheless, the five-minute wonder sold slowly during its first summer on the market. Then the second summer, sales improved dramatically, and it proved to be a very popular model for many years.[27]

Masser's freezer was enthusiastically endorsed by a popular women's magazine, *Godey's Lady's Book,* which declared that readers who could remember making ice cream by the pot freezer method would "readily recognize the difference between the smooth, rich and plastic appearance of the ice cream of the present day as compared with the granular, crystalline and icy appearance of that associated with their early recollections."[28]

American Agriculturist also endorsed Masser's, noting that many farm families had previously denied themselves the pleasure of ice cream due to the scarcity of ice and the high cost of a freezer. However, the magazine assured them that times had changed because ice was readily available in most locations and Masser's freezer could be purchased for as little as $3.00.[29]

Masser was not the only promoter to claim that his freezer worked quickly. Advertisements often promised that a freezer would produce ice cream in a very short time, even as little as two minutes. While some of these claims may have been true, others proved to be exaggerations, as in the following reminiscence of Independence Day by Elizabeth Prentiss:

We have celebrated the glorious Fourth by making and eating ice-cream. Papa bought a new-fashioned freezer, that professed to freeze in two minutes. We screwed it to the wood-house floor . . . put in the cream, and the whole family stood and watched Papa while he turned the handle. At the end of two minutes we unscrewed the cover and gazed inside, but there were no signs of freezing, and to make a long story short . . . there we all were from half-past twelve to nearly two o'clock, when we decided to have dinner and leave the servants to finish it. It came on the table at last, very rich and rather good.[30]

In addition to making extravagant claims about the speed of their freezers, manufacturers argued over whether single, double, triple, or quadruple action produced the best ice cream. In a single-action design, such as Johnson's, only one component—usually the dasher—revolved. In a double-action model, such as the Gem manufactured by the American Machine Company, the cylinder moved in one direction while the dasher turned in the opposite direction. A trade catalog claimed that the Gem froze cream in one-half the time of a single-action freezer, and a cookbook writer advised, "If you use the Gem Ice Cream Freezer, it will take only 20 minutes to make the cream." An 1894 trade catalog bragged that one wholesaler had sold 3,000 Gems during the preceding summer. Wholesale prices for the Gem ranged from $1.15 for the two-quart model to $9.80 for an 18-quart freezer with a flywheel.[31]

The White Mountain Freezer Company marketed Sands' Patent Triple Motion Freezer, which had two dashers with lifter arms, or floats, that turned in opposite directions while the cylinder also rotated. In the triple-action Fre-zee-zee, the cylinder holding the cream turned to the right, an outer beater turned to the left, and an inner beater turned "within the outer beater and in the opposite direction."[32]

For many years, Shepard's Lightning was a popular model that was advertised as a quadruple-action freezer. The Lightning had two scrapers that continually cleaned the frozen cream off the inside wall of the cylinder and a triple-bladed wheel dasher that revolved on journal bearings when the cylinder turned.[33]

The American Twin Freezer was unusual because it featured a partitioned cylinder, enabling the cook to make two flavors of ice cream simultaneously. The cylinder, which was divided into two compartments, was moved back and forth by a rocking motion of the crank. The manufacturer claimed, "Outside of the special feature of making two flavors at one freezing, it is very much less tiresome than turning a crank round and round. One can sit back in a chair with freezer alongside and rock the crank to and fro without discomfort or undue exertion."[34]

J. Tingley of Philadelphia patented a horizontal freezer, mounted on a trestle, that essentially turned Johnson's design on its side. Known as Blatchley's Horizontal Ice Cream Freezer (Tingley's Patent), its large capacity made it attractive to restaurants, saloons, and wholesale plants. The manufacturer claimed that the horizontal design saved both time and labor, that the air-tight construction saved ice, that the parts were virtually unbreakable and rust-proof, and that the ice cream was "always perfectly free of any metallic taste." However, an ice cream wholesaler who used Blatchley's offered a different perspective. "[It] worked all right if the crank shaft fitted tightly and the top screwed down correctly, but generally there was a leak somewhere, the brine leaking into the can or the mix leaking out," he recalled.[35]

For making small quantities of ice cream, there were table-top freezers, like the Hoxie or the Jack Frost, which was a rectangular box with a cylinder inside. In the Jack Frost, the salted ice was packed into the cylinder, which was suspended in a pool of cream. As the cylinder was turned, the cream froze on its outside wall and was scraped off with a knife. At least two manufacturers made toy freezers that worked just like the big ones. According to a trade catalog, "They are not simply a plaything, but ice cream can be made in them precisely the same as in larger freezers. The can when full holds nearly a pint. . . . They serve not only as a toy for children, but are a great convenience when a small amount of ice cream is wanted in the sick room or for invalids."[36]

Since some cooks continued to prefer the pot freezer method, a few manufacturers attempted to update the concept. Cordley and Hayes of New York marketed the Easy Freezer, promising "no crank-turning, no back-breaking, no time lost." Even though it looked suspiciously like a pot freezer, the manufacturer averred,

The Easy Freezer works on an entirely new principle, is made of an entirely new material, and produces ice cream as smooth as by crank-turning. The material is indurated fibre, which holds the cold; the principle is "let it freeze," but there's a mathematical calculation of diameters back of it all which renders the result absolute.[37]

Hand-cranked, patent freezers were virtually foolproof as long as the operator followed a few simple precautions, such as making sure that no salt seeped into the cylinder holding the cream mixture. Although it was easy to turn the crank quickly at the outset, manufacturers advised cooks to use a slow, even speed. "Too much speed is often injurious to the cream, and is liable to churn it into butter, or make it coarse," warned one confectioner. But most homemakers had no trouble using the patent freezers, causing the authors of *The American Woman's Home,* to lament, "There are more women who know how to make good cake than good bread—more who can furnish you with a good ice-cream than a well-cooked mutton chop."[38]

Due to the obvious advantages of the patent freezers, the public in general enthusiastically welcomed them. "The process of freezing is very much simplified by the patent freezers, which have recently come into use," was a typical sentiment.[39] Nevertheless, as the following paragraph from a cookbook shows, some people championed the old-fashioned way:

After having tried many new and patent freezers, some of the best housekeepers have come to the conclusion that the old-fashioned freezer is the best. It is well, however, to keep a patent freezer on hand, in case of your wanting ice cream on short notice; but for common use an old-fashioned one is the best, especially as servants are apt to get a patent freezer out of order.[40]

Despite this author's preference for the pot freezer, most people who have eaten ice cream made in a hand-cranked freezer, whatever the type or model, say that it was the best they ever ate. The following reminiscence is typical of the rhapsodic memories many people have of homemade, hand-cranked ice cream. Although the writer does not give the reader many details about his youth, it is obvious that he grew up on a farm around the turn-of-the-century. Making ice cream was an event that he anticipated eagerly and remembered vividly because it happened only two or three times each summer. The process, from watching his mother make the custard to the ritual licking of the wood dasher, was one of the perennial joys of summer.

To have ice cream was never a matter of caprice. Forethought was essential, and physical exertion. It was generally recognized that if mother made the custard, that was her share of the labor. The men of the household had to get the ice from the icehouse, chopping the cake out of its deep frostily steaming bed in the straw, carrying it down the ladder and cracking it up fine. They brought coarse cattle salt from the barn and made the freezing mixture. But the rest of the work was for the younger generation—each member had to stand his trick at the freezer, and how long it took! Turning in the morning, with the funny paper to help; turning in the forenoon, while everybody was at church; making the last slow, weary yet thrilling revolutions. . . . And then at last the reward, worth almost any travail, of licking off that delicious, thickly dripping wooden frame and of thinking about saucersful still to come![41]

Given the popularity of ice cream, it is not surprising that it was often the highlight of summer social events, such as the June festival or strawberry social, a tradition in many small towns. The culinary stars of these festivals were strawberry shortcake and strawberry ice cream on top of angel cake covered with strawberry sauce. Local farmers supplied the lush strawberries and rich cream that went into the hand-cranked freezer. As the handle grew harder to turn, the children hovered around the ice cream maker, awaiting the grand ceremony of licking the dasher. The lucky ones were allowed to taste a sample directly from the freezer before it was carried to the cellar or icehouse to ripen. At the social, a dime bought a serving of cake and ice cream while strawberry sauce poured on top cost another five cents. More than likely, the money was used to repair the church or pay the preacher, who offered up a prayer of thanks for the Lord's bounty and the good women who had cooked it.[42]

The Natural Ice Harvest

The growth of the natural ice industry in the United States was crucial in making ice cream a treat for the masses. Without a reliable, reasonably priced refrigerant, ice cream would have remained an expensive luxury and the soul-soothing satisfaction of licking homemade ice cream off the dasher would have been denied to countless children.

Although the details are sketchy, it is obvious that Americans began to harvest and store ice at a very early date. Excavations of ruins at Jamestown, Virginia, have uncovered pits that were undoubtedly used for preserving ice. In 1665, the English crown renewed a patent originally issued to Sir William Berkeley by Charles I, who had ruled from 1625 to 1649. The renewal gave Berkeley the right "to gather, make and take snow and ice . . . and to preserve and keep the same in such pits, caves and cool places as he should think fit." However, the patent prohibited Berkeley and his business associates from interfering with the right of "the king's loving subjects" to make and preserve snow and ice for their own personal use.[43]

Since the first artificial ice-making plant in the United States would not open for another 200 years, it is questionable exactly what the right to make ice entailed. In some locations, ice was made by leaving clay pans filled with water outside on cool nights, when the temperature would drop low enough to form a layer of ice on top. In the early morning, before the sun could melt it, this ice would be removed from the pans and transferred to a cool place for storage. It is probable that Berkeley's patent referred to a primitive ice-making process similar to this.[44]

Many colonists, especially in the warmer climates where food spoiled quickly, recognized the need for preserving winter's natural refrigerants for summer use. The first storage facilities were caves and pits covered with an insulating material, such as straw. Colonists also experimented with storing ice and snow in underground cellars, but they lost a great deal due to melting and inadequate drainage. A process of trial-and-error led to the conclusion that icehouses, designed to provide proper drainage, were more efficient than cellars. Insulated double walls, insulated double or triple ceilings, and stone floors proved to be popular features in icehouse design.

The problems George Washington encountered in preserving ice and snow at Mount Vernon illustrate the frustrations of many landowners. In June 1784, in a postscript to a letter written to Robert Morris, Washington asked for the specifications of Morris's icehouse, after complaining that his own supply of mostly snow and a little ice, harvested during the winter, had already melted.

In a return letter, Morris gave a precise description of his stone icehouse and recommended building one into the side of a hill. He stressed the importance of insulation at the top and drainage at the bottom. He sympathized with Washington because he, too, had tried to store snow one year and had lost it in June. However, he had been more successful in preserving ice, which normally lasted until October or November.

Entries in Washington's diaries reveal that in January 1785 he transported ice from a nearby river and stored it in a cellar and a dry well. On June 5, he opened the cellar, "but there was not the smallest particle remaining." Fortunately, most of the ice remained in the dry well. In late autumn of that same year, Washington supervised the building of an icehouse at Mount Vernon, and in January 1786 he harvested ice for storage there.[45]

While many landowners, like Washington, built small icehouses on their property, some families banded together to harvest ice and store it in communal buildings. In Philadelphia, a group of families shared a communal icehouse as early as the 1790s. In small towns and rural areas, homeowners were likely to have individual icehouses, but they often made harvesting a community endeavor. Like a corn husking or a quilting bee, it was an occasion for neighbors to socialize while they worked together. Because ice harvesting was hard work and involved a certain amount of danger, with men and horses sometimes falling through the ice, cooperation lightened the load.[46]

People residing in cooler climates seemingly felt less need for ice, and family icehouses were rare in New England, even among the wealthy landowners. According to one history of Boston, an icehouse was an "almost unknown luxury" there in the 18th century. Commenting on a Cambridge landowner who boasted both a greenhouse and an icehouse, the historian wrote, "Some thought a judgment would befall one who would thus attempt to thwart the designs of Providence by raising flowers under glass in winter, and keeping ice underground to cool the heat of summer." By the 19th century, ice was in greater demand in Boston, which had a commercial ice depot by 1806. The descendants of William Fletcher (1770–1853) claimed that he had been the first man to sell ice in the Massachusetts city.[47]

The extent of commercial ice trade in early America is unclear, but it is certain that many people consumed a great deal of the natural refrigerant. Ice was advertised for sale in Philadelphia newspapers as early as 1784. A Frenchman traveling in the United States in 1788 believed that the fashionable ladies of Philadelphia were susceptible to consumption because they danced too much and then drank iced water. In 1789, iced drinks were sold at Gray's Gardens in Philadelphia. Frenchmen visiting Philadelphia and Baltimore in the 1790s reported that Americans drank water with ice and that containers of ice were used to cool hotel rooms. In New York City, it was customary to serve rum punch over ice, which generally came from Collect Pond, a source of dubious purity since dead animals too large to be conveniently buried were dumped there.[48]

Isaac Weld, an Englishman who visited North America, was impressed by the widespread use of ice in Philadelphia. He wrote, "[M]eat can never be kept, but in an icehouse or a remarkable cold cellar, for one day, without being tainted. . . . Fish is never brought to market without being covered with lumps of ice. . . . Butter is brought to market likewise in ice, which they generally have in great plenty at every farm house; indeed it is almost considered as a necessary of life, in these low parts of the country."[49]

Ships leaving New York or Philadelphia for southern ports often ballasted with ice, but it is not known if such shipments were plentiful enough to provide a steady supply of ice in the South. In 1799, the brig *Favorite* transported a cargo of ice cut from a pond in New York to Charleston, South Carolina, where hotel owner Jeremiah Jessop sold ice commercially, as a sideline to his main business. A year later, ice was advertised for sale in an Alexandria, Virginia, newspaper.[50]

In 1801, an English traveler reported that he had stopped at "a tavern, where every luxury that money can purchase is to be obtained at a first summons; where the richest viands cover the table, and where ice cools the Madeira." Five years later, another Englishman wrote from Philadelphia, "Those who have never visited warm climates can scarcely conceive how pleasant the use of ice is . . . in the summer season."[51]

Hospitals were major consumers of ice because they needed to keep their patients, especially feverish ones, cool and comfortable in the summer. In Philadelphia, one of the first ice vendors was the Pennsylvania Hospital, which gathered ice from the Schuylkill River and sold the excess to the public as early as 1804. The Philadelphia House of Corrections also sold its excess ice, and New York Hospital boasted its own icehouse.[52]

In the early 1800s, a man named Turner Camac built icehouses in New Jersey to supply ice for transporting fish in wagons from the Jersey shore to Philadelphia. In 1811, Daniel George was engaged in the ice trade in Philadelphia, and Major Robert Wharton built a large icehouse there the following year, selling ice to families, a druggist who dispensed mineral water, and several confectioners who made ice cream.[53]

In 1803, Thomas Moore, a Maryland farmer, published *An Essay on the Most Eligible Construction of Ice-Houses, Also, a Description of the Newly Invented Machine called the Refrigerator.* Moore's treatise explained the basics of heat transfer and gave instructions for building an icehouse. He also described a refrigerator, or ice chest, that he used to carry his butter to market. Basically, it consisted of an oval cedar tub with an inner tin container and a cavity between the two vessels to hold ice. The vessels were covered with a wooden lid lined with cloth and rabbit skins for insulation. Moore reported that his butter brought a better price at market than the other farmers' because his refrigerator kept it harder.[54]

When Harriott Pinckney Horry visited Richmond, Virginia, she stayed with Mary Randolph, who owned a refrigerator—that is, a box inside a box with powdered-charcoal insulation between the walls. Every day an iceman delivered ice to Randolph's door to keep the contents of her refrigerator cold. The idea of a refrigerator was new to Horry, who both sketched the appliance and wrote a detailed description in her journal.[55]

In 1819, Ellen Wayles Randolph wrote that her grandfather, Thomas Jefferson, had a newfangled appliance "called a refrigerator." While the butler was ill, Jefferson insisted upon trying out the refrigerator and was rewarded with melted butter and warm wine. When the butler regained his health, he returned the butter to its proper place—a small box packed in snow.[56]

During Sarah Mytton Maury's visit to the United States, she was amazed at the widespread use of ice and at the reasonable price, which allowed even the middle class to use large quantities of it. She declared, "[O]f all the luxuries in America I most enjoyed the ice. . . . I found it a most refreshing practice to place several jugs of iced water in my bedroom during the great heats; the atmosphere became perceptibly cooled." She also extolled the revitalizing power of a cold drink after a walk or a dusty carriage ride and did not believe that drinking iced water was dangerous to one's health. "[M]any have died for yielding to the temptation," warned Frederick Marryat. Nevertheless, Maury found iced drinks to be such a pleasure that she wholeheartedly agreed with a friend who said, "Whenever you hear America abused, remember the ice."[57]

In the late 19th century, icemen carrying large chunks of ice on their backs were fixtures in America's cities—largely due to Frederic Tudor, the Yankee ice king. Tudor, who was born into a prominent Boston family, chose not to attend college but went to work in a shipping office while he was in his early teens and became involved in the spice trade. Following a voyage to the West Indies, he became convinced that there was a market for ice in the tropics. In the winter of 1806, he hired men to harvest ice from a pond near Boston and chartered a ship. Although his eventual goal was establishing a regular ice trade between Boston and Havana, Cuba, he decided that it would be better to begin with small ports. So he ordered the captain of his chartered brig to sail to the French island of Martinique.[58]

In March, Tudor reached Martinique with 130 tons of ice but could not procure a warehouse for his cargo. Frantically, he buttonholed the proprietor of the Tivoli Gardens, an eating and drinking establishment, and suggested that the man sell ice cream to his patrons. Although the owner insisted that ice cream could not be made in such a hot climate, Tudor was determined to try it and set to work freezing the cream. The first night, as word of the exotic treat spread like wildfire, the astonished proprietor sold more than three hundred dollars' worth of ice cream to curious customers. Although the proprietor had been skeptical at first, "after this he was humble as a mushroom," wrote Tudor.[59]

Despite the natives' enthusiastic acceptance of ice cream, Tudor lost a substantial amount of money on this venture. He was discouraged, but he was far from giving up. In his journal, he wrote, "He who gives back at the first repulse and without striking the second blow . . . has never been, is not and never will be a hero in love, war, or business."

Tudor returned to Boston convinced that he could profitably export ice if he could find a better way to pack and insulate his cargo. His experience in Martinique had also demonstrated the need for insulated warehouses to store his cargo once it reached its destination. While he was regrouping and planning his next step, Congress passed the 1807 Embargo Act in an effort to protect United States ships from involvement in the European wars. Tudor managed his father's farm and experimented with different types of insulation while American commercial shipping all but ceased.[60]

As soon as normalcy returned to the shipping industry, Tudor traveled to Cuba and persuaded the Spanish colonial government to grant him a monopoly to import ice for the next six years. Returning to Boston, he borrowed money to buy a ship and to purchase lumber to build a large icehouse in Cuba. Then he established a depot in Havana and began supplying the island city with ice. When the War of 1812 disrupted shipping, Tudor was jailed in Massachusetts because he was unable to pay the interest on his loan. He managed to gain his release and subsequently fled from Boston, "pursued by sheriffs to the very wharf." In Cuba, he reopened his depot, promoted the consumption of ice and ice cream, and watched sales climb gradually.[61]

When his business was well established in Cuba, Tudor sailed to Martinique and persuaded the government to give him a 10-year monopoly on ice imports. After returning to Boston, he purchased the rights to harvest many nearby lakes, including Thoreau's Walden Pond. He also continued his experiments with insulation, trying rice chaff, wheat, tan bark, coal dust, and pulverized cork before he hit upon the perfect material—pine sawdust. In addition to dramatically slowing evaporation, pine sawdust had the advantage of being a cheap, plentiful by-product of New England's numerous sawmills.[62]

Circa 1820, Tudor built an icehouse in Charleston, South Carolina, and began selling ice there. Soon he was shipping to other Southern cities, including Savannah and Mobile. Later, he would transport ice to South America, the East and West Indies, Persia, and India.[63]

Because Tudor realized that wider demand for ice increased his profits, he hired carpenters to build refrigerators, or ice chests, and promoted their use. He ordered his agents to aid in establishing businesses selling ice cream, and he told doctors about the therapeutic benefits of ice packs and cool liquids. He also broadcast handbills extolling the virtues of ice for preserving food and promoted the sale of carbonated water, which tasted better cold. He gave barkeepers free ice for up to one year if they agreed to sell iced drinks for the same price as warm ones, but some consumers were suspicious because they thought ice disguised bad liquor or diluted the effects of alcohol.[64]

Naturally, Tudor's success encouraged others to enter the ice business, and a major industry developed around natural ice. Ice from Maine was shipped to large cities along the Atlantic seaboard, including New York, Philadelphia, Baltimore, Savannah, and Washington, D.C. Ice from Boston was transported to domestic markets all the way from Philadelphia to Galveston, Texas. Harvests from Rockland Lake, the

Hudson River, Saratoga Lake, Lake George, and Lake Champlain were sold in New York City. Ice for major metropolitan areas in New Jersey came from lakes in the northern portion of that state. Baltimore consumed ice from the Susquehanna River as well as from the New England states.[65]

Lake Erie, Cleveland, Sandusky, and Toledo were hubs of the ice industry in northern Ohio. Cincinnati's ice came largely from nearby sources, including the Little Miami River, Mill Creek, and the Miami Canal. A significant portion of Chicago's supply came from a large man-made lake formed when speculators drilling for oil struck artesian waters. Chicago also bought ice from harvests on rivers and natural lakes in Indiana and Wisconsin as well as Illinois. Because Wisconsin's lakes produced an unusually clear, pure product, that state's ice was especially marketable and was sold as far south as Mississippi and Louisiana.[66]

San Francisco received its first shipment of ice from Alaska in July 1850, initiating a trade that flourished for many years. In addition, ice harvested from Lake Tahoe and the Truckee River was sold throughout California. It was hauled by rail to San Francisco and then loaded onto wooden-hulled schooners for the trip to San Diego. Isadore Louis, a Russian cobbler who became a prosperous entrepreneur, owned San Diego's first large icehouse. He has also been credited with introducing ice cream to that southern California city.[67]

New Orleans residents first bought ice from owners of Mississippi River flatboats, who packed it in hogsheads before heading South, and from ship captains, who used it as ballast. Then in 1819, John Blake and Richard Salmon petitioned the city council for permission to establish the first large-scale commercial icehouse in the Crescent City. In June of that year, a newspaper ad announced that a large shipment of ice had arrived from the North and was being sold on a subscription basis. For $5, each subscriber received tickets redeemable for a month's supply of ice, a pail for carrying the ice home, and a "cellarett" for storing several pounds of ice, food, and beverages. The advertisement declared that the attractive cellaretts were "designed to grace the parlors of the most fastidious." If the subscriber did not want a cellarett, the ice pails, wrapped in layers of flannel, could be used for storage.

Less than a month later, a second advertisement warned readers that subsequent ice shipments would be cancelled unless more subscribers were found. At the same time, Salmon announced that he had hired a cook to make ice cream. Apparently, the ice cream sold well because Salmon soon reported that a new shipment of ice would arrive in August. Exactly what happened after this is unclear. However, on December 31, the city council authorized the city attorney to take possession of the property where Blake and Salmon's icehouse was located.[68]

Tudor may have supplied Blake and Salmon's ice, although this is not certain. It is certain that Tudor regularly shipped ice to New Orleans during his heyday. Several sources state that, when the very first shipment of northern ice arrived in the Crescent City, the residents dumped it overboard because the mayor feared that it was contaminated and might cause an outbreak of consumption. At least one source states that this was Tudor's ice, but the date of the incident is unclear.[69]

The natural ice industry was a boon in areas where cold weather normally idled farmers, fishermen, and other seasonal workers. Many men were grateful for the extra money, and laborers often traveled long distances for a few weeks' work. The job required minimal skills, a stout back, and a willingness to work long hours under harsh conditions. Young boys were usually hired for the most odious task, following behind the horses to clean up the droppings.

Ice harvesting was a simple operation that required a lot of man- and horse-power. It began when the ice was 6 to 36 inches thick, depending on the geographical location and the weather conditions. First, the ice was scraped to remove the snow and, if necessary, planed to give it a level surface. Holes were bored to test the thickness and to allow any standing water to run off. Using an implement resembling a farming plow, the ice field was divided into large squares until it had the appearance of a giant checkerboard. This plow, which had a row of progressively longer cutting teeth running from front to back, was drawn by a horse and grooved the ice down to a depth of about 3 inches. Normally, squares 22 x 22 inches were preferred, but larger sizes were standard in some markets, especially when the ice was thin.

A second plow, with longer teeth, was driven back and forth along the grooves, deepening them, until the squares could easily be detached with hand tools, such as a saw, a chisel, or a breaking-off bar. The first squares that were removed cleared a wide channel to the warehouse. Then large sections of squares, called rafts, were broken off and floated to the icehouse. In some cases, a worker would stand on the raft and guide it, using a float hook, a long pole with a spike on one side for pushing and a hook on the other for pulling. Sometimes other men would be stationed along the channel with ice hooks to assist the rafter. In other cases, a horse or a team would tow the rafts to the icehouse. On rivers, harvesters liked to cut ice above the warehouse, in order to gain the advantage of going with the flow in floating it to the storage site.

When the rafts arrived at the icehouse, they were separated into smaller sections and pushed or pulled along an inclined plane to the entrance. Normally, the door or entranceway stretched from the ground all the way to the ceiling of the warehouse. When a layer of ice had been laid down, that part of the entranceway was boarded up and another layer was started. When the industry was in its infancy, pulleys powered by a horse were used to hoist the ice above the level of the inclined plane into the icehouse; later, the horse was replaced by a steam engine.[70]

When the ice harvesting industry was in its heyday, enormous icehouses, each holding 10,000 to 90,000 tons of ice and painted a glaring white to reflect the sun, dotted the banks of many Northern lakes and rivers. At one time, the state of Maine alone boasted 244 large icehouses. It was customary to store ice near the harvest site in the winter and move it as needed via ships, barges, or trains during the warmer months. At the destination site, it would normally be stored in another warehouse until it was needed. According to industry statistics, ice usage grew dramatically from 1806 until 1886, when the United States natural ice harvest peaked at 25 million tons. The magnitude of the retail ice business is illustrated by the fact that more than 1,500 ice wagons regularly serviced customers in Brooklyn and New York City in 1895.[71]

A refrigerator was a curiosity in the early 1800s, but iceboxes were commonplace by the end of the century. Each day the late-19th-century housewife placed a card in her front window to tell the iceman how many pounds she needed. Some homeowners added a small back porch onto the house just for the icebox, so the iceman could deliver the daily supply even if no one was home. In that simpler, gentler era, the homemaker left the money to pay for the delivery on top of the icebox, without worrying that someone would steal it. The iceman was a familiar, and generally trusted, figure in the neighborhood, even though he was often a character in ribald jokes. Prosperous ice dealers prided themselves upon their handsome delivery wagons and the appearance of their uniformed drivers.

As the 20th century approached, ice harvesters conserved winter's bounty, the natural ice industry prospered, and the ice barons luxuriated in their wealth. Despite the opening of artificial ice plants in at least 20 United States cities, the natural ice industry seemed invincible. Industry executives declared that artificial ice was both impure and too expensive. Even though natural ice was sometimes contaminated with industrial waste, sewage, or horse manure, industry trade associations had the chutzpah to attack artificial ice as being unsanitary. Moreover, natural ice advocates confidently declared that the cost of manufacturing artificial ice precluded the possibility that it could ever successfully compete with nature.[72]

However, even the ice barons had to admit that artificial ice had one distinct advantage over the natural refrigerant—consistency of supply. The occasional mild winter was disastrous for the natural ice industry. Moderate temperatures in 1895 resulted in a famine for ice harvesters, and prices soared to unprecedented heights. The winter of 1906 was even worse, because less than half of the normal crop was harvested in many regions and none was cut in others. Only seven years later, many ice cream plants had to close due to a scarcity of natural ice.[73]

As the technology for producing artificial ice improved, its benefits could not be denied. Even some of the large natural ice firms, such as the Knickerbocker Ice Company of Philadelphia, opened artificial ice plants. Meanwhile, others attempted to improve their productivity by replacing horses and hand tools with gasoline-powered equipment. By 1911, the United States boasted nearly 2,000 artificial ice plants serving the general market, in addition to the dedicated plants that supplied meat packers, breweries, and other businesses requiring large quantities of ice.[74] As mechanical refrigeration became more efficient, technology inevitably replaced natural ice in industrial applications, including ice cream manufacturing, until it was taken for granted. Although the ice cream industry as a whole was slow to modernize, wholesalers gradually converted their plants to circulating brine and then to ammonia refrigeration.

It was only a matter of time until ice harvesting was a forgotten skill and empty icehouses decayed along the riverbanks.

3

Wholesalers and Heavyweights:
1850–1900

The Surplus Cream Problem

In the second half of the 19th century, the ice cream industry grew in a new direction as wholesalers entered the business. The traditional ice cream makers who produced small quantities, such as the confectioners, were threatened by the advent of the wholesalers who operated on a larger scale. The bulk manufacturers experimented with new ingredients, and consumers enjoyed new flavors. Children on city streets ran after the hokey-pokey man to spend their pennies on the cheap ice cream he sold from a cart or wheelbarrow. Proper hostesses served ice cream for afternoon teas and ladies' luncheons. Ice cream sodas, milk shakes, and sundaes became the rage at soda fountains. Per capita consumption soared as nearly everybody ate ice cream.

Jacob Fussell, a dairyman in Baltimore, is generally acknowledged to be the father of the wholesale ice cream industry in the United States. Fussell (rhymes with "muscle") was born February 24, 1819, at Little Falls in Harford County, Maryland. He came from a clan of Quaker farmers and tradesmen tracing their lineage back to Solomon Fussell, who had migrated to the colonies from Yorkshire County, England, nearly a century before Jacob's birth.

As a teenager, Jacob Fussell was apprenticed to a stove fitter. After completing his training and failing in his efforts to establish his own stove business, Fussell was given an opportunity to go into the dairy business. One of Fussell's acquaintances, an older Quaker, had loaned money to a dairyman/ice cream caterer, who had defaulted on the debt. The elder Quaker had no desire to operate a dairy business, but he did not want to lose his money either. So he asked Fussell to run it, and the arrangement worked out profitably for both men.[1]

In 1851, Fussell was servicing milk routes in Baltimore, selling dairy products from farms in York County, Pennsylvania. Then, as now, "country fresh" products were popular because they were perceived as pure and healthy. In American cities, public awareness of the dangers

51

of inferior dairy products had created a demand for unadulterated milk. In New York City, reformer Robert Hartley exposed the health threat posed by milk from urban swill dairies, where cattle were confined in stables, fed distillery slops, and rarely, if ever, grazed on grass. A subsequent investigation by the New York Academy of Medicine revealed that swill milk was a significant factor in the high infant mortality rate in that city. Other municipalities had similar problems with their milk supplies. In Boston, for example, an inquiry proved that virtually all dairy dealers routinely sold adulterated milk. Many watered down their milk and added cornmeal, chalk, or plaster of Paris to improve the color.[2]

Astute urban dairymen, taking advantage of two expanding industries—natural ice and railways—advertised that their products were shipped into the city each morning directly from the farm. Fussell received his merchandise from dairy farms located near the Northern Central Railroad in Pennsylvania. Every day, hundreds of cans of milk were shipped to Baltimore from Seven Valleys, Larue, Hanover Junction, Glen Rock, and other small towns along the line. Before daylight, scores of dairy farmers drove their wagons filled with heavy milk cans to the station, where the railroad agent tagged each can and loaded it onto the 5 A.M. train for Baltimore.[3]

A few of Fussell's customers also bought cream, but both the demand and the supply were unpredictable. Fussell found that enough cream for one day was too much for another, and disposing of surplus cream became a major problem for him. Fortunately, his recent experience with ice cream catering suggested a solution. He decided that he could make a profit if he turned the surplus into ice cream and sold it for significantly less than the prevailing retail price of 60 cents per quart. Accordingly, he advertised himself as a "country produce dealer" selling "ice cream at 25 cts. per quart, delivered in moulds or otherwise, day or night."[4]

In the beginning, Fussell faced a dilemma that has confronted many manufacturers: whether goods should be produced where they will be sold or where the raw materials are generated. Since preventing ice cream from melting was a problem in the days before mechanical refrigeration, producing it at the point of sale seemed like a good idea. However, the raw materials were also perishable and were cheaper in rural areas.

After consideration, Fussell decided to manufacture his ice cream in Seven Valleys (sometimes called Sevenvalley). In the winter of 1851–52, he traveled to the small Pennsylvania town, built and equipped a factory, and filled an icehouse for the coming summer. For the next two years, Fussell's ice cream was manufactured in Seven Valleys, packed in ice, and shipped, via train, to Baltimore. According to one account, Fussell began his venture using two dishpans to make ice cream by the pot freezer method, producing only two quarts per day. However, another source states that he used a patent freezer with a flywheel.[5]

Although Fussell was able to produce his ice cream more cheaply in Seven Valleys than in Baltimore, he found it difficult to supervise sales and deliveries in the city while simultaneously running the factory in Pennsylvania. Moreover, the weather sometimes caused a supply-and-demand problem. Ice cream sales were very seasonal, with the vast majority of the demand in the summer. Even a few days of cool weather could severely reduce orders. Since communications between Baltimore and Seven Valleys were slow, Fussell was sometimes left with an oversupply in the city because the plant, which had no way of knowing that the ice cream was selling slowly, shipped too much. Likewise, Fussell had no way of increasing a day's output to meet an unexpected rise in demand.[6]

After two summers, Fussell decided to abandon the Pennsylvania plant and manufacture his product in Baltimore. However, that was not the end of the ice cream industry in Seven Valleys, because the farmers had learned that making ice cream could be lucrative. A local resident—probably Daniel Henry, a flour miller who had an icehouse on his property—took up where Fussell left off, continuing to operate an ice cream plant and shipping most of the output to Baltimore via railroad. For many years, "there was hardly a train running south on the Northern Central that did not carry the familiar green tubs of Seven Valleys' ice cream."[7]

Daniel's grandson David Henry and Winfield Bott operated the Seven Valleys ice cream business immediately after the Civil War. By 1870, Henry had purchased Bott's share of this business, which he later turned over to his son-in-law, Noah Lau. The Bott family opened their own ice cream plant, the Seven Valley Steam Ice Cream Manufactory. A third manufacturer, Benjamin Klinedinst, also shipped ice cream from Seven Valleys to Baltimore. For one Independence Day, Lau and Klinedinst pushed their manufacturing capacity to the limit, loading three railroad boxcars with ice cream headed for the Maryland city. The Seven Valleys ice cream industry prospered until the advent of mechanical refrigeration.[8]

In 1856, Fussell left a partner in charge of his Baltimore operations and opened a factory in Washington, D.C. During the Civil War, army sutlers were eager to buy his entire Washington output for resale to the troops. Despite his devotion to the Northern cause, he refused to sell to them because he knew that the civilian trade would be more reliable in the long run.[9]

During this period in his life, Fussell was active in politics and the antislavery movement. Although he was normally soft-spoken, he was a radical Abolitionist who made impassioned speeches that stirred strong emotions in his listeners. Following one of his inflammatory public addresses, an irate lynch mob charged through the front door of his office while he hustled out the back door just ahead of the pack.[10]

This political activism contrasted sharply with Fussell's quiet home life, where he enjoyed telling stories to his children and playing chess or checkers. He had five children with his first wife, Anna Elizabeth Taylor, a cousin of author Bayard Taylor. Caroline Krafft, who married the widowed Fussell in 1864, bore three children and outlived him by nearly a quarter-century. Although Fussell kept a daily record of every penny he spent and had a reputation for frugality, his family lived well and he gave freely to charities. Following the Civil War, he financed Fussell Court, a housing project with brick residences for newly freed slaves.[11]

Having prospered in both Baltimore and Washington, Fussell decided to expand his operations northward and opened a business in Boston in 1862. His success soon came to the attention of Tudor & Company, the shipping concern owned by Yankee ice king Frederic Tudor. The natural ice exporting business was in full swing in Boston, and Tudor's company saw an opportunity to expand its trade in South America by opening an ice cream manufacturing plant in Brazil. Tudor offered Fussell unlimited capital to start a business in Brazil, but the ice cream entrepreneur was not willing to "depart from a land where dollars were plenty and yellow fever unknown."

Tudor persisted, asking Fussell if he had a young man in his employ who might go to Brazil. But Fussell had no such employee and was, in fact, looking for a younger man to run his Boston business because he planned to move on to New York City. So the ice king tried another tactic, asking Fussell to train a Tudor employee to go to Brazil. Fussell agreed to do so for the princely fee of $500. The man was chosen and with only a few hours' instruction was pronounced ready to make ice cream. At that point, Fussell felt that he had fulfilled his part of the bargain and played no further role in the project. (The Tudor employee may have been Osgood Carney, who was the supercargo of the barque *Madagascar,* which took Tudor's first shipment to Rio de Janeiro. Tudor instructed Carney to build an icehouse and establish an ice cream business in the Brazilian capital.)

In 1863, Fussell moved to New York City and started a business on Fourth Avenue near Twenty-third Street, becoming the first major ice cream wholesaler in the metropolis. Shortly after he opened his plant, a committee from the Associated Confectioners of New York came to his office, demanding that he sign an agreement to fix prices. Fussell refused to sign, even though it angered the confectioners, who threatened to force him out of business. Despite their animosity, Fussell's New York trade prospered.[12]

Circa 1870, in order to expand his New York City operations, Fussell took in three partners—Stephen Dunnington, Nathaniel V. Woodhill, and James Madison Horton. Operating as Jacob Fussell and Company, this firm sold ice cream for $1.00 per gallon to hotels, festivals, and other customers ordering quantities of five gallons or more. Smaller quantities cost $1.20 per gallon. The firm's pricing policy stipulated that "while there must be no discounts, no donations or no subterfuge used to gain customers," special terms were permissible for church fairs and other charitable ventures.[13]

Eventually, Horton bought out the other partners and changed the firm's name to J.M. Horton Ice Cream Company. Meanwhile, Fussell's son operated an ice cream plant under the family name and competed with Horton for many years. In 1893, Horton claimed that he sold three-fifths of all the ice cream consumed in New York City. Two years later, he employed 250 workers and owned 250 wagons.

Horton's business grew rapidly, supplying transatlantic ocean liners and railroad dining cars as well as many public festivals and private social events in New York City. On Christmas Day, 1891, the steamer *Hamburg American Packet* left New York for an around-the-world voyage with 1,000 bricks of Horton ice cream in its cold hold. Five years later, a New York newspaper reported that all steamers leaving the city for Europe or the Southern and West Indian ports carried a supply of ice cream. Each steamer had a special refrigerator, a large double-walled wooden box lined with zinc, that held several hundred one-quart bricks of ice cream. A mixture of cracked ice and salt kept the ice cream frozen for weeks.[14]

After Fussell sold his business to Horton, he decided to return to Washington to live. However, his second wife preferred New York City and refused to move with him. Although the couple never legally separated and the family claimed that there was never a serious quarrel, Fussell deeded his New York residence to his wife and returned to Washington alone. When he died at the ripe old age of 93, he was living in Washington and his will was probated there. Nevertheless, the State of New York felt that at least part of Fussell's considerable estate should be subject to death taxes in the Empire State. Court papers related to the tax matter revealed that Fussell had visited New York only twice after he moved to Washington—once to vote and once for a Thanksgiving dinner. He preferred to live among "the friends of his youth . . . and only few of his friends ever journeyed farther from their home than the Capital City."[15]

The Pioneers

After the Civil War, the number of ice cream wholesalers increased dramatically. They came from diverse backgrounds; some were experienced businessmen; others had no particular expertise; but they all shared an entrepreneurial spirit. Some ice cream ventures began as a natural sideline for companies already in the ice or dairy business. Others started from scratch. The new manufacturers built an industry by trial and error and watched wholesale ice cream output climb to more than five million gallons in 1899.[16]

Jacob Fussell taught the business to a number of men, including Perry Brazelton, who opened three ice cream plants in the Midwest. On a trip west, Fussell stopped in Mount Pleasant, Iowa, and went to the local bank to transact some business. There he met Brazelton, the town banker, and the two immediately formed a strong friendship. After Brazelton lost his personal fortune in the Panic of 1857, he traveled east looking for a new job and spent the winter with his friend Fussell. Brazelton observed Fussell's business operations and learned to make ice cream. In the spring, he moved to St. Louis, where he established his first ice cream plant. When he was offered a good price for this business, he sold it for a substantial profit and went to Cincinnati, where he repeated the process. Then he moved to Chicago, where he opened another ice cream plant. The Great Fire of 1871 destroyed his building, but Brazelton was back in business within three weeks.[17]

In 1866, as the United States began to recover from the Civil War, William Breyer started a business in Philadelphia, hand-cranking ice cream in his kitchen and selling it to his neighbors. Demand grew quickly, and in only a few months he was traveling the streets of Philadelphia in a horse-drawn wagon, delivering his ice cream to an expanding clientele. Before his death in 1882, he had opened six retail stores, producing ice cream for all of them in his back room and transporting it in a wagon pulled by Old Peacock, a white horse familiar to many Philadelphians. After Breyer's demise, his wife and sons continued the business and in 1896 opened Breyer's first large manufacturing plant.[18]

Lawrence, Kansas, became the site of that state's first wholesale ice cream plant immediately after the Civil War, when A.M. Field opened for business. Only two years later, in 1868, William Weideman followed Field's lead, establishing his factory in the same town. Weideman shipped ice cream to Topeka, which did not have its own wholesale plant until 1882, when Henry C. Scott went into the business. That same year, Nicholas Steffen, who was in the bakery and confectionery business, started producing ice cream on a commercial scale in Wichita. In 1889, the firm of Steffen & Bretch was formed and began shipping ice cream to nearby towns. By 1902, the company was shipping its products as far as Fort Worth, Texas, and Roswell, New Mexico.[19]

The experience of Frank M. Wright of Manteno, Illinois, was in many ways typical of the dairymen who diversified into ice cream manufacturing. The Wright family owned about 150 cows and shipped the milk to Chicago. When the price of milk dropped, the family made cheese and butter, which was sold in Chicago and New Orleans. Later, Wright learned how to make ice cream from a Chicago wholesaler who bought sweet cream from him. Then Wright began manufacturing his own ice cream, selling it along the Illinois Central and the Big Four railroads. He was so successful that he subsequently opened factories in Kankakee, Paxton, Champaign, Mattoon, and Gibson City.[20]

As the number of wholesalers proliferated, they began to make substantial inroads into the confectioners' markets. It was only natural that the confectioners viewed their new competitors with both trepidation and contempt. Many deprecated the competition by claiming that the wholesalers were selling mostly fluff because they whipped too much air into their cream. Moreover, confectioners tried to scare consumers by telling them that the factories used suspect chemical flavorings. The following letter of advice to a young confectioner, printed in a trade magazine, catches the flavor of the confectioners' reaction:

Your whole aim and effort, as a beginner, should be to make an honest article, pure and unadulterated, as to ingredients; and a quart for a quart, not a sham puffed-up article with no soul or body in it. People don't want to pay for atmospheric air instead of ice cream. My advice is for you to let the slop-shop, cheap-John factorymen's processes severely alone; do not try to make the fradulent and depraved wares of the factories . . . which are no creams but only frothy, watery slop and slush and still viler "flavorings," whose make-up is only known to the devil's chemical emissaries.[21]

Although many wholesalers were experimenting with new ingredients and formulas, the confectioners' criticism was too harsh. Most wholesalers were producing a good product for a reasonable price, even if they did modify traditional recipes. Nevertheless, purists decried the wholesalers' use of condensed milk, corn starch, colorings, egg yolks, gelatin, and packaged flavorings. Moreover, most wholesalers sold ice cream with a lower butterfat content than that in traditional recipes, and their product was fluffier, causing some consumers to complain that they felt like they were eating air.[22]

For wholesalers, the most popular flavor was vanilla, but some also produced chocolate or fruit flavors, using either fresh fruits or extracts. Albert D. Sidwell, a wholesale pioneer in Iowa, remembered making only three flavors:

The flavor used in the earlier years was just vanilla and was secured by the purchase of the vanilla bean and putting the powder direct from the bean into the cream. The use of the powder in this form made the ice cream show up all full of specks, and people thought there was dirt in it. However, that was the best we had, so it was used until a satisfactory vanilla oil was discovered. This was about the only flavor used, except a fresh peach or strawberry in season.[23]

Most manufacturers followed standardized formulas but varied their mixes a little from day to day, depending on the availability of raw ingredients. The following recipes were used in George Schmid's factory in Jersey City, New Jersey:

About 10 quarts of pure cream, 10 quarts of milk, and about eight pounds of sugar (granulated) are first mixed together. If the ice cream is to be flavored with strawberry, about six to eight drops of pure red coloring and one-fourth pint of essence of strawberry is added. A quantity of gelatine dissolved in about a quart of warm water is then added to this. . . . Chocolate ice cream is made by dissolving about one and one-fourth pounds of chocolate cakes into about one quart of hot water, which is added to the milk and cream in the same manner. For vanilla flavoring about one-half pint of the extract is used for a can containing 40 quarts of ice cream.[24]

While wholesalers generally took pride in producing pure ice cream that was not watered down and contained no fillers, a few were not so scrupulous, as is evident from the recollections of a Milwaukee manufacturer:

During the first season that I made ice cream, which was a summer business entirely at that time, we would start with enough material on hand to make 200 gallons of ice cream. If it turned out to be particularly hot and we found that 200 gallons would not be enough, we used to do what was then known as "stretching" the mix. The elasticity in the mix was provided by water. . . . The mix was never standardized and we used whatever material we happened to have.[25]

Then, as now, vanilla was the top-selling flavor by an overwhelming margin. The vanilla bean that is most desirable commercially is a member of the orchid family, is native to Mexico, and grows on the *Vanilla planifolia*, a perennial climbing plant that reaches 100 feet or more in height. The Aztecs believed that vanilla gave them strength, prevented fever, and eliminated fatigue. Early in the 16th century, a European explorer discovered the plant and reported his findings. Subsequently, European physicians endorsed it as a stimulant, an aphrodisiac, an antidote for poisons, and a flavoring agent for bitter medicines.[26]

After a *Vanilla planifolia* flower has been pollinated, two months are required for the pods to reach full growth, and another seven to ten months must elapse before the beans are ripe enough to pick. The vanilla bean is an odorless, tasteless pod that must be "cured" before it is used for cooking. In Mexico, the traditional method of curing the beans was a time-consuming process requiring a great deal of patience. First, the pods were placed on blankets and exposed to the sun during daylight hours. Soon the pods began to darken and wrinkle. In a week or two, they reached a dark brown or nearly black hue, had a strong aroma, and were pliable even though they had a tough and leathery texture. Then came perhaps the most important step in the process—the drying, which required from six to ten weeks. When fully dried, the pods were tied in bundles and carefully packed to preserve the flavor and protect them during shipment.[27]

During the 19th century, the price of vanilla fluctuated from high to outrageous because the crop was unpredictable. Efforts to transplant and cultivate the *Vanilla planifolia* failed until botanists discovered that it could be successfully cultivated if pollinated by hand, a delicate operation in which a small stick or sliver of bamboo was used to raise the stigma and press the pollen out of the anther. Then the plant had to be constantly nurtured, and the pods had to be painstakingly picked because carelessness could damage a pod or destroy immature ones. Although cultivating vanilla was a tedious, labor-intensive chore, the use of slaves made it lucrative for planters in the West Indies, Madagascar, Reunion, and Mauritius.[28]

Jefferson's preference for vanilla ice cream and the sale of vanilla at the pleasure gardens indicate that the flavoring was well on its way to becoming an American favorite by 1800. By the 1840s, vanilla was commonly available in United States cities, even though the price was often very high. In 1886, a grocer's trade publication noted, "It is the most perplexing of all products to deal with, being so easily liable to injury. It is kept in vaults prepared for the purpose, but these must not be below the surface of the ground, otherwise the bean will become mouldy and spoiled by moisture; neither will it answer to store it in upper chambers, for in that case a sort of dry rot will attack it. It must be watched and tended like a baby."[29]

Due to the high cost of chocolate, it was used sparingly by wholesale ice cream manufacturers. *Theobroma cacao*, the cocoa tree, is a native of the dense tropical forests of the Amazon and thrives only in very hot, humid climates. The Mayans and Aztecs cultivated cocoa long before its introduction to Europe. Montezuma consumed up to 50 jars per day of a concoction called *chocolatl*. Because the Aztecs believed that the cocoa tree was of divine origin, the scientific name *theobrama* means "food of the gods." The tree's melon-like fruits change from green to yellow-orange or purple-red when ripe, giving it the appearance of a gaudy Christmas tree. The fruit contains a pinkish pulp with pale purple-pink beans arranged in a column around the central core.[30]

Columbus took some cocoa beans home to Europe but only as a curiosity. Don Hernando Cortes, who was the first European to recognize cocoa's commercial value, sent beans back to Spain along with instructions on cooking them. Although the Spanish tried to keep chocolate as their own secret treat, its use had spread throughout Western Europe by the mid-1600s. Across the Atlantic Ocean, advertisements for chocolate appeared in newspapers in Charleston in 1747, Annapolis in 1749, and New York in 1758. In 1772, a Philadelphia newspaper advertised for sale an "almost new" commercial chocolate mill with everything needed "for carrying on the chocolate-making business." Six such factories were operational in the City of Brotherly Love around the end of the 18th century.[31]

Despite the abundance of chocolate in America, very little was used to flavor ice cream. Most went into chocolate drinks until the mid-19th century, when chocolate candy gained favor with the general public. After the Civil War, the American market for chocolate expanded tremendously. In 1868, a New York City guidebook noted that street vendors sold all kinds of chocolate candies. By 1891, the Baker factory in Dorchester, Massachusetts, was producing five tons of pure chocolate daily, marketing both powdered cocoa and solid chocolate that could be grated, shaved, or cut up for cooking.[32]

Although vanilla and chocolate prices remained high, there was good news for wholesalers regarding sugar. In the early 19th century, white sugar was expensive because refining it to remove its natural brown color and strong taste was difficult and time-consuming. Since most of the United States' sugar was imported from the West Indies, tariffs added to the price. Gradually, the supply increased as cultivation expanded in the West Indies, South America, and the southern United States. Largely due to slave labor and the use of steam-powered machinery in the refining process, sugar prices dropped and consumption rose. In the late 1850s, United States companies began using centrifugal machines to produce soft, granulated sugar, which eliminated the need to pulverize it for ice cream.

Producing a stable, uniform ice cream was a problem for wholesalers making large quantities. It was sometimes said that "the top of the can of ice cream is bad, the middle lovely, and the bottom terrible." Cornstarch was commonly used to stiffen the mixture and give it body, but it was not the only additive wholesalers tried. Some manufacturers experimented with adding egg whites to their mixes, although the whites had a tendency to make the texture tough and rubbery. Moreover, they were too expensive.[33]

Circa 1880, the Thomas W. Dunn Company, which was in the business of selling gelatin, had an overstock because the United States government had recently prohibited the use of the stabilizer in oleomargarine. One hot summer day, Dunn stopped at a little Greek ice cream parlor to have a dish. When he saw the melting ice cream on his plate, he was struck by a sudden inspiration. Soon he was selling gelatin to ice cream manufacturers as a stabilizer for their products, although many were secretive about using it because it had a dubious reputation. After gelatin received government approval as a food in 1906, its use became even more prevalent in wholesale ice cream.[34]

In the latter half of the 19th century, many wholesalers also regularly added condensed milk to their mix as a substitute for raw milk or cream. Although some confectioners criticized this practice, Gail Borden's preserved milk was actually safer than fresh dairy products since pasteurization was still a generation away.

In 1851, Borden was returning to the United States from the London World's Fair. While pacing the deck of the ship, he became aware of two annoying sounds—the feeble lowing of seasick cows in the hold and the wailing of hungry babies in steerage. He angrily demanded that the captain do something about the situation. But the sailor merely reminded him that seasick cows gave no milk and preserved milk was not palatable—hence, the hungry, crying infants. Borden, who was an inventor and entrepreneur—albeit an impecunious one—decided then and there to find a way to preserve milk.

When the widowed Borden arrived in New York, he sent his four children to live in a Shaker colony in upstate Lebanon while he rented a cellar in Brooklyn. His early experiments with milk produced nothing drinkable. Then, while visiting his children, he observed the Shakers boiling fruit preserves in a vacuum pan, a spherical tank from which most of the air had been pumped. This led him to an exciting discovery: in a vacuum pan, milk boiled at a substantially lower temperature than under normal conditions. This allowed him to boil milk without discoloring it or giving it a scorched taste. Although he knew nothing about bacteria, he believed that milk was "a living fluid," that something in the air soured it, and that boiling it in a vacuum shielded it from this airborne contaminant. When Borden added sugar, which had long been used as a food preservative, to the boiled milk, he discovered that it remained potable more or less indefinitely.

Armed with his new knowledge, he applied for a patent in 1853, but it took him three years to satisfy the patent commissioners' requirements. When he finally received his patent, he opened a condensery in Wolcottville, Connecticut, and attempted to sell his new product in New York City. However, he found few customers because consumers were not accustomed to the taste of condensed milk. Reluctantly, he closed his small factory.

Undaunted, he then spent a year raising additional funds and opened a new factory in Burrville, Connecticut. This venture also seemed destined for failure until Jeremiah Milbank, a financier and wholesaler grocer, agreed to go into partnership with Borden. Capitalizing on yet another exposé of New York City's swill dairies, the new partners advertised the purity of their milk and the rigid standards of cleanliness in their country condensery. Sales and production soared.[35]

Low Tech

Surprisingly, the proliferation of wholesale ice cream plants was not accompanied by dramatic advances in manufacturing technology. Despite the blossoming demand for ice cream, methods of production changed little during the last half of the 19th century. Most wholesalers relied on manpower, and the industry as a whole advanced very slowly.

The experiences of John W. Miller, who worked in the ice cream business for more than 60 years, mirrored the evolution of the early technology. Miller began freezing ice cream in a candy kettle placed inside a wooden washtub filled with ice and salt—both of which came in blocks and had to be crushed with an axe and stamper. In the beginning, he produced only two flavors, lemon and strawberry, and made his own food coloring. Red coloring was obtained by grinding cochineal between two stones; yellow was made by soaking saffron in alcohol; burnt sugar created a brownish hue. He added corn starch to the mix "to make the ice cream stand up."[37]

From the makeshift candy-kettle freezer, Miller graduated to a tall metal can with a tight-fitting cover and a wooden crossbar handle. "This, filled three-quarters of the way up with mix, was packed in a tub of ice and salt, turned right and left for a while, then the frozen mix was scraped from the sides and the process continued until we had ice cream," he recalled. "This ice cream was then beaten smooth with a wooden spatula and we called the job finished."

Next, Miller used a single-action hand-cranked patent freezer, which was replaced by a patent freezer with a dasher and scraper. Later, he progressed to a triple-action freezer and then to Blatchley's (Tingley's patent) horizontal model. The Blatchley's was soon discarded because it leaked, and a heavy-duty hand-cranked freezer designed for industrial use took its place. Miller and another man cranked this freezer by hand, although some of his larger competitors utilized steam power, with two-speed pulleys, to turn similar freezers. In 1887, Miller visited the Palmer House in Chicago and saw a freezer run by an electric motor for the first time.[37]

The recollections of Albert D. Sidwell, whose family pioneered in the ice cream industry in Iowa, paralleled Miller's in many respects. The Sidwell family began making ice cream by the pot freezer method, progressed to a small hand-cranked freezer with a dasher, and then used larger-capacity patent freezers with flywheels. The next step was to use a horse-powered tread mill to turn the freezer and finally to replace the horse with a gasoline engine.[38]

The first ice cream freezers intended specifically for industrial use were simply larger, sturdier versions of the familiar patent freezers used in homes. For example, Blatchley's advertised its 3- to 8-quart horizontal freezers for family use and 12- to 40-quart sizes for ice cream saloons and wholesalers. North Brothers Manufacturing of Philadelphia sold freezers that held up to 20 quarts for either home or commercial use. But it also made 32-quart freezers especially for factories.[39]

Experience quickly suggested some modifications to make the patent freezers more suitable for wholesale operations. Manufacturers soon began mounting their freezers on platforms, and they replaced the crank with a manual flywheel, which increased the leverage and made turning easier. Later, they rigged up freezers with pulleys and drive belts, powered by steam boilers or gasoline engines, to turn the dashers. Although the advantages of the belt-driven "power freezers" were obvious, they were not foolproof because the belts sometimes slipped—generally, at the most inopportune time.[40]

The White Mountain Freezer Company advertised 25- and 50-quart power freezers operated by pulleys, with a choice of double- or triple-action. The 25-quart model could freeze ice cream in 20 minutes while the larger model finished in 30 minutes. If the manufacturer preferred, he could operate several freezers at once using a countershaft, which hung over the freezers to start and stop them.[41]

The following description of a plant using power freezers was published in *Ice and Refrigeration* in 1892:

Descending into the cellar work room of the typical ice cream factory, the visitor finds himself surrounded by countless boxes, vats, tanks, casks or other receptacles filled with ice, near which are groups of busy workers preparing the rich, raw cream for the freezers. The cream having been properly flavored, it is poured into cans holding several gallons each, which are then conveyed to the whipping wheels.

Then blades, or whippers, are inserted into the cans, the covers clamped tightly on, and the can attached to the machinery. A rasping squeak, a subdued roar, a crushing, grinding noise of ice, and the cans are whirling furiously in their icy beds, and the whippers are doing their work. This continues for ten minutes, when the cans are removed to make way for others.[42]

Whether a plant used hand-cranked or power freezers, ice cream manufacturing was not an occupation for weaklings. From Memorial Day to Labor Day, ice cream men routinely worked 14 to 16 hours daily Monday through Saturday and a half-day on Sunday. Most ice cream factories were small businesses, and many were one- or two-person operations. Morris Lifter, who owned an ice cream plant in Philadelphia, remembered, "It was my regular schedule each day to get up in the morning, make the fire under the boiler, feed and curry the horse, make the mix, and if I was not actually freezing the cream, I was delivering it."[43]

Wholesalers enhanced the demand for all types of equipment needed in making ice cream and occasionally inspired inventors to create new products. A typical supply house advertised ice cream freezers, packing cans, carry-out cans and pails, cedar tubs, brass bung holes, brick and fancy ice cream molds, lemon squeezers, packaging boxes, ice axes, tin and copper measuring cups, strainers, ladles and spoons, scoops, trowels, ice caves (insulated boxes for hardening ice cream), ice breakers, steel ice chisels, ice-crushing machines, and insulated boxes with shelves for carrying molded ice cream.[44]

The ice cream industry became a major market for metal and porcelain cans, which were needed for storing the ice cream while it hardened as well as for delivering it. Dipping, or transferring the ice cream from the freezer to the can, was done by hand. Recalled one ice cream pioneer, "We had to make our product in a tub and dasher type of freezer, and when it was partly frozen we had to dip it into five- or three-gallon shipping cans. . . . It took a good Frenchman to dip 500 gallons a day, and it would nearly freeze his hand stiff."[45]

The partially frozen cream was usually transferred to porcelain-lined iron packing cans that were placed in cedar tubs packed with ice and salt. Manufacturers had to be careful that the packing cans were kept cold enough to prevent the cream from becoming soft but not so frigid that the cream became rock hard. As needed, the cream was transferred to small tin packing cans with one- to four-quart capacities for the retail trade. When ice cream was left in a metal container for too long, it became tainted. "The best tinned cans, if the creams are kept for a longer time, cause an unpleasant metallic taste, while poorly tinned cans spoil and discolor the creams," warned one manual.[46]

Wholesalers also enhanced the demand for delivery wagons and mules. Both the wagons and the animals had to be sturdy and reliable because breakdowns were costly. Corrosion of metal wagon components, due to exposure to brine, was a chronic problem. Sidwell's experiences as a small-town wholesaler demonstrated the importance of the delivery wagon. Most of Sidwell's output was transported via wagon to Iowa City's drugstores, which sold ice cream only on one or two days each week. But the delivery wagon, pulled by two horses wearing sleighbells to attract attention, also made two trips a week to the nearby towns of Stone City and Marion. As the wagon rolled through residential areas, housewives brought their dishes to the driver to be filled with ice cream for dinner. For the convenience of customers who did not have a container handy, the deliveryman carried wooden dishes. "A strip of wood split from the side of the dish made a convenient spoon," Sidwell recalled.[47]

In addition to the manufacturing and delivery equipment, ice cream factories needed huge quantities of ice and salt. For example, a single large ice cream factory could use 100,000 pounds of ice daily during the peak summer months. Sudden increases in salt prices or warm winters producing little ice were a serious threat to such plants. Therefore, it is not surprising that some large wholesalers bought icehouses and even salt mines to insure themselves against disruptions in their supplies. Reid Ice Cream, for instance, owned salt mines in upstate New York and harvested its own ice from private lakes.[48]

In the late 19th century, two major developments in the dairy field had significant implications for ice cream wholesalers. In 1867 came the invention of the centrifugal cream separator, which eliminated the need for setting milk aside for 12 to 24 hours to allow the cream to rise to the top. The centrifugal separator shortened the process to one hour for 300 pounds of whole milk and, moreover, produced a greater quantity of cream. This new separator enabled dairies to produce greater volumes of cream with a more consistent butterfat content.

The second development was the invention of a centrifugal butterfat tester by Dr. Stephen Moulton Babcock of the University of Wisconsin in 1890. The Babcock tester scientifically determined the butterfat content of milk, replacing the old rule-of-thumb methods. The essential principle of the Babcock process was that sulphuric acid added in the proper proportion dissolved all components of milk except the fat, permitting precise measurement of the fat content. Before the Babcock tester, buying milk or cream was largely guesswork, complicating the job of ice cream makers, who could not be certain of the quality of their raw materials.[49]

Factory operators had to be trained to use the Babcock tester, which led to the opening of the University of Wisconsin's Dairy School, the first specifically for dairy education. The need for better-trained workers also led to the introduction of the first university course in ice cream making at Pennsylvania State College in 1892. At least three more colleges—Iowa State, Purdue, and the University of Illinois—were soon teaching similar courses.[50]

Plain or Fancy

Molds had been a popular way of serving ice cream as early as George Washington's time, but they became even more fashionable during the second half of the 19th century. Cookbooks often included instructions to help housewives use molds purchased from the local general store or a mail order catalog. Confectioners, caterers, and chefs vied with one another to create the most elaborate, decorative forms in ice cream. They could purchase fancy molds from wholesale suppliers, such as Schall and Company, but many chose to make their own from plaster of Paris or thin sheet copper. Even wholesalers, who were noted for their mass-produced cream, made fancy forms to satisfy that segment of their clientele who wanted something showier than a brick of ice cream.[51]

A *plombierre*, which was often ordered for parties, was made in a round mold, like a cannon ball, with a center of fruits and nuts surrounded by ice cream. *Plombierres*, which were often large enough to serve 35 to 40 guests, were covered with chopped nuts or hand-dipped in chocolate for a glossy finish. Fancy molds shaped like animals—such as turkeys, doves, geese, and elephants—were popular, as were ice cream cakes, called society puddings in the trade. The traditional towers, pyramids, and melons were always in demand as were baskets filled with ice cream molded into fruits, vegetables, or flowers. Fresh or artificial leaves and stems were sometimes added to make fruits and flowers appear more natural. Food coloring mixed with syrup was brushed on to enhance the colors of molded ice cream, as needed.

Ice cream in the shape of an organization's insignia, such as a Masonic emblem, could be ordered for club meetings. Hearts, clubs, spades, and diamonds were available for card parties. The Eiffel Tower and the Statue of Liberty were both recreated in miniature in ice cream, but the popularity of such molds was fleeting, limited to the brief time the new sensation was in the headlines.[52]

Holidays created a demand for appropriate molds, such as pink hearts for Valentine's Day. For Washington's Birthday, at least one popular confectioner offered three-cornered hats made of wafers filled with ice cream and hatchets decorated with candied cherries and angelica. For St. Patrick's Day, the same fellow suggested pistachio ice cream frozen in harp shapes or Irish potatoes made of chocolate or caramel ice cream. He recommended colored ice cream eggs for Easter and red-white-and-blue ice cream for Independence Day.[53]

"Great competition existed between dealers, and what one lacked in flavors he made up in shapes, the dealer with the largest assortment of molds having the largest trade," remembered Miller, whose recollections offer an intriguing glimpse of the flights of fancy possible with molds. The Vienna Bakery from Vienna, Austria, had a concession to make ice cream and fancy baked goods at the Centennial Exhibition in Philadelphia in 1876. In order to learn their secrets, Miller worked at the concession for several months, without pay, gaining experience in making everything from *petits* to *pièces montées* (large mounted pieces). The Viennese confectioners combined candy with ice cream to create goblets, cups, saucers, and bowls that resembled Bohemian glass. They sailed ice cream ships on spun-sugar waves and made ice cream chicks that roosted inside spun-sugar nests filled with ice cream eggs. Other noteworthy creations included log cabins constructed of ice cream and ladyfingers; frozen plum puddings soaked in brandy; individual ice cream fruit molds filled with sweetened fruit pulp; Lalla Rookh (French vanilla ice cream flavored with cherries, apricots, dates, and Madeira) served in edible candy cups; and an ice cream Mount Vesuvius, with a walnut shell encrusted in the peak to hold alcohol that was set ablaze just before the volcano was served.[54]

After the exhibition, Miller traveled across the continent and settled down in Oakland, California, working for a catering firm "where everything that could be made in ice cream was produced." A few of the more memorable orders included ice cream elks' heads with papier-mâché horns for the opening of an Elks Club; ice cream footballs for a reception after a game between Stanford and the University of California; and an ice cream replica of the battleship Oregon for a banquet honoring naval officers returning from a round-the-world cruise.[55]

After gaining all this experience, Miller went to work for a wholesaler, supervising the fancies department. In most factories, the fancies department was a little apart from the main freezing room, where large batches were produced. An engineering journal reported, "In another place are the men who make and freeze the French glaces, ices and more expensive forms of ice cream, and those who also mold the ornamental works in ice cream which so often adorn the banquet tables of public occasions or elaborate private entertainments—statuettes in cream and ornamental pieces in various colors." In the fancies department described in the journal, the mixture was whipped in small batches in copper kettles nestled in an ice-and-salt bath until the cream appeared "not unlike a ball of cotton in its snowy fluffiness." Then it was sweetened, flavored, partially frozen, molded, and frozen again.[56]

Transporting fancy ice cream molds without damaging them was a problem that prompted manufacturers to design various types of carrying cases. A typical case contained a series of trays or shelves spaced far enough apart for each shelf to hold a standard-sized mold. The case had a water-tight lid and could be placed inside a large receptacle filled with ice and salt to keep the molds frozen during delivery.

Although the fancy forms attracted the most attention, brick molds were the bread-and-butter of ice cream factories. The process of making bricks was simple, although there were some variations from one factory to another. In Schmid's plant, ice cream was packed in rectangular metal forms, covered, and stored in a bath of ice and salt for about three hours. Then the forms were taken out and dipped in a pail of warm water, to loosen the cream from the sides. After the covers were opened, the loosened brick of cream was removed from the form, placed in a pasteboard box, and packed in ice for delivery. Multicolor bricks were made by stacking different flavors on top of one another.[57]

Wholesalers sold single-flavor and Neapolitan bricks, which generally included vanilla, chocolate, and strawberry, although other flavors were sometimes used. Fancies in different flavors and colors could be ordered from wholesalers, but the greatest experimentation with flavors came from confectioners, caterers, and professional chefs. It seemed as if no fruit or vegetable was unsuitable for flavoring ice cream and no combination too outrageous.

Many ice cream makers experimented with less familiar, therefore more exotic, ingredients. For example, Miller's customers especially liked his gumdrop-pistachio nut combination. Tutti-frutti, a name derived from an Italian term meaning "all fruits," was a bestseller in the 1870s. It contained a combination of colorful chopped candied fruits, such as cherries, apricots, raisins, pineapple, and English currants. One of the most bizarre flavors was Irish moss. Not surprisingly, the recipe noted that the seaweed must be "rinsed well to cleanse it of sand and a certain foreign taste."[58]

In culinary circles, the pace was set by the chefs at Delmonico's in New York City. From humble beginnings, the Swiss immigrant Delmonico family had built an impressive restaurant dynasty and a reputation for simply the best food anywhere. The first Delmonico venture was a wine store located on the Battery, but the brothers soon opened a small shop on William Street, where they served coffee, chocolate, wines, spirits, pastries, candy, and ice cream. This place was so successful that they converted it into a full-fledged restaurant and hired a French chef. Whenever they needed more space or a more fashionable address, the Delmonicos opened at a new location, and at times New Yorkers had their choice of more than one Delmonico restaurant. Regardless of the location, Delmonico's remained *the* place to eat for those who could afford it.[59]

Charles Ranhofer, the most renowned of the Delmonico chefs, was very innovative in creating new ice cream flavors and dishes. Ranhofer's impressive repertoire of ice cream flavors included caramel, chocolate, chestnut, asparagus, cinnamon, ginger, lemon, strawberry, cherry, currant, raspberry, peach, truffle, pistachio, tutti-frutti, pumpernickel rye bread, apricot, nectarine, pineapple, burnt almond, angelica, rice, and white coffee.[60]

Ranhofer was famous not only for his ice cream flavors but also for the presentation. For example, he had two versions of asparagus ice cream; one was actually flavored with asparagus while the other was a vanilla-pistachio combination. Regardless of which recipe he used, he liked to mold the ice cream into individual asparagus spears and tie them together with pink ribbon. Cookbook author Mary Henderson was probably referring to Ranhofer's creation, or a variation, when she wrote that guests "at handsome dinners in large cities" might "see a perfect imitation of asparagus with a cream dressing, the asparagus being made of the *pistache* cream, and the dressing simply a whipped cream."[61]

Another of Ranhofer's unusual presentations was a stuffed tomato—actually a combination of burnt almond ice cream and strawberry water ice frozen in a tomato-shaped mold. He made mushrooms of maraschino ice cream, dipping the stalks in grated chocolate to give variations in color. His fetish for imitating common foods in ice cream also extended to potatoes, which were fashioned of chestnut ice cream and rolled in grated chocolate, with slivers of almond for eyes. Tin molds shaped like ears of corn were filled with hazelnut ice cream or lemon water ice. Lemons and bananas were hollowed out, filled with ice cream, and decorated with ribbons for a festive presentation.[62]

For a centerpiece, Ranhofer might create a hen with chicks or eggs in a nest, using sponge cake, chocolate icing, spun sugar, and burnt almond ice cream. Another favorite centerpiece was an ice cream Bacchus sitting on a miniature wine barrel, made of chocolate ice cream, resting on a platform of pistachio ice cream. A more understated but elegant presentation required making a hexagon-shaped box of dough, decorating it with icing, and filling it with a rich ice cream flavored with pistachios, candied fruits, raisins, and kirsch. When the diner removed the lid from the pretty box, he discovered the ice cream inside.[63]

Ranhofer created truffle ice cream for a special dinner party in 1867. Three of the wealthier members of New York society—Leonard Jerome, William Travers, and August Belmont—decided to outdo one another by hosting the most sumptuous dinner party imaginable. Naturally, each chose Delmonico's for the occasion and commanded the chef to make his dinner the best, regardless of the cost. Even Ranhofer's considerable culinary talents were strained to the utmost by the task.[64]

Why Ranhofer decided to make truffle ice cream for one of these dinners is unknown. However, it is certain that the novel flavor created a stir. Always mindful of presentation, Ranhofer froze a rich ice cream flavored with truffles in chocolate-lined, truffle-shaped molds. After the ice cream was removed from the molds, he rolled it in a powder made from truffle peelings and vanilla seeds. One author characterized this dish as "a triumph of skill and imagination over taste and good sense." But social arbiter Ward McAllister, who attended the dinner, remembered that the truffle ice cream was "strange to say, very good." The contest to host the best dinner was declared a tie, but the real winner was Delmonico's, which had enhanced both its coffers and its reputation with the three lavish meals.[65]

Ranhofer is often credited with inventing baked Alaska to commemorate the United States' purchase of Alaska from Russia. Although dishes combining the frigidity of ice cream with the warmth of baked pastry were known long before that event, Ranhofer's creation was unusual. Sometimes called Alaska-Florida, it featured a tall inverted cone-shaped mold of ice cream, half banana and half vanilla, which was placed on a cake base that had been hollowed out and filled with apricot marmalade. The dish was kept frozen until the last possible minute, then covered with meringue, quickly browned in a hot oven, and served immediately.[66]

George Augustus Sala, who ate baked Alaska at Delmonico's, reported, "The nucleus or core of the *entremets* is an ice cream. This is surrounded by an envelope of carefully whipped cream, which, just before the dainty dish is served, is popped into the oven, or is brought under the scorching influence of a red hot salamander."[67]

An alternative history of baked Alaska traces it to experiments in heating and cooking conducted by Benjamin Thompson (1753–1814). Born in Woburn, Massachusetts, Thompson became a renowned scientist both in the United States and in England, where he was rewarded with the title of Count Rumford. His studies of the resistance of egg whites to heat resulted in the browned meringue that eventually became the topping for baked Alaska. Even this alternative account acknowledges that baked Alaska was popularized at Delmonico's.[68]

Although Ranhofer was New York's most celebrated culinary artist, he had several notable rivals, including Oscar Tschirky, or Oscar of the Waldorf, who did not actually cook but specialized in planning and arranging magnificent meals. Oscar's culinary philosophy emphasized the sensual indulgence of food in a proper, decorous manner. He created sumptuous menus for royalty and several United States presidents as well as the celebrities and socialites of his era.[69]

One of Oscar's most acclaimed dinners was prepared for Charles Steinway, the piano manufacturer, and 31 guests. The menu included fancy deviled eggs; oysters; green turtle soup; mousse of bass, with cucumbers; breast of chicken with Madeira sauce; oyster crabs with mushrooms; saddle of lamb, braised with ham, served with potatoes and French peas; sherbet; terrapin served Philadelphia style; canvasback duck with currant jelly; celery salad with mayonnaise dressing; fancy ice cream; small cakes; and assorted fruits.

Records show that Steinway and his friends also consumed two quarts of champagne, three quarts of amontillado, 6 bottles of chablis, 7 bottles of Rauenthaler Berg, 6 bottles of Berncasteler Doctor, 3 bottles of medoc, 2 bottles of Chateau Mouton, 4 bottles of Chambertin, 2 bottles of Madeira, 25 bottles of Pommery, and 47 quarts of Apollinaris seltzer water! There is no record of how they felt the next morning.[70]

On the spur of the moment, Oscar created a simple ice cream dessert called the Lillian Russell, which was very popular for a time. One night Diamond Jim Brady, a gourmand notorious for his incredible overindulgence, escorted Russell, a famous actress-singer, to the Waldorf-Astoria for dinner. Russell, who had no small appetite herself and had the good fortune to live in an era when ample figures were admired, could not decide whether she wanted cantaloupe or ice cream for dessert. She finally decided to take both. Upon Oscar's instructions, the waiter soon returned to her table with a melon-half filled with ice cream. Although the combination is still served occasionally, the name Lillian Russell has fallen into disuse.[71]

At Home or Away

Not everyone could afford to eat at Delmonico's or the Waldorf, but almost everyone could afford to eat ice cream in the second half of the 19th century. The middle class served ice cream at home and frequented ice cream parlors or saloons, while those with only pennies to spend bought the frozen treat from street vendors.

Ice cream was hawked on the streets of New York City in the early 19th century, but the number of vendors in big cities exploded after the Civil War. Historians often lump all of them together under the category of hokey-pokey men, although many were not men and some were not selling hokey-pokey, which specifically referred to cheap ice cream or ice milk. Since street vendors were part of the informal economy, the sources that usually provide facts about business history offer virtually no data about them. However, the sparse information available indicates that ice cream hawkers were a familiar sight in large American cities and some small towns in the second half of the century.

In New Orleans, vendors of both sexes balanced heavy wooden pails, packed with ice and ice cream, on their heads as they strolled barefooted through the narrow streets of the French Quarter. In general, they sold delicious ice cream, even though their standards of sanitation were quite low. Typically, the New Orleans vendor carried a small towel in one hand and a large spoon and a basket, containing two glasses, in the other. When a paying customer approached, he set his pail on the ground, filled one of the glasses, and waited while the consumer ate. Then he wiped the glass with the towel, returned it to the basket, positioned the pail on his head, and resumed his route. His more fastidious customers brought their own glasses—a gesture that he appreciated because he did not have to wait while they ate.[72]

The following description of Philadelphia's ice cream hawkers indicates that they also sold a quality product:

The countryman . . . sells an excellent article. It is really country ice cream, fresh from the farm, and although cried and sold in the streets, the market, and the public squares, it will please the most fastidious palate. The loudest criers . . . are the coloured gentlemen, who carry the tin cans containing it, about the streets on their shoulders. They sing a most laughable, but scarcely intelligible song in praise of their lemon ice cream and vanilla too. . . . [I]t is by no means unpalatable; and considering the half price at which the coloured merchants accommodate their juvenile customers, it is a pretty good fip's worth.[73]

This passage suggests that the quality of the ice cream sold on Philadelphia's streets generally was superior to the hokey-pokey hawked in other cities, where hokey-pokey peddlers routinely sold ice milk. Very little, if any, cream was required in the hokey-pokey recipes published in trade magazines or the free cookbooks given away by freezer manufacturers. Typically, these recipes called for milk, condensed milk, sugar, vanilla extract, cornstarch, and gelatin. Sometimes they also included instructions for molding the hokey-pokey, slicing it into small blocks, and wrapping it in tissue paper—in short, preparing it for sale.[74]

Linguists agree that "hokey-pokey" denoted inferior ice cream, but that's about all they agree on. Some etymologies trace the origin of the term to *O, che poco*, an Italian expression meaning "Oh, how little!" or "Oh, how cheap!" At least one dictionary has suggested that the term is related to *orche-porchem*, Yiddish for tramp or vagabond. However, the majority of linguists believe that "hokey-pokey" is a corruption or anglicization of "hocus pocus," the familiar phrase used by jugglers and magicians.[75]

Exactly when "hokey-pokey" entered the English language is uncertain, and unfortunately there are few clues. One of the earliest published usages appeared in a British magazine in 1884, when it was described as "a curiously compounded beverage." The following year, a book stated, "Hokey-pokey is of a firmer make and probably stiffer material than the penny ice of the Italians." In 1888, another British periodical related an anecdote suggesting that the term was related to the Italian phrase *O, che poco*. An American cookbook published in 1892 referred to "another type of ice cream (called Hokey-Pokey) which you can buy on the New York streets from the sons of sunny Italy." This book, written by a well-known confectioner, included a recipe for lemon hokey-pokey.[76]

Whatever the origin of the term, it lent itself to the catchy, nonsense phrases popular with street vendors. Among the familiar street cries were the following:

> Hokey-pokey, pokey ho.
> Hokey-pokey, a penny a lump.
> Hokey-pokey, find a cake; hokey-pokey on the lake.

Here's the stuff to make you jump; hokey-pokey, penny a lump.
Hokey-pokey, sweet and cold; for a penny, new or old.

If these cries were not enough to attract attention, many hokey-pokey men also rang bells as they made their way along the streets.[77]

Children, who were the biggest market for the cheap treat, borrowed the term for a jump-rope rhyme: "Hokey, pokey, penny a lump; The more you eat, the more you jump." A variation—"Hokey-pokey, penny a lump, the more you eat, the more you pump"—could also be heard on city streets. Some linguists have suggested that this was chanted derisively at children eating ice cream by those who had none.[78]

Many hokey-pokey men pushed their cans of ice cream along the streets in wheelbarrows, but some had small carts pulled by goats or even wagons pulled by horses. Hokey-pokey vendors made their ice cream at home or purchased it from wholesaler manufacturers, who sometimes rented carts or provided them free to the street vendors. While some hokey-pokey peddlers traveled a regular route each day, others sold their wares from a booth or stand. (In Northern cities, when the weather turned cold, many of them hawked hot chestnuts and "miggies," charred yams or potatoes. In Los Angeles, the hokey-pokey peddlers sold hot tamales when the weather was cool.)[79]

As the largest United States city, New York naturally had the biggest population of street criers or patterers, with representatives from virtually every immigrant group, even though the stereotypical hokey-pokey man was Italian. A New York guidebook described the patterers as "that large class of people who hawk their wares upon the street, or get a living at a stand. Some of them do a thriving trade, others barely eke out a miserable existence. Take them all in all, and they are a very curious class of people, interesting to study."

In New York City, many of the street vendors were individuals who could not find other types of employment—such as the handicapped, the elderly, young girls, and midgets. In fact, respectable citizens generally looked down on able-bodied men who hawked goods on the streets, feeling that they were lazy and should be employed in more manly occupations. The guidebook reflected this attitude, saying, "Some of these men are middle-aged, able-bodied fellows, quite strong and healthy enough to be clearing up land in the West or laying bricks at five dollars a day. For some unaccountable reason, they prefer to remain in New York, living from hand to mouth, and doing nothing to improve themselves, mentally, worldly, or financially."

The guidebook reported that, although male vendors predominated, a large number were women "from the oldest gray-haired grandmother, tottering on her cane, down to the young woman of sixteen." There were "numerous little girls struggling to get a living, too, from three-years-old upwards." Although patterers hawked everything from matches to men's clothes, female vendors typically specialized in flowers or foods, such as ice cream, lemonade, doughnuts, buns, tropical fruits, and sweetmeats. Not surprisingly, the guidebook declared that the female vendors were not pretty. To put it bluntly, they were "a very ugly-looking set," because working on the streets was a hard life that quickly took its toll.[80]

The vendors in each section of the city generally reflected the character of that area. Park Row and the Bowery were the favorite locations for "the cheapest sort" who sold "every kind of low-priced article, from a dog-eared volume to a decayed peanut." These vendors specialized in ice cream made with sour milk; soda water without fizz; "lemonade without lemons; songs without sentiment; jokes without point; cigars innocent of tobacco; and all manner of shams."[81]

On a hot summer day in the city, there were "swarms of children surrounding the ice cream vendors. . . . Little boys with pennies exchanging their wealth for small daubs of ice cream on squares of brown paper, which they linger over in long drawn-out licks of epicurean joy." However, not everyone's heart was warmed by the sight of street urchins "as early as seven o'clock in the morning . . . crowded around the hokey-pokey cart or the soda water stand." Some social critics felt that lower-class parents were being frivolous and indulgent when they allowed their children to buy such treats. "Thriftless, but affectionate, is the lower class parent. Shoes the child must do without, for the father has not quite enough money to purchase them. But here is five cents to buy hokey-pokey. That much he can afford," observed one newspaper editorial.[82]

Since hokey-pokey was neither made nor sold under exemplary sanitary conditions, vendors became adept at dodging public health inspectors. In many cities, the hokey-pokey men and their product came under the close scrutiny of reformers and health officials. Even Philadelphia, which was noted for premium ice cream, had problems with unsanitary practices. Mary Engle Pennington, a remarkable woman who was denied a baccalaureate in chemistry by the University of Pennsylvania due to her sex, nevertheless managed to complete a doctorate and became head of Philadelphia's municipal bacteriological lab. After devising a system for inspecting cattle and dairies to insure that the city's milk supply was safe, she turned her attention to the hokey-pokey peddlers. Since the existing laws did not extend to the street vendors, she used her powers of persuasion to convince the hokey-pokey men to adopt basic sanitary procedures, such as washing their utensils in boiling water.[83]

The public health concern also extended to ice cream saloons and other establishments serving ice cream. In New York City, reformer John Mullaly warned residents about adulterated milk, saying, "The greatest proportion is used by hotels, restaurants, and in the manufacture of all kinds of confectionery. In the summer season particularly, there is a great demand for it in the form of ice cream." Three decades after Mullaly wrote those words, contaminated dairy products were still a problem, and newspapers still printed periodic reports of illness or even death due to ice cream. In one noteworthy case, more than 100 individuals became sick after eating ice cream from a shop in Brooklyn on July 4, 1884. Although such cases were rare in relation to the amount of ice cream consumed, they received enough publicity to make the public aware of the danger.[84]

Despite dire warnings about adulterated food, ice cream parlors and saloons were fashionable, especially with prosperous middle class patrons who enjoyed the ambiance as well as the food. In 1860, a women's magazine reported, "Every village, however humble in size or rank, has its ice cream saloon." Both "ice cream parlor" and "ice cream saloon" denoted retail establishments where ice cream and other treats were sold. It has been suggested that the difference between them was simple: a parlor had carpets while a saloon had bare floors. As a general rule, both were decorated with ornate tables, gilt-framed pictures, and gleaming mirrors. Normally, both had a candy counter on one side of the center aisle and a soda fountain, where ice cream was sold by the saucer, on the opposite side. In some establishments, ice cream was served in the rear of the building, with a small bakery occupying one side of the front and the candy and soda fountain on the other. During the winter months, many proprietors temporarily converted their ice cream parlors to oyster bars, serving oysters, sandwiches, cake, and coffee.[85]

Every large city had one or two famous ice cream parlors that set the standard for the rest. In New York City, Thompson's on the corner of Broadway and Lispenard Street had a reputation for serving the very best ice cream. In Philadelphia, Parkinson's and Isaac Newton's were recognized as first-rate. At Parkinson's, where ice cream was served in long-necked champagne glasses, the most popular flavors were lemon and vanilla. One patron wrote, "In the summer season, immense quantities of the finest ice cream are sold in Philadelphia. Indeed the city vaunts itself on producing the best ice cream in the world; and strangers generally give the preference to that which is sold at such establishments as Parkinson's and Isaac Newton's over any which is to be found in our other great cities."[86]

Parkinson, who also owned Parkinson's Broadway Saloon in New York City, claimed that he had originated pistachio ice cream. However, at least one early English cookbook had included a recipe for pistachio. Parkinson hated the fact that the American public generally believed French cuisine to be superior to their own native foods. "So deeply rooted is this sentiment in the public mind . . . that when an American confectioner or caterer makes any invention in his craft, he feels that to secure its sales, and to establish its popularity, he must give it a French name," lamented Parkinson, whose own menu included *biscuit glace.*[87]

Trade catalogs advertised furniture, including special tables, for parlors and saloons. The favorite table design was rectangular with two legs supporting one end and one ornate leg placed at the mid-point of the opposite end, which was often curved—a configuration that supposedly allowed more people to be seated comfortably. These handsome, sturdy tables were typically made of black walnut, ash, or cherry and boasted glossy tops of marble or polished wood.[88]

Of course, parlors and saloons were not the only commercial establishments featuring ice cream. Steamships served ice cream, as did trains after dining-car service was initiated following the Civil War. A menu for the steamer *United States*, which was built for the Ontario and St. Lawrence Steamboat Company circa 1831, included ice cream for dessert. In the 1840s, the standard price for a serving of ice cream on a steamboat was six cents. Traveler Theresa Pulszky complained about the "Western fare" served on steamboats in the 1850s. "Instead of giving a few, cleanly prepared, plain dishes, the table is covered with dainties, with jellies and creams, ices, French sauces and sweets," she lamented.[89]

Ice cream was a standard item on the menus of dining cars, which catered to passengers who had the time to enjoy a leisurely meal as the train chugged along the rails. But not all trains had dining cars, and some passengers did not want to eat on the train, anyway, preferring to wait for a stop to eat—which often proved to be a regrettable decision. The diaries and letters of early rail travelers were filled with accounts of the nightmarish experience of hopping off a train, quickly ordering a meal at an eatery beside the tracks, and bolting down the badly cooked food before the train pulled away. According to a newspaper, "It is expected that three or four hundred men, women and children . . . shall rush out helter-skelter into a dismal, long room and dispatch a supper, breakfast or dinner in fifteen minutes." Noted one rail passenger, "All ate as if for their very lives."[90]

The lack of decent eateries at train stops motivated Fred Harvey to start one of America's first restaurant chains. Harvey, an English immigrant, began his career as a dishwasher and soon became a partner in a restaurant in St. Louis. When his partner absconded with all the money, Harvey went to work as a sorting clerk on a railroad mail car and then held other railway jobs, where he was exposed to the lackluster cuisine available to train passengers. He realized that there was a market for good food served in pleasant surroundings in or near the railroad station, where passengers could relax while they ate and feel refreshed when they continued their journey. With a new partner, he opened three eateries along the Kansas Pacific line and, after that partnership dissolved, launched a chain of dining establishments along the Atchison, Topeka, and Santa Fe Railway. His restaurants were noted for cleanliness, efficiency, and the Harvey girls, smiling waitresses wearing spotless white aprons. In the 1880s, a typical Harvey restaurant offered a 75-cent special with puree of tomato soup; stuffed whitefish with potatoes; a choice of mutton, beef, pork, or turkey; chicken turnovers; shrimp salad; a choice of rice pudding or apple or cranberry pie; ice cream; cake; fruit; cheese and crackers; and French coffee. The larger Harvey establishments had their own dairy farms and ice cream plants.[91]

The bicycling craze of the late 19th century created a clientele for roadhouses, big barn-like structures with patios and gardens enclosed by fences decorated with colorful Japanese lanterns. A journalist depicted the scene at a typical roadhouse in New York City, as follows:

It seems an indescribably busy place at night. Bicyclists dismount to discuss whither next they will go, to have their punctures mended, their tires blown up, their chains tightened, or some other one of their ceaselessly recurring repairs made. They sit at the tables on the piazza or in the gardens and drink according to their tastes. Here waiters run, pushing straws down into a mass of ice and lemon; here they balance foaming glasses of beer with such nicety that the foam does not fly; again it is innocuous ice cream that they bear.[92]

Despite the growing number of roadhouses and other commercial establishments serving ice cream, many people preferred to eat at home. The manufacture and sale of serving dishes and utensils specifically for ice cream reflected both the popularity of the food and the prosperity of the middle class. Ice cream knives, made of sterling silver or silver plate, featured serrated cutting edges and broad, curved blades. Ice cream forks had three wide prongs and were curved like spoons.[93]

China ice cream sets consisted of matching individual dishes and a large platter that was the right shape and size for holding a brick of ice cream. An 1894 wholesale catalog offered seven different sets in a range of prices. The cheapest set, which consisted of twelve saucers and a platter, cost $1.35 wholesale. The most expensive was a reception set for $3.00, decorated with clusters of flowers, gold-edged leaves, and a gold border. The following year, the Montgomery Ward and Company catalog advertised ice cream dishes made of bon ware, "light in weight, but very strong and serviceable." The catalog recommended bon ware "highly to those in search of something extra nice in tableware for use on extra occasions."[94]

Women's magazines, cookbooks, and etiquette manuals advised homemakers about how and when to serve ice cream. *Godey's Magazine and Lady's Book* recommended Masser's Self-acting Patent Ice-Cream Freezer to its readers and explained the importance of ice cream, as follows:

Ice-cream has now become one of the necessary luxuries of life. A party, or a social entertainment, could hardly be thought of without this indispensable requisition. Other delicacies might be omitted, by substituting other articles in their stead, but nothing can supply the place of ice-cream. It would be like breakfast without bread, or a dinner without a roast.

The Home Manual recommended the following menu for an afternoon tea: thin slices of bread and butter; sandwiches; fancy biscuits or cake; tea, coffee, or chocolate; bouillon; salted almonds; ice cream; cakes; candies; punch; and lemonade—but no wine of any kind. For an afternoon reception, the manual suggested oyster salad, pâtes, boned turkey, ice cream, bonbons, and coffee. *The Table: How to Buy Food, How to Cook It, and How to Serve It* stated that ice cream should be served on cold dessert plates "with fancy paper underneath" and should be eaten with dessert spoons or forks.[95]

The Civil War affected every aspect of American life and was especially hard on the South, but many people still managed to enjoy little luxuries, like ice cream. In some locations, ice cream and strawberry festivals were a favorite means of raising money for soldiers relief funds. Diarist Mary Chestnut wrote about eating ice cream to celebrate an exchange of Union and Confederate prisoners of war. "There was ice cream for all and to spare," she noted. On July 4, 1865, the Lindell House in St. Louis was the site of an extravaganza to celebrate the fall of Vicksburg and the opening of the Mississippi River. Politicians and the social elite dined on salmon, ham with champagne sauce, cold ornamental dishes, Supreme of Chicken a la Pre de Pois, Timbale de Servilles a la Milanaise, and ice cream. For such upper-crust affairs, it was fashionable to use ice cream and spun sugar to create cannon, forts, turrets, and other military symbols.[96]

Samuel Eliot Morison, who wrote an extensive memoir of his childhood in Boston in the last quarter of the 19th century, grew up in a family that entertained often. His extended family hosted everything from very formal dinners for visiting dignitaries to Daughters of the American Revolution luncheons and card parties. Ice cream was almost always on the Morisons' menu. After playing whist, the Morisons' guests enjoyed oysters, game, ice cream, and champagne. At a luncheon for the Warren and Prescott Chapter, DAR, the ladies nibbled on turkey salad, chartreuse of grouse, creamed oysters, lobster farci, dainty sandwiches, ice cream, and water ices.

In the tradition of Boston's elite, both Morison's father and grandfather belonged to a dining club. When the Morisons hosted this club, they served oysters, radishes, soup, roe shad, cucumbers, creamed chicken, string beans, filet of beef, Brussels sprouts, mushrooms, Roman punch, duck, celery and lettuce salad, cheese and olives, ice cream, coffee, and wine. When Morison's young friends were invited for an afternoon of fun, they ate sandwiches, pink and white ice cream, cake, and milk. Reluctantly, Morison gave up his daily ice cream soda when he became a teenager and suffered from the malady that has plagued adolescents of all eras—pimples.[97]

Records of White House entertaining reveal that the First Families shared the Morisons' taste for ice cream. At President James Buchanan's inauguration, the refreshments included oysters, chicken salad, jellies, mutton, ham, tongue, ice cream, and pâtes. Although Democrat Buchanan and Republican President James Garfield had little in common personally or politically, their inaugural cuisine was definitely similar. The provisions for Garfield's inaugural ball consisted of turkey, oysters, ham, chicken salad, biscuits, jellies, ice cream, and cake. For President Ulysses S. Grant's second inaugural, the weather was so cold that the champagne and ice cream were frozen solid. But the guests did not seem to notice because they only wanted hot drinks.[98]

During Grant's administration, his daughter Nellie was married in the East Room of the White House. Following the ceremony, the bridal party, the immediate family, and intimate friends were seated in the State Dining Room, while the other guests were relegated to nearby parlors. After a substantial meal, Nellie's wedding cake was served along with ice cream, water ices, chocolate pudding, and chilled fruits.[99]

The next White House wedding was on June 2, 1886, when President Grover Cleveland married Frances Folsom, the daughter of his former law partner. After observing the ceremony in the Blue Parlor, the small group of guests followed the couple into the family dining room, where the wedding supper was served. The guests were not seated but mingled as they munched on croquettes, game, salads, ices, creams, and champagne.[100]

Ellen Maury Slayden, the wife of a Texas politician, observed Washington society during several presidential administrations. Although she enjoyed her status as a a congressional wife, she was often disdainful of the women she met. "The Washington Smart Set, like others I have glimpsed, is too much concerned with smartness to be interesting," she wrote. In her diary, she described many social events, including the following luncheon during the McKinley era:

I went to a ladies' luncheon where 12 overdressed and overfed women, with not even one little man to leaven the lump, sat down to a table beautiful and expensive but too much beribboned for my taste—ribbon and gravy are so incompatible. Broad pink satin strips ran diagonally across, with big bows, like a little girl's sash, at each corner. . . .

We were offered ten courses, all wonderful to behold, especially the ice cream—pink roses falling out of a pink sugar umbrella into spun-candy snow.

Slayden also related the anecdote of a Western senator at a dinner party who heaped ice cream on the fancy Brazilian-point doily on his dessert plate and was preparing to stuff the well-laden doily into his mouth when she rescued him with as much tact as was possible in such an embarrassing situation.[101]

While ice cream made an elegant dessert for formal occasions, such as inaugural balls, it was also appropriate for informal events, such as Sunday school picnics and the Fourth of July. Reminiscences about Independence Day often depict making and eating ice cream as an integral part of the patriotic celebration. Catherine Bigham Brode's recollections of the holiday in Chatsworth, Illinois, are typical of small-town America. A parade, orations, fireworks, and picnics attracted Chatsworth's entire population from the oldest to the youngest. Brode remembered:

As soon as the daily chores about the place were finished, the younger members of the family were off to join the crowds that filled the main streets. Each had his precious dime tucked away in a pocket but, fearful that it might disappear, it would be handled every few minutes until the choice between lemonade, ice cream or firecrackers had been made.[102]

Like Brode, many authors have written nostalgically about the simplicity of life in America when most families lived on farms or in small towns. Some of the most elegant memoirs have been written about the pure pleasures of growing up in an era before Teenage Mutant Ninja Turtles and Mighty Morphin Power Rangers. Not surprisingly, eating homemade ice cream is often part of those memories, as in the following:

It was a great time for children. In summer, when ice cream (and it really had cream, not thin milk) would be made at home, there was always the dividing-up of the labor between the kids, each doing a fixed number of turns with the crank. And afterward, there was the sharing of the ice cream left clinging to the dasher. Nothing in a dish, eaten with a spoon, was as full of flavor as that remnant, hardly five minutes old. Chances were that we could look across from the back porch and see the cow that had given us the cream and the tree that had given us the nuts. The chances were just as good that we had milked that cow and gathered those nuts.[103]

For children, ice cream marked the climax of the traditional end-of-school picnic, but it was also popular at more elaborate, adult picnics. George Wymberley Jones De Renne of Savannah wrote an account of a picnic that he hosted in 1878, when he chartered a steamer, *The Centennial*, for $50 to take a group of friends on a day cruise down the river. He carried aboard bamboo rocking chairs for the ladies, napkins, plates, dishes, tumblers, wine glasses, knives, forks, spoons, saucers, and other necessities. His picnic provisions included boned turkey, sandwiches, crab salad, chicken salad, rolls, orange sherbet, strawberries, strawberry ice cream, snowball pound cake, champagne, sherry, whiskey, and plenty of ice. It proved to be a very pleasant outing. "The weather was perfect and nothing untoward happened," he wrote in his diary. What more could one ask on a picnic?[104]

While Easterners and city residents could enjoy ice cream regularly, there remained remote areas where the treat was largely unknown. Although residents in some small frontier towns could buy ice cream from soda fountains, drugstores, bakeries, or candy kitchens by the 1850s, many other frontiersmen had never tasted it.[105]

The first record of ice cream in Montana Territory was in 1869, when it was served on the steamboat *Nile*, piloted by Capt. Grant Marsh. On the way to Fort Benton, the *Nile* stopped at Fort Peck and took on some ice from a supply the soldiers had harvested the previous winter. After leaving the fort, the steamboat stopped for fuel and picked up two backwoodsmen as passengers, X. Beidler and Liver Eatin' Johnson. One night, the *Nile*'s cook served ice cream for dinner. Neither Beidler nor Johnson had ever seen or even heard of it before. Biedler, though suspicious of the frozen delicacy, did not want to appear ignorant, so he pretended that he had eaten it previously. However, Johnson blurted out, "Where in ——— does this stuff come from?" "Shut up, you fool," replied Beidler. "It comes in cans."[106]

Despite the contrived punch line, this anecdote was probably based on fact. The 1867–1920 city directories for Helena, Montana's capital, list no ice cream parlors. And Helena was not unique in this respect. In many remote areas, ice cream remained a rarity until the turn of the century or even later.

As the 20th century neared, ice cream found an unlikely champion in the person of James J. Corbett, a professional boxer. Corbett, who was called Gentleman Jim due to his proper manners and clean living, was not the stereotypical pugilist. While working as a bank clerk in California, he tried amateur boxing and soon turned professional.

In 1892, the hard-drinking, bombastic heavyweight champion John L. Sullivan, who had a habit of swaggering into bars and declaring, "I can lick any sonofabitch in the house," announced that he would defend his title. In issuing his challenge, he named three men he would like to fight, with Corbett being his third choice.[107]

Although Corbett was not Sullivan's top choice, he was the first to put up money and thus secure a fight. On September 7, 1892, in New Orleans, Corbett knocked out Sullivan in the twenty-first round of the first heavyweight title bout fought with padded gloves under the Marquess of Queensberry rules. The arena shook with thunderous applause as the humbled Sullivan pulled on his dressing robe and left the ring. In striking contrast, Corbett's exit drew few cheers because he had beaten a national hero. Also in stark contrast to Sullivan, Corbett celebrated his victory by drinking milk, because he wanted to set a good example for young men.[108]

Corbett attributed his victory to clean living and his training regiment, which was somewhat unconventional. Part of his routine was eating ice cream every evening, even though boxing fans generally felt this was not properly manly. In his autobiography, he remembered, "Then, I formed the habit of going down to the most popular ice cream parlor about ten o'clock at night and eating a couple of plates of ice cream, to the accompaniment, which I could hear, of sarcastic remarks from observers in the place."

Nevertheless, Corbett persisted in eating ice cream with regularity, even after a doctor, "a well-known authority from Philadelphia," told him that it was unwise.

Corbett successfully defended his title until March 17, 1897, when Robert Fitzsimmons knocked him out in a championship bout in Carson City, Nevada. After the defeat, Corbett returned to San Francisco, his hometown, via train and promptly went to bed while his family held a post-mortem in an adjoining room. When he called for his wife, they assumed that he wanted her to send for a doctor. Instead, he said, "I'd appreciate it if you'd get me a quart of ice cream."[109]

As the first heavyweight champion to publicize his love of ice cream, Corbett's example may have inspired a later legend, Gene Tunney, who believed that dairy products were very important in a boxer's diet. Accordingly, he consumed one quart of ice cream and two quarts of milk every day. After leaving the ring where he had defeated Jack Dempsey, Tunney was asked how he would like to celebrate. According to press reports, he replied, "If you don't mind, I think I'll have a little ice cream."[110]

With everyone from street urchins to presidents and heavyweight champions eating ice cream, it is no wonder that the frozen treat was becoming ever more popular and people were inventing new ways of consuming it.

i. The cherubs are making ice cream in *sorbetières* in this detail from the frontispiece of *L'art de bien faire les glaces d'office* by Emy. *(Courtesy The Winterthur Library, Printed Book and Periodical Collection)*

2. In this magazine illustration, the woman is selling fruit and ice cream at a stand on the waterfront. (*Harper's Weekly, Sept. 18, 1875*)

3. Ice harvesting. After the ice was grooved and scored, workers sawed it into large blocks. (*Scribner's Monthly, Vol. IX, 1875*)

4. A middle class Victorian visit to a fashionable ice cream parlor.

5. This Tufts soda fountain created a sensation at the 1876 Centennial Exhibition in Philadelphia. (*Pharmaceutical Era, June 1, 1892*)

6. This ad for the Lightning hand-cranked freezer appeared in the women's magazines in 1899.

NO ZINC SURFACE in Contact with the Cream.

NO ZINC SURFACE in Contact with the Cream.

White Mountain Freezer.

(TRIPLE MOTION.)

THE LEADING ICE CREAM FREEZER OF THE WORLD.

Features of Especial Merit are:

A strong water-proof tub, bound with heavy, galvanized iron-hoops; gearing completely covered, so that nothing can get between the cogs; Cans made of the very best quality of tin-plate; **beaters of malleable iron,** and **tinned;** all castings attached to tub nicely galvanized, to prevent rusting; and, above all, **it is the only Freezer in the world having the triple motion — three simultaneous motions** — and this fact alone is sufficient to commend it to every one in want of a first-class ice cream Freezer.

All material used is of the highest possible grade, and workmanship the very best.

"Frozen Dainties."

A book of Choice receipts for Ice Cream, Sherbet, Water Ices, etc., packed in every Freezer.

For prices and other information enquire of

7. The retailer could print his name and address on the foot of this White Mountain freezer trade card.

8. Trade cards, like this one for White Mountain ice cream freezers, featured attractive pictures on the front side and information about the product on the back.

9. A pretty girl eating ice cream was a popular subject for calendar art.

10. Plain soda fountains, like the one in this magazine illustration, were often found in small towns where stores could not afford the faddish, ornate models.

11. Movie stars Eddie Quillan and Sally O'Neil shared an ice cream soda in *The Sophomore*, released in 1929. (*Courtesy The Museum of Modern Art, Film Stills Archives*)

12. An ice cream sandwich and a cold drink were a popular snack at crossroads stores in rural America.

13. Children run down the street to catch the Good Humor truck. (*Courtesy Good Humor–Breyers Ice Cream*)

14. The success of Good Humor and Eskimo Pie prompted many manufacturers to market novelties.

15. Valley Farm's Bing Crosby brand was promoted as "the cream of the stars."

16. In this 1934 photo, a worker was filling ice cream cartons in a plant on Long Island. (*Courtesy Good Humor–Breyers Ice Cream*)

17. Customers lined up to buy the cone with the curl on top at Dairy Queen. (*Courtesy International Dairy Queen, Inc.*)

18. The teenagers in this 1941 photo were hanging out at the soda fountain in Olmstead Falls, Ohio. (*Photo by Walter Kneal*)

19. The menu at Seattle's Igloo drive-in included a special ice cream sundae called the Boeing Bomber. (*Courtesy Ralph Grossman*)

20. Ben and Jerry's first shop was a converted gas station in Burlington, Vermont. (*Courtesy Ben and Jerry's*)

4

Sodas, Sundaes, and Other Innovations: Soda Fountain Treats in the 19th Century

Setting the Stage

Today it is hard to imagine the novelty and excitement surrounding the first soda fountains. However, in the days before air conditioners, refrigerators, and artificial ice, a glass of cold bubbly water was truly an epicurean delight. Imagine how a glass of icy water must have tasted on a humid August day to a man laboring outdoors in the blazing sun, a woman wearing a long dress and several layers of petticoats, or a clerk in a stifling office without even an electric fan to stir the air. Placed in that perspective, it is not surprising that a very prosperous industry developed around a product as simple as frigid, effervescent water.

The American soda fountain evolved from an ugly spigot protruding above the drugstore counter, to ornate marble towers dispensing soda water in hundreds of flavors, to chrome-and-tile eateries where customers, perched on swiveling stools, consumed ice cream, sand-wiches, and soft drinks. In its heyday, the soda fountain served as the neighborhood social center, attracting people of all ages. It represented a unique combination of respectability, prosperity, and camaraderie. It was, in many ways, quintessentially American.

Although naturally carbonated waters have bubbled up from springs and spas since time immemorial, artificially carbonated drinks are a relatively modern invention. In the early 18th century, a Belgian chemist named Jean Baptiste Van Helmont coined the word "gas" to describe a mysterious substance he had observed. This gas seemed to be every-where. It collected in mines, escaped from burning charcoal, formed wherever fermentation was in progress, appeared as a result of respiration, was imprisoned in calcareous minerals, and animated naturally effervescent waters. Later, Joseph Black would name it "fixed air" while Antoine-Laurent Lavoisier would label it "carbonic acid."[1]

A Frenchman, Gabriel Venel, is credited with making the first artificial carbonated water. In 1750, he reported to the French Academy of Sciences on his research, which included producing seltzer water by mixing two drams of soda and marine acid in a pint of water. Seventeen years later, Joseph Priestley produced a carbonated beverage by pouring water back and forth between two small vessels held in a layer of carbon dioxide over the fermenting mass in a brewery vat. He also impregnated water with fixed air, using sulfur acid and chalk. Although Priestley failed to interest others in producing carbonated water, an early biographer of his friend Thomas Jefferson said that the clergyman-scientist "not only did all he could to assist the birth of the nation, but he invented the national beverage."[2]

In 1770 a Swedish chemist, Tobern Bergman, became interested in producing artificial mineral waters because he noticed that natural waters imported from Germany relieved colic. He invented an apparatus to generate carbonic-acid gas from chalk using vitriolic acid. Then he impregnated water with the carbonic acid and added various minerals in an attempt to imitate natural springs.[3]

In the early 1800s, Professor Benjamin Silliman of Yale began manufacturing and bottling small quantities of carbonated water. In 1807, Henry Thompson of Tottenham, Middlesex, was granted a British patent for impregnating water with gas. Two years later, an American, Joseph Hawkins, invented machinery to produce soda water. Around the same time, Simmons and Rundell of Charleston, South Carolina, invented a process for saturating water with fixed air. Patent office indexes indicate that the first United States patent for a mineral water apparatus was issued to Samuel Fahnestock in 1819. In 1836, Robert Boston and T. Bryant were granted a patent for a soda fountain.[4]

Circa 1810, Dr. Phillip Syng Physic of Philadelphia, impressed with Bergman's claims regarding the beneficial effects of artificial mineral water, decided to manufacture it. He collaborated with Townsend Speakman, a pharmacist, to fabricate an apparatus that utilized sulphuric acid and sodium bicarbonate to make carbonic gas, which they used to impregnate water. Then they added medicinal salts.[5]

As scientists gained experience in producing soda water, it became obvious that there were two essential ingredients: an acid and a carbonate. Trial and error revealed that sulphuric acid was superior to any other for making carbonated water. Pulverized marble, whiting (powdered calcium carbonate), and bicarbonate of soda were all used for the carbonate, with ground marble eventually emerging as the preferred material.[6]

One of the first soda water fountains was operational in 1808 in Philadelphia, where a merchant dispensed mineral water that was "prepared underground" and transported "through perpendicular wooden columns, which enclose metallick tubes." In 1810, a fountain operator in

New York City sold seltzer waters that were reputed to cure obesity. The habit of drinking mineral water quickly became popular, and a British visitor to Philadelphia in 1819 observed that "the first thing every American who can afford five cents . . . takes, on rising in the morning, is a glass of soda water."[7]

In this early period, sodium carbonate was often dissolved in water impregnated with carbonic acid to enhance its effervescence. But this apparently proved unsatisfactory, because the technique fell into disuse. In 1821, a Philadelphia doctor noted that the liquid sold at apothecaries under the name of soda water had "a wrong appellation" because it contained no soda.[8] A later critic agreed that soda water was an "accidental and inappropriate name . . . fastened upon it by an obscure manufacturer, who either derived his gas from bicarbonate of soda, or thought to improve the acidulated liquid by adding a little soda to it." This writer predicted that the word "carbonade" would "be universally adopted in a few years." Aerated water, marble water, and carbonic acid water were also promoted as more precise terms, but soda water survived all the alternatives.[9]

Soda water might never have become the American national beverage if John Matthews had not emigrated from England to the United States in the 1830s. As a teenager, Matthews had been apprenticed to Joseph Bramah, a creative soul who invented the permutation bank lock, a hydraulic press, and a type of seamless lead tubing. From Bramah, Matthews had learned how to construct an apparatus to make carbonic acid gas.[10]

In New York, Matthews manufactured generators of cast-iron lined with lead, in which he produced carbonic acid gas by the action of oil of vitriol (sulphuric acid) on marble dust and purified it by passing it through a water chamber. From this chamber, it traveled to a reservoir of cast-iron lined with block-tin, in which the gas was combined with water by means of a revolving agitator or by manually rocking the reservoir, which was mounted on trunnions in a cast-iron frame. To produce an appropriately bubbly water, it was necessary to rock the reservoir for 15 to 30 minutes. The resulting liquid was dispensed through a simple draft-tube projecting from a counter. To keep the beverage cold, the reservoir was packed in ice or the reservoir and the draft tube were connected by means of a coil of pipe placed in an ice box. As the beverage traveled through the coil, it was cooled by the surrounding ice. To imitate the flavor of natural mineral waters, salts were added after the water had been drawn.[11]

The use of marble chips was one of Matthews's innovations. Bramah had used whiting and chalk, but marble was easy to obtain in

New York. When Matthews's demand for chips increased, he arranged to acquire all the marble scrap from the building of St. Patrick's Cathedral—a cache that eventually produced an estimated 25 million gallons of soda water.[12]

The pressure from producing the gas sometimes caused a noisy explosion, and Matthews developed an unusual method of coping with the problem. A strong, intelligent ex-slave named Ben Austen was one of his first employees. When the pressure had to be measured, Austen simply placed his thumb on the pressure cock and when there was enough force to blow his thumb away, Matthews concluded that the water was fully charged. Fortunately, more accurate and less dangerous methods of monitoring the pressure would be invented as the industry matured. Austen, "who was a Methodist and very devout," became well known to many New Yorkers because he also sold soda water from a portable fountain on a small cart that he pushed around the city.[13]

The frequent explosion of primitive generators inspired some unknown bard to compose a macabre ditty that was often recited by soda fountain workers:

> John Blount
> Bought Fount.
>
> Weak, Thin
> Washed Tin.
>
> Fount Bust,
> John Dust.

Regulating water pressure was also a problem in the beginning. Because the water pressure was forceful and unpredictable in the first fountains, when the spigot was opened water sometimes spurted out, dousing everything in its path. One industry pioneer remembered that the soda water poured out "with sufficient force to rebound to the ceiling." He described the operation of drawing water from the spigot or draft arm as follows:

To each of these arms a rubber nozzle was attached, against which the nose of a bottle, made for that purpose, was held in such a manner as to form an air tight joint, thus making it possible for the druggist to fill the bottle with water from the fountain without experiencing the inconvenience arising from a sputtering, spurting, and uncontrollable single stream directed into an uncovered glass, and this arrangement had the further advantage of permitting soda to be drawn without the loss of a great amount of gas. . . . When the bottle was filled the druggist would pour its contents into a glass, secure in the knowledge that no injury would come to his ceiling.[14]

In the first fountains installed in shops, only the draft tube or spigot—called a gooseneck due to its long, curving shape—protruded above the counter. In an attempt to make these faucets more attractive, the curved portion was sometimes fashioned into a bird's head, complete with eyes and a beak, where the water poured out. Goosenecks quickly became old hat in a faddish industry, but manufacturers continued to sell them to country stores and small drugstores that could not afford trendy, upscale models.[15]

In this formative stage of the industry, most soda water was sold in pharmacies. One trade journal described the early business as follows:

Partially on account of the recognized medicinal properties of soda water and partially because of the marked absence of swell confectioners' shops in those days, its sale, in the populated places, may be said to have been confined to apothecary stores; in the rural sections the general store, perhaps, had a pair of uncleanly draught tubes set on a corner of its well-laden counter.[16]

Although the gooseneck was adequate for its intended purpose, manufacturers soon began marketing decorative metal urns that sat on top of the counter. In both gooseneck and urn fountains, the unsightly mechanical works remained concealed beneath the countertop or in the basement. The urn, which had a removable lid, often served as a reservoir for ice, helping to cool the water as it was dispensed. The first decorative soda fountain in New York City was an urn on a stand outside the Barnum Museum.[17]

The Tontine Coffee House in New York City was one of the first firms to install several urn fountains. According to a contemporary description, "The cisterns are placed in the cellar, and the waters are conveyed to the bar in block-tin tubes, which pass up into mahogany pillars, crowned with gilt urns. . . . The pillars with their urns stand a foot apart, and the middle one is raised above the others." From this description, it is easy to see how the urn fountain evolved into the marble column fountain, which resembled an architectural pillar with a base and a capital.[18]

In the late 1830s, a novel idea—flavored soda water—propelled the business in a new direction and greatly enhanced the beverage's popularity. Historians believe that the first flavored soda water was served in Philadelphia and have identified two possible originators. One was Elie Magliore Durand, a pharmacist who was the father of the modern drugstore because he diversified his business by selling cigars and soda water as well as medicines. The other was Eugene Roussel, who sold French perfumes and mineral waters in a small shop that catered to an exclusive clientele.[19]

Roussel, who sold his mineral water in bottles, reportedly used lemon as his first flavoring. His success quickly spawned no less than six additional flavored mineral water dealers in Philadelphia. Within a few years, Roussel's bottled water was being shipped to New York City, where it was sold by John Tweddle, who had competition from at least two more shops. As demand grew, bottled mineral waters were served in ballrooms, saloons, and concert halls in New York. It was not uncommon for each of the city's two largest ballrooms, Niblo's Garden and Tammany Hall, to order 200 dozen bottles for a special event.[20]

Whether Durand or Roussel first thought of flavoring soda water, the idea caught on immediately. Soon, most fountain operators were keeping bottles of syrup on hand to spice up their drinks. The inventory of flavors grew from a few basic choices to literally hundreds in the late 19th century. Vanilla and fruit flavors were industry standards from the beginning. As demand grew, operators experimented with more exotic tastes, such as celery tonic, ginger, nectar, pepsin, sarsaparilla, root beer, champagne, and claret. Phosphates were made by adding a dash of citric or tartaric acid solution to the mixture of syrup and carbonated water. Commercial bottled syrups were available, but some soda fountain operators preferred to make their own syrups, using fresh fruits.

Matthews's original machinery, with improvements, became the standard for the soda fountain industry in the United States. In Philadelphia, Charles Lippincott went into the soda water business in 1832 and subsequently began to manufacture marble dispensers. A few years later, A.D. Puffer and A.J. Morse, both of Boston, started manufacturing soda fountains. Puffer received the first patent for a soda-water cooler, while Morse manufactured a vertical copper generator and portable copper tanks for storing and transporting beverages. Toward the end of the 1830s, William Gee, who had been an apprentice under Matthews, established his own business and patented several devices, including a blow-off cock for generators and a pump for forcing water into the fountain against pressure.[21]

In 1848, the Galena and Chicago Union Railway inaugurated the Windy City's first train service, and the City of Chicago constructed its first municipal building. That same year, Josiah H. Reed opened Chicago's first soda fountain. The generator was shipped from New York, while the remainder of the fountain was fabricated, according to

Reed's specifications, in Chicago. Since many Chicagoans had never seen a fountain, "for many days it proved a wonder and was a shrine at which many worshipped."

Reed found that the demand for soda water at times exceeded the capacity of his single marble-box fountain, so he decided to add another. Because "many ladies disliked to take soda where they were liable to encounter a crowd," he installed the second one on the opposite side of his store, "especially dedicated to the requirements of the fair sex." Men were never served at the ladies' fountain unless they were accompanied by a woman.

Reed prided himself on serving very cold, highly charged soda water and was rewarded with a business that sometimes reached two thousand glasses per day, even though Chicago was basically still a frontier town. The flavors, which were stored in elegant cut-glass decanters in an ice chest under the counter, were limited to sarsaparilla, lemon, vanilla, strawberry, and raspberry. A Reed employee later recalled, "There was a single public cab for hiring purposes, and a ride in that vehicle, with a drink of soda after, was considered quite an event in one's life."[22]

It is impossible to pinpoint when soda fountains were introduced in most states, but it is certain that the industry moved west with the settlers. Although a soda fountain was not likely to be the first amenity in a frontier settlement, many of the more prosperous towns had fountains as early as the 1850s.[23]

In that same decade, Gustavus D. Dows—who worked as a clerk in his brother's drugstore in Lowell, Massachusetts—revolutionized the soda water industry with a new fountain that was ingenious, simple, and practical. Dows marketed a design that incorporated several technical advances and dispensed eight flavors directly from the fountain, which was basically a rectangular box with a cooler for the soda water, a large spigot for controlling the water flow, and metal containers for the syrups. The flow from each syrup container was controlled by a silver-plated faucet, which became a distinctive Dows trademark because each one was topped by an eagle that served as the lever for opening and closing it.[24]

Another of Dows's innovations was building an ice shaver into his fountain because clerks often complained that preparing shaved ice by hand was too time-consuming. In his fountain, a block of ice was stored inside the box and the operator turned a crank on the outside to shave off slivers, which fell through a slot into a glass. The new storage arrangement for water, syrup, and ice made "the coldest and most delicious glass of soda water that had ever been produced up to that time." As with other designs, Dows's white marble box sat on the counter that concealed the machinery.[25]

The draft tubes in Dows's box had soft rubber nozzles, which allowed the operator to hold the bottle snugly against the spigot while it was being filled, preventing carbonation from escaping from the water. With the advent of the marble fountain, consumers tended to disparage the urns and goosenecks, "imagining that soda from them was not as good as from the marble."[26]

In subsequent models, Dows improved his design by inventing the first double-stream draft tube, which enabled the operator to choose either a fine, forceful stream or a broader stream with less pressure. This provided more flexibility and control, so that the water could be poured directly into a tumbler, eliminating the bottle if the operator so desired. Although the principle behind this new draft tube was really rather simple, a trade magazine reported that "some of the druggists in the rural sections of New England, on first viewing the workings of this draught cock arrangement, had a lurking suspicion that Mr. Dows was a conjurer, and some of them did not hesitate to say so."[27]

Dows installed his first fountain in Lowell, but he soon moved to Boston to test the waters in the big city. When he set up the Dows Ice Cream Soda Apparatus in a location that seemed less than promising, skeptics declared that no soda business had ever been done, nor ever could be done, in that neighborhood. Nevertheless, his first season's sales greatly exceeded his highest expectations. Elated, he applied for a patent and opened a small manufacturing firm the following year. Orders for his fountain poured in from virtually every northern state.

Dr. Z.S. Sampson, Boston's leading druggist, was the first to buy a Dows fountain. Subsequently, Sampson gave an enthusiastic endorsement to Dows' apparatus, declaring that his soda water sales had increased from $500 to $16,000 per year. Sampson's aggressive advertising campaign was at least partially responsible for his success. He plastered Boston with signs proclaiming that a person who failed to taste a glass of Sampson's soda would "miss one-half the pleasure of his life."[28]

Sampson also utilized tokens, a promotional tool that was popular for many years. Some fountain operators sold tokens, which looked like movie theater tickets or were metal coins inscribed with the name of the store, in bulk, offering a discount to customers who bought them. Tokens, whether paper or metal, offered an obvious advantage to regular soda drinkers and saved the clerk the trouble of making change. Sometimes several stores would cooperate in issuing tokens that could be used at different fountains in the same city. Bliss & Sharp of Chicago sold tokens that were left in the store by the purchaser and filed in a large drawer near the fountain. This drawer was divided into numerous small compartments, each of which was labeled with a customer's name. Although Bliss & Sharp's tokens entailed no discount, they were a convenience for regular customers and for the clerks.[29]

In the 1860s, the Puffer fountain added a new draft tube that permitted soda water and syrups to be drawn through the same nozzle. Puffer also introduced a revolving water gauge and a pressure regulator that controlled the water pressure while bottles were being filled, preventing breakage.[30]

Around the same time, Puffer added another first, the hot soda apparatus, to his list of innovations. Like cold-water models, the early hot soda machines were unattractive, primitive affairs that evolved into more efficient, ornate fixtures. Hot soda was never as popular as cold soda, but it did become a significant money-maker for some stores, particularly in colder climates. In 1892, a trade publication stated, "During the last dozen years the demand for hot soda has grown amazingly, and now every dealer is compelled to be able to cater to a winter as well as a summer demand." In many stores, hot chocolate was the most popular flavor. Fountain operators with good hot chocolate formulas guarded them closely and even refused large amounts of money for their recipes.[31]

In 1863, James W. Tufts, a druggist in a small town near Boston, wanted to buy a soda fountain from Dows but discovered that there was a waiting list. Impatient, Tufts designed and built his own, a rectangular marble fountain, which utilized metal cooling cylinders that kept the water at very low temperatures. The syrup containers were positioned in the rear of the box and connected with the faucets by means of coolers passing beneath the ice.[32]

Tufts apparently intended to build only one fountain for himself, but his design attracted so much favorable comment that he decided to go into manufacturing. He called his first model the Arctic, a reference to its major selling point—the very cold temperature of its soda water. His first factory was an assembly plant, where components that had been made in other locations were put together—an unusual arrangement at the time. Tufts, who had other business interests, regarded soda fountains as a sideline in the beginning. Later, his fountain business would employ 600 skilled laborers, 50 salesmen, 65 clerks, and "designers of no small number."[33]

Near the end of the Civil War, it was estimated that there were only 15 soda fountains in Chicago. But Tufts and other manufacturers targeted the city as a major market and expanded their efforts to sell their products there. They were so successful that at least 200 soda fountains were operating in Chicago at the time of the 1871 fire. Only a handful were operational after the disaster, and the fountain business was slow to recover. The aftermath of the fire "forced the people to study more closely the policy of economy and forego for a time those little luxuries with which they had been wont to indulge themselves." Therefore, in the decade following the fire, few Chicago businesses were willing to invest in expensive soda fountains.[34]

In 1867, the American soda water industry was represented at the Exposition Universelle in Paris. Dows left his family in charge of his manufacturing concern while he went to France to supervise the operation of a soda fountain and restaurant at the exposition. All the restaurant furnishings, from the ranges to the piano, were manufactured in the United States, and the cuisine was thoroughly American. Even the waiters were transported from the United States to Paris for the fair. Although the Europeans were lukewarm about American food in general, the cream soda was a big hit. "It was popular with the mass of the people, and even kings and emperors often partook of the delicious draught," according to a report given to the United States Senate.[35]

Even though Dows lost a substantial amount of money on his venture at the Exposition Universelle, he was convinced that there was a market for American products in Europe. In the next few years, he spent much of his time abroad, establishing a soda fountain industry in England and France. His efforts were quite successful in London, where the British queued up like "long files of clerks after stamps at the New York post office."

When Dows returned to Boston, he discovered that his rivals had been busy in his absence. Several new manufacturers had entered the business, and the competition was fiercer than ever. Nevertheless, Dows optimistically moved his workers into a larger factory. Later, he even diversified into bottling ginger ale as well as making fountains. Then financial problems forced him to sell off most of his assets. In 1875, a disastrous fire ruined what was left of his business, which was grossly underinsured. Although he lived for another 11 years, he never recovered financially.[36]

In 1868, Matthews was reputed to be the world's largest soda fountain manufacturer. Most of the fountain makers understood the value of promotion, and advertising was a big factor in Matthews's success. One of his better-known advertising slogans went as follows: "Youth as it sips its first soda experiences the sensations which, like the sensations of love, cannot be forgotten." Although Madison Avenue would probably not be impressed by this slogan, it coupled romance with selling a soft drink, just as today's commercials do.[37]

In 1870, John Matthews died, but his business was continued by his family. Four years later, the first patent was granted for the Matthews steel fountain, which was a marked improvement over previous cast-iron and copper models.[38]

In 1869, Tufts introduced the cottage-style fountain, which was more an innovation in architecture than in technology. He added a slanted roof to the box, making it look somewhat like a cabin or a dog house, as it was sometimes called. Until that time, white Italian marble had been the industry norm, but Tufts offered his new cottage fountain in different colors of Tennessee, Vermont, and New York stone.[39]

Response to the new style was so favorable that Tufts soon offered a French cottage, a slightly more ornate version with a vase of flowers on the roof. Then, pressure from competitors who were marketing their own cottage fountains prompted Tufts to design a grandiose version that resembled a castle. The larger size of these new fountains allowed operators to dispense up to 20 syrups and to provide faster service.

Tufts's architectural embellishments started a trend toward more decorative fountains with a hint of the exotic and the fantastic. In the coming years, designers would borrow elements from Gothic, Roman, Byzantine, Egyptian, and Oriental architecture to create fancy fountains with imaginative names: the Transcendent, the Nonpareil, the Titania, the Spectre, the Meteor, the Frost King, the Icefloe, the Avalanche, and the Cathedral—to name only a few. Soda gushed from tombs, temples, and turrets adorned with cupids, wild animals, knights, and partially clothed nymphs. Now customers were drawn into a shop to marvel at the splendor of the fountain as well as to drink the soda water.[40]

In urban areas, the installation of the latest fad in fountain architecture guaranteed a brisk business—at least until a competitor opened a more ornate model. The impact of a fancy new fountain in Chicago was typical. "The new fountain was a great curiosity, it was talked about all over the city and out of the city, and many were tempted to drink from the new affair out of curiosity to see how it worked," reported a trade magazine. The reporter quoted the fountain's owner as saying that "it is the grossest error imaginable to suppose that there is any economy in having a small and unpretentious apparatus."[41]

While the fancy fountains were quite expensive, costing thousands of dollars, manufacturers continued to sell more modest models for small stores. For example, the Tufts catalog advertised a generator, a four-gallon steel fountain, and a silver-plated dispensing tube for only $140. A system with a larger generator, a six-gallon fountain, four syrup faucets, and one water faucet cost a mere $237. Puffer suggested a system costing $345 for small businesses. Some stores leased their fountains from manufacturers or distributors, enabling them to have a more elaborate system than they could otherwise afford. The popularity of leasing varied from city to city. In Chicago very few fountains were leased, but the number of rented fountains outnumbered owned ones in St. Louis.[42]

The 1876 Centennial Exhibition in Philadelphia provided a unique chance to promote soda water because temperance advocates persuaded fair officials to ban alcoholic beverages. Seizing the opportunity, Tufts and Lippincott joined forces to pay $50,000 for an exclusive concession, and each operated 14 of his fanciest fountains. Fairgoers were favorably impressed by Lippincott's black-marble Minnehaha model, which was ornamented with silver pillars, bronze dolphins, a lion's head, bronze urns, and fluted basins. Another popular Lippincott fountain featured variegated marble, alabaster statuary, bronze urns, a silver crown, and a silver bouquet-holder.[43]

As the *pièce de résistance* for the exhibition, Tufts built the most ornate tower-of-marble fountain ever seen. The structure, which was 33 feet high and weighed 30 tons, reportedly cost $25,000. It did an enormous business and, according to some sources, made a substantial profit. Although Tufts claimed that it did not make money, he nevertheless believed that the venture had been successful because it was an excellent advertisement for the industry.[44]

Soda water sales at the Centennial were stimulated by the stifling heat that plagued Philadelphia that summer. An English visitor, who obviously belonged to the group that believed consuming cold foods was unhealthy, reported, "I was nearly dissolved by the heat . . . one is compelled at considerable risk to be continually eating iced creams and drinking 'arctic waters.' "[45]

After the exhibition, Tufts's huge soda fountain proved to be a white elephant because no buyer could be found and it had to be warehoused for a few years. Then it was moved to Coney Island until 1885, when it was purchased by a department store, the Famous Clothing Company of St. Louis. There it proved to be a popular attraction, and customers traveled many miles just to say that they had enjoyed a glass of soda water from it. On November 17, 1891, fire destroyed the Famous Clothing Company, ending the saga of the centennial fountain.[46]

In the late 1880s, the Low Art Tile Company, owned by J.G. Low of Chelsea, Massachusetts, began producing marble fountains with tile facades. The first Low's fountain, which was installed in a drugstore in New York's Fifth Avenue Hotel, attracted a great deal of attention in an industry where novelty was a major drawing card. Noted primarily for their aesthetic qualities, Low's fountains typically had bas relief designs in colored tiles ranging "from pale yellows and delicate grays, through the entire scale to intense, lustrous browns and vigorous tones of green and even black."[47]

In 1891, a major magazine declared, "Soda water is an American drink." That same year, the four largest fountain manufacturers merged and organized the American Soda Fountain Company to serve as an umbrella corporation. The four subsidiaries—James W. Tufts, A.D. Puffer & Sons, Charles Lippincott & Company, and the John Matthews Apparatus Company—continued to operate separately, but they effectively created a trust to monopolize the industry and control prices. Only a few smaller manufacturers, including Otto Zweitusch of Milwaukee, Bennett and Gompers of New York, the Robert M. Green Company of Philadelphia, and the Iron-Clad Can Company of Brooklyn, managed to stay in business.[48]

In 1892, the four manufacturers in the American Soda Fountain Company had equipment sales of more than $3 million. That same year, the St. Louis Automatic Refrigerating Company used liquefied ammonia gas to cool fountains and make ice. Proponents claimed that ammonia refrigeration saved time, labor, and money because clerks did not have to repeatedly fill the fountain with ice. The St. Louis company appears to have been the first to use this type of refrigeration in soda fountains. About this same time, the American Carbonate Company began operating in New York City, furnishing liquid carbonic acid gas in portable wrought-iron cylinders for use in carbonating beverages.[49]

In 1895, it was estimated that there were 50,000 to 60,000 soda fountains in the United States. In the words of a trade magazine, the soda fountain manufacturers' "names are known throughout the United States and their agents are everywhere." Tufts declared that "soda water, which a few years ago was a novelty and luxury, is now looked upon as a necessity."[50]

In the last decade of the 19th century, New York City alone had hundreds of fountains operating in drugstores, department stores, haberdasheries, confectionaries, and dairy-kitchen restaurants. Thirsty residents could buy their soda at all types of fountains, from the small portable ones pushed along the streets on carts to the world's largest soda fountain—the 40-foot long Riverside, built by Matthews for a Sixth Avenue drugstore.[51]

Two of the busiest fountains in New York City were located in pharmacies near the Brooklyn Bridge. "The stream of soda water, flavored in every conceivable way, that runs all day—and all night— from the fountains of these two pharmacies into the thirsty throats of the multitude is prodigious," declared a trade publication. "Night and day an army of soda water clerks are busy drawing and mixing the sparkling beverage, cold in summer and hot in winter, the effervescent flow never ceasing." The menu at these fountains included almond, anise, apple, apricot, banana, birch beer, blackberry, blood orange, calisaya, champagne cider, cherry, chocolate, cinnamon, Java and mocha coffee, cognac, coriander, cream soda, currant, excelsior bouquet, ginger, ginger ale, gooseberry, grape, green gage, grenadine, hoarhound, julep, lemon, Persian and Bavarian mead, mint julep, mulberry, nectar, nutmeg, orange, orange flower, orange sherbet, orris root, peach, peach cider, pear, pear cider, peppermint, phosphate, pineapple, plum, quince, raspberry, raspberry cider, root beer, rose, sarsaparilla, sherbet, strawberry, tonic beer, vanilla, wild cherry, and wintergreen. Customers could also order egg phosphates, milk shakes, or koumyss (a fermented milk beverage).[52]

As is obvious from the preceding list, the number of soda water flavors proliferated over the years, with operators advertising "strange combinations with stranger names." In addition, many fountain operators dispensed common medicines. According to a trade journal, "No well-regulated fountain is now complete without a list of such remedies as bicarbonate soda, seidlitz powders, bromo-caffeine, aromatic spirits ammonia, and tincture ginger." Quinine, antipyrine, and phenacetine were also sold at fountains.[53]

In most locations, a glass of flavored soda water cost a nickel throughout the 19th century and well into the 20th. Although some of the posher fountains charged a dime for a glass, most operators felt that five cents was a fair price. In large cities, department store fountains often charged only three cents per glass, but the drugstore's stiffest competition came from confectioners who had fountains in their shops. Of course, all soda fountains charged more for fancy drinks requiring fresh fruit or ice cream.[54]

Fountains were a social center for young people, serving in a genteel fashion the function that singles bars would serve much later. In a subtle, refined manner, soda fountains promoted romance. Not surprisingly, some fountain owners, such as the Huyler's chain, sought to capitalize on this by cultivating a clientele of stylish young women. Consider, for example, the following description of a Huyler's in New York City:

The fountain at Huyler's is the shrine before which the Vassar girl bows down in worship. The gently sparkling liquid, with its soft lumps of frozen delight, has a peculiarly soothing effect upon the membrane of the Vassar girl's graceful throat, and there is no more inspiring sight these days than is afforded by a group of these fair young creatures seated before a fountain, gracefully delving with the long, slender spoon and giving little gurgles of delight on successfully fishing from the foamy depths frozen particles of delicious chocolate or fruity strawberry.

Huyler's strategy of catering to young women worked very well, prompting a trade journal to describe the chain's sales as "phenomenal" and to proclaim that "the ice cream soda habit and the summer girl are inseparable."[55]

Throughout most of the 19th century, the United States had an active temperance movement, which became more visible and more vocal after the Civil War. The Prohibition Party, the Women's Christian Temperance Union, and the Anti-Saloon League all arose in the latter half of the century to advance the cause of sobriety. Aggressive leaders like Carry Nation, "the Kansas smasher" who did not hesitate to threaten saloonkeepers with "hatchetation," drew public attention to the movement. More importantly, responsible temperance leaders realized the significance of political power and successfully organized their followers into large voting blocs.[56]

As the temperance movement evolved, so did the attitude of the soda fountain industry toward abstinence. Alcoholic beverages, especially wines, were ingredients in some of the more popular, traditional fountain drinks. When the public first began to take the temperance movement seriously, the soda fountain industry was divided over whether to continue using alcoholic ingredients. However, as the movement gained momentum, the industry climbed aboard and, as a group, enthusiastically promoted the soda fountain as an alternative to the saloon. In 1892, a trade publication stated unequivocally, "No successful soda fountains sell ardent spirits in their soda."[57]

As the reformers gained strength, urban soda fountains took choice business locations away from saloons—much to the delight of the prohibitionists. By 1906, confectionaries or drugstores operating soda fountains could be found on one or more corners at every principal intersection in Chicago. In New York City, temperance leaders beamed as the number of soda fountains surpassed the number of bars in the Modern Gomorrah.[58]

"Temperance sired the soda fountain, and the ladies of the movement selflessly mothered it in the fond hope that it would someday vanquish the bar," according to one writer. Even though this statement exaggerates the importance of the temperance movement to the industry, soda fountains definitely profited from their image as a wholesome alternative to saloons. Male patronage increased as men looked for a substitute for strong drink. Fountain owners responded by promoting unflavored mineral waters and tart, pungent drinks that appealed to masculine tastes. Heavy, hearty drinks took their place on the menu alongside the traditional sweet, frothy concoctions favored by women and children. In 1892, a magazine noted that the demand for sour drinks and plain mineral water had grown dramatically over the past decade.[59]

Raw egg drinks—such as egg flips, egg phosphates, and egg creams—were so popular with men that they were sometimes called temperance eggnogs. The egg phosphate craze reached "sublime proportions" in Boston, and in New York City the drugstore in the Astor House was famous for its egg phosphates. "Here are stacked huge piles of eggs, apparently one for every man, woman and child of the population. But they do not remain long enough to outlive their usefulness, as they are turned into phosphate in a surprisingly short time."[60]

Men were also good customers for malts, or malted milk. Malted milk was a trademark name coined and registered by William Horlick of Racine, Wisconsin. Horlick's powder, made with dry evaporated milk and malted cereals, was originally promoted as a source of nutrition for infants and invalids, but some druggists used it to flavor soda water and ice cream sodas.[61]

As the soda fountain industry profited from the temperance movement, industry publications proudly pointed to the fountain's contribution to sobriety. "The soda fountain has become quite an important factor in the temperance question," wrote one magazine. "There is no doubt, whatever, that the increasing popularity of this business and the number of drinks brought out to tickle the palate of the thirsty man have made serious inroads in the business of the saloon."[62]

The Marriage of Ice Cream and Soda Fountains

The marriage of ice cream and soda fountains had a certain inevitability about it, even though soda fountain owners often resisted the idea. For many of them, it was a shotgun wedding because they felt it was more profitable to serve drinks only and leave the more time-consuming concoctions to restaurants and confectionaries.

The enduring relationship between ice cream and soda fountains began with the invention of the modern ice cream soda. In the 1850s, and perhaps even earlier, fountains served ice cream sodas, a drink that enjoyed tremendous popularity and staying power, despite the faddish nature of the business. But the name was deceptive because there was no ice cream in this drink, which consisted of shaved ice, sweet cream, syrup, and soda water. "People doted on this mixture and the man who made the best ice cream soda in Boston commanded the best patronage; best both in quality and number," declared a trade magazine.[63]

"Ice shaved almost as fine as snow flakes," an essential for this drink, was prepared by hand on an ice planer—"a most awkward and time-consuming machine," according to the same magazine. A small block of ice was scraped back and forth across the blades of the planer, with the slivers falling into a cup. To protect his fingers, the worker wore a special insulated glove or used small ice tongs to hold the block.[64]

This early ice cream soda seems to have been indirectly responsible for the invention of the modern ice cream soda, although it is impossible to identify the father of the newer treat with certainty because several versions of its birth have been published over the years. The principal claimants have been Fred Sanders of Detroit and Robert M. Green of Philadelphia, but J.C. Kirkbride of St. Louis and G.A. Guy of Seattle also believed that they had been present at the conception. Unfortunately, the details surrounding the claims of Kirkbride and Guy seem to have been lost. Yet another account stated that two anonymous newsboys in New York City had been the motivating force behind the creation of the ice cream soda. Of the various claims, Green's has been given the most credibility by historians.[65]

Version No. 1: Green was a soft drink concessionaire at the Franklin Institute's semicentennial celebration in Philadelphia in 1874. He had planned to operate a very elaborate soda fountain built in New York but, for unknown reasons, had to settle for a small box fountain. Green, of course, routinely served traditional ice cream sodas. However, one day he ran out of sweet cream and was unable to procure more right away. So, he bought two small pitchers at a neighboring pottery exhibit and hurried to Henry Snyder's confectionary, where he purchased vanilla ice cream, intending to use it in lieu of the cream after it had melted. When he returned to his fountain, he found a few customers waiting and was forced to use the frozen cream because he did not have time for it to thaw.

Green wrote his recollections of the event, as follows:

To note the effect of the new drink, I personally dispensed the first glass, watching at the time, with considerable anxiety, I must confess, the effect upon the first drinker of the ice cream soda. The result was entirely satisfactory, but people were slow to try the new novelty. An occasional chance passerby would stop and relish the new food drink, pass on and leave more than room for the next comer. But even so, the first day's receipts amounted to eight dollars.

Green's receipts skyrocketed to $400 per day before the celebration closed, which convinced him that he could make a fortune in the soda fountain business. Elated, he opened his own fountain manufacturing plant in Philadelphia.[66]

Version No. 2: One suffocating day in Detroit, drugstore owner Fred Sanders discovered that all the cream in his shop had soured. As fate would have it, the heat had filled his store with thirsty customers, most of whom wanted a sweet cream soda. As an experiment, Sanders measured some fruit syrup into a glass, added a scoop of ice cream, and topped it off with soda water. One sip prompted the customers to demand more. Sources do not agree on the date of this incident in Detroit, placing it as early as 1858 or as late as 1878.[67]

Version No. 3: In 1872, two newsboys regularly patronized a New York City confectionary, where they spent their pennies on gumdrops and all-day suckers. One day, because they were bored with the same old treats, they decided to create a new gastronomical delight. With the sufferance of the proprietor, they added a half-penny slice of pineapple to a glass of ice cream and then poured soda water over it. In another experiment, they poured ginger ale over ice cream and strawberries. They also tried cold coffee over ice cream. Finally, the proprietor said, "Here, boys, take all the stuff you want, make me a good drink, and it won't cost you a cent." So, they mixed one of their new concoctions for him. He liked the taste and set about perfecting it. The result was the ice cream soda.[68]

Although the patrimony of the ice cream soda is in doubt, there is no doubt that it quickly became a classic, eliciting sighs of rapture from many a consumer. In 1893, an American magazine sedately called it "our national beverage." A more enthusiastic writer declared, "[T]he ice cream soda is king." A newspaper editorial noted, "The ice cream soda is a characteristically American product along with baseball, skyscrapers, hot biscuits, Sandwich glass, Vermont maple sugar, Negro spirituals, rough-riding cowboys, and hooked rugs."[69]

Will Rogers, upon tasting his first ice cream soda as a youngster in the Oklahoma Territory, told a friend, "[I]t's the finest thing that you ever tasted in all your life. You will think that you have died and gone to heaven." A multitude of youngsters before and since have agreed with him, as in the following recollection of a childhood trip to the soda fountain:

The day is hot, and the street outside is quiet. A fly buzzes insistently somewhere; the dusty, lazy summer drifts in at the screen door. But the ice cream sodas are miracles of coolness, coloring their tall glasses delicately pink, rich brown, or pale yellow. Perhaps they represent an extra reward for a faithfully-tended woodbox or well-kept chicken pen; again, they may be in the nature of a crowning triumph to that good report card. Or just an expenditure from the small allowance given by loving parents. At any rate, childhood, with all its capacity for enjoying the present moment, is consuming them; and they are appreciated.[70]

Of course, it is impossible to please all of the people all of the time. So it is not surprising that a few individuals found the ice cream soda to be a problem. A Pennsylvania woman sued her husband for divorce, claiming that he spent too much time drinking sodas. According to the divorce papers, she owned a poultry farm that he was supposed to manage, but he neglected the chickens while he was at the fountain spending their money on ice cream sodas. She was granted a divorce. On the other hand, in a Chicago domestic dispute the court ordered the husband to eat ice cream sodas. The husband, who was accused of pulling his wife's hair every time he became intoxicated, was given a year's probation on condition that he consume ice cream rather than booze.[71]

The birth of the sundae, which was called a college ice in some locations, is even more obscure than that of the ice cream soda, but the sundae probably originated in the 1880s. A dictionary copyrighted in 1890 did not contain an entry for sundae, but a manual for soda fountain operators published in 1897 contained a recipe for a peach sundae and also noted that pear, orange, raspberry, and other fruit flavors could be made with syrup or fresh fruit. In 1900, eight flavors of sundaes were included in a trade paper's list of treats that every small fountain should serve.[72]

A manual published circa 1900 noted, "The introduction of ice cream with crushed fruits in the form of sundaes or college ices has opened a broader horizon for the soda fountain." It included an illustration of a sundae serving set, consisting of a metal cup with two handles, a glass, and a long spoon on a small tray. It advised the fountain operator to promote cherry or claret phosphate, ice water, or ginger ale as the proper drink to go along with a sundae. The author noted that the sundae was steadily gaining popularity and quoted the manager of a New York soda fountain as saying, "I am sorry it is, for a sundae requires so much time for service and cleansing the dishes and spoons afterward. But the public must get what it wants."[73]

Several towns and stores have sought to claim the honor of serving the very first sundae. However, all of the accounts are anecdotal, and none of the claimants have produced any convincing documentation.

Among the towns believed to be the birthplace of the sundae are Buffalo, New York; Evanston, Illinois; Two Rivers, Wisconsin; and Ithaca, New York.

Version No. 1: Stoddard Brothers, which was the first drugstore to install a soda fountain in Buffalo, was famous for its nickel ice cream soda. According to the recollections of one of the Stoddards, "One Sunday, when the store ran out of soda water, my Uncle Charles suggested the clerks serve two scoops of ice cream with syrup on top. It was hurriedly named a 'sundae' and became very popular." The date was 1885 or later.[74]

Version No. 2: In 1881, Edward C. Berners owned a popular ice cream parlor in Two Rivers, Wisconsin, where a dish of plain ice cream sold for a nickel. One night a customer named George Hallauer ordered a dish of ice cream and, hankering for something different, asked Berners to pour chocolate syrup over it. Berners protested that the syrup, which was used to flavor sodas, would ruin the ice cream. But Hallauer insisted, and he liked the new concoction so much that he ordered a second dish. Other customers were intrigued by his idea and tried it. As news of the new treat spread, Berners received many orders for it.

Soon confectioners in nearby Manitowoc heard about the treat. One of them, Charles W. Giffey, made a trip to Two Rivers to see what all the fuss was about. He ate one of Berners's new treats and loved it, but he was concerned about the cost. Stores could not make money serving ice cream with chocolate syrup for only a nickel. The two businessmen discussed the problem and decided that they would serve the new treat only on Sunday, as a loss leader.

What seemed like a logical solution soon encountered an illogical little girl who came into Giffey's shop and ordered the new dish on a weekday. After he explained to her that the treat was only served on Sunday, she declared that it must be Sunday because she wanted one. Unable to argue with such a determined customer, Giffey filled her order.[75]

Version No. 3: Around the turn of the century, government officials in a southern state decided to enforce the blue laws. Selling sodas was prohibited, but an ingenious druggist came up with a way to circumvent the law by adding a few berries to a glass of ice cream soda and calling it a "sundae." In some versions of this story, the druggist lived in Virginia, but other accounts do not name the southern state.[76]

In many locations, the question of what soda fountains could serve on Sunday continued to be a problem well into the 20th century. However, in some states, businesses successfully argued that ice cream should be exempt from the blue laws. In Pennsylvania, for example, a shopkeeper who was arrested for selling ice cream on Sunday was acquitted after he argued that ice cream was regularly prescribed by physicians.[77]

Version No. 4: Several sources state that the ice cream sundae originated in Ithaca, New York, but there is no agreement on the details. According to one legend, the sundae was invented at the Christiance and Dofflemyer soda fountain circa 1896. Another states that the name "sundae" was first used in 1897 at the Red Cross Pharmacy, which was directly opposite the barroom of the Ithaca Hotel. Since the bar was closed on the Sabbath, erstwhile patrons meandered across the street to the drugstore where they bought the distinctly Sunday treat.[78]

Yet another legend credits the innovation to a young minister who habitually dropped into an Ithaca drugstore for a dish of ice cream following his Sunday sermon. One Sabbath Day in 1891, ice cream did not appeal to him, nor did the proprietor's suggestion of soda water. However, the clergyman felt that a combination of the two might satisfy him. Therefore, he ordered a dish of ice cream with cherry soda syrup on top. The dish was so good that he decided to name it, and Sunday seemed appropriate.[79]

Version No. 5: Evanston, Illinois, was a "Methodist-minded" town, where the Sabbath was strictly observed and reports of men working on Sunday would prompt a published rebuke in the local newspaper. The pious townspeople resented the dissipating influence of the soda fountain and believed that selling sodas on the Sabbath distracted people from spending the day in reverential quietude. Community officials, yielding to popular sentiment, passed an ordinance prohibiting retail sales of ice cream sodas on Sunday. Some ingenious fountain operators managed to obey the letter of the law by serving ice cream with syrup but no soda on Sunday, which soon became the common name for the new dish. When Evanston's pious citizens objected to calling a frivolous treat by a sacred name, the spelling was changed to "sundae."[80]

According to sources published in Evanston, the sundae originated in the 1880s at Garwood's drugstore, which was also an innovator in curb service. William C. (Deacon) Garwood came up with the idea of placing an electric signal bell on the trunk of a big shade tree, which could be reached by a carriage driver. When the driver rang the bell, a clerk responded, took the order, and later delivered the ice cream or soda water to the customers, who were waiting comfortably in the shade of the tree.[81]

Exactly when the spelling of Sunday was changed is not known. The variations "sundi," "sundhi," and "sundaye" appeared in some early publications. The phenomenal success of the sundae prompted at least one drugstore to introduce a mondae (a combination of a sundae and soda water), but the trend does not seem to have reached tuesdae through saturdae in most locations.[82]

Another late-19th-century serving innovation was fried ice cream, a fad that proved to be less enduring than the soda or the sundae. Fried ice cream, called Alaska pie or Alaska fritter, was introduced at the 1893 Chicago World's Fair. It was prepared by dipping a cube of hard ice cream into a thin fritter batter and then plunging it into hot lard or oil. Although it sold briskly at the fair, it did not become a classic.[83]

A treat that was introduced a few years later did become a classic. Ice cream sandwiches were popularized in New York City, where hokey-pokey vendors sold them as early as 1899. According to a contemporary description, the vendor would place a thin, oblong wafer in a small tin mold, cover it with ice cream, place another wafer on top, and close the mold to press the sandwich together. These ice cream sandwiches originally sold for two or three cents, but children protested that this was too expensive. "The penny is a convenient and fairly abundant coin for constant use, and they desired a penny sandwich," explained a newspaper. So the vendors switched to smaller wafers and reduced the price to one cent.[84]

A book of soda fountain recipes, published circa 1900, stated that ice cream sandwiches "have become very popular." In 1903 a women's magazine noted, "Ice cream sandwiches are new, but many are afraid to attempt them as they seem difficult to manage; they are very simple, on the contrary." The magazine gave instructions for making the sandwiches at home, but many consumers preferred to buy them at ice cream parlors and saloons, which had begun to sell a fancier version of the street treat.[85]

Milk shakes joined the growing list of serving innovations in the late 19th century, but the circumstances of its birth, like those of the sundae's, are obscure. A dictionary copyrighted in 1890 defined "milk shake" as follows: an iced drink made of sweetened and flavored milk, carbonated water, and sometimes raw egg, mixed by being violently shaken by a machine specially invented for the purpose. The milk shake seems to have been one of those heartier drinks that appealed to men, and one source states that it was a favorite of students at the University of Wisconsin in the 1880s. Supply catalogs and trade magazines advertised milk shake machines, which were cranked by hand and usually made two glasses of the concoction at one time.[86]

A manual for soda fountain operators, published around the turn of the century, stated that wherever the milk shake "has been properly introduced, it has immediately become extremely popular." Interestingly, a trade paper printed in April 1900 urged soda fountains to "revive the old-time milk shake." This suggests that the milk shake was already old hat or, as in the case of the ice cream soda, there may have been an old and a new drink known by the same name.[87]

By the end of the 19th century, customers expected soda fountains to serve ice cream sodas and sundaes, even though fountain operators complained that these new treats reduced their profits. A trade magazine spoke for many fountain owners when it asserted, "The introduction of ice cream as a soda-water adjunct was a grievous mistake, for it not only takes longer to serve it but also takes longer to consume it, thus materially limiting the output on crowded days."[88]

Nevertheless, ice cream had come to stay at the soda fountain.

The Scoop on Dippers

Until the late 19th century, it seems that no one felt the need for a special utensil to serve ice cream because any large spoon would do the job. However, once an inventor demonstrated that there was a better way to scoop up ice cream, the industry quickly grasped the benefits of the new utensil as if it were the proverbial better mousetrap.

Not surprisingly, the first mechanical ice cream disher, or scoop, was invented by a confectioner, William Clewell of Reading, Pennsylvania. Clewell's design, which was patented in 1878, featured a small conical bowl attached to a metal handle. The server scooped the ice cream into the bowl and then released it by rotating a small key-shaped mechanism that protruded from the top and turned a scraper around the bowl's interior wall. Both hands were required to operate the disher, which delivered a compact, attractive serving of ice cream to the customer's plate. At first, Clewell's disher was manufactured by a Philadelphia tinsmith, Valentine Clad. Later it was produced by another Philadelphia firm, Thomas Mills & Brother.[89]

In the 1890s, the Kingery Company of Cincinnati, makers of Crystal Flake Ice Cream Powder, marketed the first one-handed "rapid" disher. Invented by E.C. Baughman, this dipper featured a squeeze-handle that left one hand free and enabled the user to dip ice cream faster. In addition, its German silver plating made it more sanitary than earlier tin and steel scoops.[90]

One of the most prolific disher inventors was Edwin Walker of Erie, Pennsylvania, who patented at least nine designs between 1905 and 1915. Before he began inventing scoops, Walker was a founding partner in a manufacturing firm that produced ice shavers, lemon squeezers, cork screws, and milk shake machines. His first ice cream dipper was a cone-shaped device with a brass loop handle. One of the earliest disher manufacturers to utilize aluminum, Walker patented a special dipper for sundaes that left an indentation, the size of a cherry, in the top of the scoop of ice cream.[91]

Walker's major competitors were Raymond Gilchrist of Newark, New Jersey, and Rasmus Nielsen of Troy, New York. Nielsen held at least ten patents for dishers, and three major disher manufacturers were located in his hometown. While other manufacturers emphasized economy and ease of operation, Gilchrist relied on quality, advertising his dishers as "better than need be." In fact, he was so confident that his product was superior that his trade ads actually bragged that his dippers cost more. In the 1920s, Gilchrist's firm became a subsidiary of the Scoville Manufacturing Company and in the 1930s was merged with Hamilton-Beach, another Scoville subsidiary.[92]

Without doubt, John Manos of Toronto, Ohio, invented the most romantic ice cream dipper, which produced a heart-shaped scoop of ice cream to be served in a special heart-shaped bowl. A confectioner, Manos wanted an ice cream novelty that could be made fresh at the soda fountain to compete with prepackaged treats. In 1925 Manos, who persuaded a local engineer to help him with the details in return for a small share of the profits, received two dipper patents for slightly different designs. Then he contracted with a machinist in Cincinnati to produce the dippers and a firm in Wheeling, West Virginia, to make the molds for the heart-shaped serving dishes. The clear-glass dishes were etched with either a bird design or a Greek motif, which Manos hoped would appeal to the large number of Greek-Americans in the confectionery business. A set with a scoop and two dozen dishes cost $8.25 wholesale. Although Manos received orders from Canada and Australia as well as the United States, he stopped marketing his design in 1928 and opened a restaurant, which failed in the Depression.[93]

During the Depression, confectioners and soda fountain operators suffered because their products were luxuries that many consumers could not afford. In this era of small profits, disher manufacturers emphasized economical designs that gave more servings per gallon. The harsh economy was largely responsible for the phenomenal success of the Zeroll dipper invented by Sherman Kelly of Toledo, Ohio. While vacationing in West Palm Beach, Florida, Kelly observed a young woman serving ice cream and noticed that she had blisters on her hand from repeatedly digging the scoop into the hard, frozen cream. He decided to invent a device to make the job easier.

Kelly's solution was a nonmechanical dipper with a sealed cast-aluminum handle filled with "a nontoxic defrosting fluid." As the server scooped up ice cream, heat from his hand warmed the fluid, which in turn slightly thawed the ice cream, permitting it to be easily removed from the scoop. Because Kelly's design was practical and economical, it was immediately popular with Depression-plagued confectioners. It had no moving parts, eliminating breakage and the need for repairs. Moreover, it rolled the ice cream into a loose ball, rather than compacting it, which allowed the dispenser to get more servings from a gallon.

The Zeroll's early success was halted by the advent of World War II, because aluminum was needed for wartime uses. After the war, the Zeroll Company was one of the first to obtain aluminum, enabling investors, including Kelly's son, to revive the business. The new management introduced variations on the basic Zeroll design, in order to capitalize on the growing home market for ice cream scoops.[94]

The Depression also boosted the sales of another disher, the Sky-Hi. This cylindrical dipper produced a tall, slender serving of ice cream that appeared to be larger than an ordinary one, even though it was no bigger than that of a normal scoop from a conventional dipper of the same size. (Dippers were sized by the number of level scoops to a quart; for example, a No. 24 produced two dozen scoops per quart.)[95]

The Missouri Association of Ice Cream Manufacturers vigorously promoted the use of the Sky-Hi dipper, claiming that it could boost cone volume by 300 to 500 percent. In advertisements the manufacturer, Perfection Equipment Company, assured retailers, "There's as much money to be made as ever, only nowadays it has to be scientifically extracted." Consumer advocates might have argued that the Sky-Hi dipper was more optical illusion than science. Nevertheless, many ice cream sellers reported that it helped their sales.[96]

More than 240 ice cream dishers were patented between 1878 and 1940, attesting to the great variety possible for a simple piece of equipment. While the basic round scoop became the staple of the industry, intriguing designs were created for special functions, such as making ice cream sandwiches or pie a la mode. Ice cream sandwich dippers were square or rectangular, forming a block of ice cream to fit between two wafers. Harlen P. Gardner of St. Louis patented two triangular dishers for forming a wedge of ice cream to top a slice of pie. Gilchrist manufactured an oval-shaped scoop especially for banana splits.[97]

Despite the great variety of scoops on the market, Baskin-Robbins decided to develop its own dipper in the 1960s because Burt Baskin wanted to insure uniformity of servings among the chain's stores. Baskin's ideal was a scoop that, when properly used, would dispense equal portions of ice cream to all customers. In addition, it must be made of an alloy that would resist corrosion and pitting in many different types of water, since it would be used throughout the United States. After five years of experimenting with different designs and materials, Baskin-Robbins signed an exclusive contract with a manufacturer to produce the dippers. Unfortunately, that company soon went bankrupt and another manufacturer had to be found. Despite the problems, Baskin was pleased with the final product—a scoop that yielded an attractive, neat ball of ice cream weighing 2.5 ounces, standardizing servings from coast-to-coast.[98]

5

Flappers, Doughboys, Blind-Pigs, and Eskimo Pies: 1900–1939

From Prohibition to Depression

In the early 20th century, ice cream junkies gleefully succumbed to new temptations, including waffle cones, Eskimo Pies, Good Humor bars, Dixie cups, and dozens of other novelties. The ice cream industry added new flavors to the traditional favorites and extended its distribution to new outlets, including the corner grocery store. The industry also had its share of problems—most notably, decreasing consumption and falling profits during the Depression.

The temperance movement continued to gain momentum in the early 20th century, culminating in the passage of the Eighteenth Amendment and the Volstead Act, with national Prohibition going into effect in January 1920. Even before then, numerous state and local governments had passed laws prohibiting the sale of alcoholic beverages. Consuming liquor had become decidedly unfashionable in many circles, especially the middle class, which had appointed itself as the arbiter of respectability. On Main Street USA, saloons closed their doors while soda fountains and pool halls did a booming business. Barkeepers and breweries looked for alternate sources of income. In Chicago, for example, "Hinky Dink" Kenna, a well-known saloon-keeper, and "Bathhouse John" Coughlin, the political czar of the first ward, opened an ice cream parlor when the Eighteenth Amendment went into effect. Meanwhile, Anheuser Busch and several other major brewers switched to manufacturing ice cream.[1]

As men sought alternatives to having a drink at the local saloon, many ate ice cream more often. "The day has gone by when a man laughs at the matinee girl at the soda fountain or ice cream table, for he has forever sworn off the beverage that intoxicates," reported a trade journal. "In the Wall Street district, the numerous ice cream places are monopolized by the men, and the gilded cafes are silent in the heated times."[2]

111

Estimated annual consumption of ice cream was 260 million gallons during the first year of Prohibition. It fell slightly in 1921 and then climbed steadily, reaching more than 365 million gallons in 1929. There seemed to be no limit to how high consumption could go—until the Great Depression hit. In 1930, ice cream production fell nearly 12 percent, and consumption continued to slide for the next three years as the United States economy stagnated. In 1934, ice cream production finally began to rebound. Although some industry executives feared that the end of Prohibition would adversely affect ice cream consumption, production actually rose after repeal, probably because the general economic conditions were a more decisive factor than the end of Prohibition.[3]

Changes in lifestyle and technology, such as automobiles and better refrigeration, dramatically affected ice cream consumption during the first half of the 20th century. The growth of automobile travel stimulated ice cream sales as roadside stands appeared in cities and along heavily traveled highways. In urban areas, the best locations for stands were near, but not at, major intersections on the outskirts of town. On the open road, slight elevations or long curves, where the driver had to slow down, were prime locations because it was important that the driver see the stand in the distance and prepare to stop. In all cases, plenty of parking was essential. Interestingly, an industry survey showed that two-thirds of these wayside stands were operated by women, and a substantial number were owned by the elderly.[4]

The concept of chains of stands with unique buildings that were themselves advertisements for ice cream was popularized in southern California, where drivers could stop at igloos, icebergs, ice caverns, huge ice cream freezers, and giant inverted waffle cones. Like some early hamburger outlets, many of these could be easily disassembled and reassembled, enabling the owner to move if there was not enough traffic or the landlord raised the rent on the lot.[5]

The Big Freezer was, in many ways, a typical chain. It was concentrated in the Los Angeles area, although it had a few outlets in Pennsylvania, New Jersey, Florida, and even Cuba. Each store, which resembled a hand-cranked ice cream freezer, was painted white with red hoops and a red handle. The first freezers had been painted a dull brownish color to imitate wood, but the company decided a more striking color scheme was needed. When the freezers were repainted, sales immediately improved. Likewise, the freezer handle was stationary until the company decided it would attract more attention if it revolved, and a motor was installed for that purpose. In the first week after the handles began to rotate, sales doubled. The Big Freezer's flashy facade caught the eye and promoted ice cream because there was no doubt about what was sold inside.

The Big Freezer differed from soda fountains and ice cream parlors because it sold only packaged ice cream and had no tables. Customers took their purchases home or ate in the car. Although the metal buildings had mechanical refrigeration, there was no plumbing. Since there were no dishes to wash, sinks were not needed and the absence of plumbing connections simplified relocation. The bare-bones freezers did not even have cash registers, and employees were trusted to keep track of each day's receipts.[6]

One of the best-known of all roadside chains, Howard Johnson's, began as a small business in Wollaston, Massachusetts. Johnson returned home after serving in France during World War I and began selling cigars, just as his father did. After a few years, he decided to start his own business and opened a drugstore with a newsstand and soda fountain. At first, he bought his ice cream from a local manufacturer, but he did not like the taste of the artificial flavoring. Johnson's mother, who had owned a herd of Jersey cows when he was boy, had made ice cream on Sundays, using her own rich cream and fresh strawberries. Remembering the incomparable taste of homemade, he decided to freeze his own and hired an ice cream maker from Boston to teach him the trade.

When Johnson felt that he had learned all he needed to know, he froze his first batch and proudly served some to a customer. Trying to sound casual, he asked the customer how it tasted and was crushed when the man replied that it was gritty. Disappointed but determined, Johnson improved his skills and was soon producing excellent ice cream. He experimented with different recipes and, when he found just the right combination of ingredients, wrote the formula in his notebook. He made all the ice cream by himself in his basement until the chore became too much for one person. Then he swore an employee to secrecy and revealed the contents of his notebook to this trusted assistant.

Ice cream sales soared until Johnson could not meet the demand in his little shop, which seated only 10 people. To ease the crowding, he decided to sell some of his ice cream on Wollaston beach, where he set up a tiny stand. Since he had no delivery truck, he had to load drums of ice cream into a taxi. Soon the taxi was making several trips to the beach each day. Sometimes the crowds at the stand were so huge that police were needed to keep order. Johnson, who was already a hero among Wollaston's children for selling oversized ice cream cones at his fountain, sold 14,000 cones at the beach one blistering August day.[7]

This first stand led to a chain of stands, painted bright orange to catch the eye, on beaches and roads in the Boston area. In addition, Johnson opened a short-order restaurant serving hot dogs, hamburgers, fried clams, and ice cream in the Granite Trust Company building in Quincy. Although this restaurant was not immediately profitable, he felt that he had a viable concept. His restaurant business suddenly picked up when Eugene O'Neill's *Strange Interlude* opened at a nearby theater. The convoluted tale of lost love, lust, and deceit had been banned in Boston. Naturally, Bostonians flocked to Quincy to see it. During the dinner intermission, which was necessary because the nine-act play ran more than four hours, Johnson's cash registers rang regularly.

In 1935, Reginald Sprague, a former schoolmate, offered to sell Johnson a property in the Cape Cod village of Orleans. Because the land bordered a popular tourist route, Sprague thought it would be a good spot for an ice cream stand. But Johnson had a better idea. He persuaded Sprague to build and operate a restaurant, purchasing his ice cream and other products from Johnson. Thus, the first Howard Johnson's Restaurant was franchised.

This restaurant was immediately successful, and Johnson quickly signed up more franchisees. Although the restaurants were built primarily with the franchisees' money, they were designed by Johnson's architects, led by Joseph G. Morgan. Each building had certain standard features, with modifications to accommodate the needs of individual franchises. The basic style "consisted of Georgian architectural elements applied to a building whose shape, while not Georgian, was in character with New England's past." The restaurant roofs were painted bright orange to identify them with Johnson's ice cream stands. The standard restaurant interior was divided into two sections, the main dining room and the dairy, where quick meals, ice cream, and other desserts were served at a counter. In the early restaurants, the counter stools were portable so they could be moved out after lunch to make room for the afternoon hordes coming to sample Johnson's famous 28 flavors.[8]

By the fall of 1940, more than 130 Howard Johnson's restaurants had opened, mostly in the Northeast. They were a comforting stop for travelers because the food, service, and cleanliness were predictable. Johnson once explained that he had the measurements for making an ice cream soda marked on the glasses at each restaurant "so every customer would know he was getting just the right amount of syrup and just the right amount of cream. No matter where he was—Quincy, Route 40, Chicago." Similarly precise standards were applied to virtually every aspect of the chain's operations and printed in a manual, commonly called the Bible. Howard Johnson employees acted as itinerant customers to monitor franchises, and the council of franchisees reprimanded restaurant managers who failed to follow the manual.[9]

As ice cream wholesalers sought new markets during the Depression, the potential of grocery store sales became the subject of a lively debate. Grocery stores had traditionally sold little or no ice cream because it was a luxury item reserved for confectionaries and soda fountains. Marketing ice cream in groceries would transform its image from an expensive treat to an everyday food—a very desirable change when American families were counting every penny. However, some ice cream manufacturers worried that high-volume buying and selling by grocery chains would drive down prices and profits for the entire industry.

Recent improvements in both household and commercial refrigeration had made grocery store sales more practical. In 1930, approximately 850,000 refrigerators were sold in the United States, exceeding sales of iceboxes for the first time. The numbers continued to climb steadily, reaching 1.5 million in 1935 and 4 million in 1941. However, early refrigerators were not designed for storing frozen foods and could accommodate only one or two frozen packages in the coldest part of the interior, near the unit's evaporating coils. The first dual-compartment, dual-temperature refrigerator was not marketed until 1939. Another major obstacle was the absence of frozen food cases in grocery stores. Before grocers could sell ice cream, they would have to install cabinets to display the product.[10]

One of the first companies to plunge boldly into the grocery market was the New York Eskimo Pie Corporation, which by 1930 had developed a merchandizing scheme for grocery store sales. Recognizing the limitations of refrigerators and iceboxes, the company decided that it must provide a storage container along with the ice cream. Therefore, it manufactured ice cream in cylindrical molds to fit inside Thermos vacuum jars refrigerated with solidified carbon dioxide. Large vacuum jars were supplied to the grocer for storing the product, while smaller ones were available for taking the ice cream home. Ice cream would stay frozen for up to 24 hours if the jar was placed in a refrigerator or about seven hours without the benefit of refrigeration. Shoppers were required to make hefty deposits on the vacuum jars to insure their return to the store.[11]

The novelty of ice cream in groceries was evident in a 1930 ad for a Detroit chain. Under the headline "National Groceterias Now Sell Ice Cream," several paragraphs of text explained that the chain had decided to stock ice cream for the shopper's convenience and gave the following instructions for buying it: "Just lift the transparent lid of the new type ice-cold self-serve cabinet, take the flavor (always three kinds) and size you want, and be on your way in a minute."[12]

In 1931, the Great Atlantic and Pacific Tea Company experimented with ice cream in its stores in northern New Jersey. The following summer, the chain sold ice cream in its outlets in New York City and the surrounding area, stocking novelties as well as a variety of flavors in pint cartons. The A&P gave shoppers insulated bags to protect their purchases from the heat. At least three other New York chains experimented with ice cream sales that same summer, as did a number of stores in Massachusetts, Connecticut, and Washington, D.C.[13]

While manufacturers debated the desirability of grocery store sales, everyone agreed that two other types of distribution were harmful. The Depression had created a new class of street peddlers who hawked almost everything, including ice cream. Because these peddlers had virtually no overhead, they sold cheap ice cream that took sales away from parlors and soda fountains. In response to demands from wholesalers and retailers, many local governments decided to license these roving ice cream vendors, giving the community more economic and sanitary control over them. Another problem was the bootlegger, the small manufacturer who did not comply with government regulations and thus was able to supply retailers with cheaper ice cream, diverting sales from manufacturers who maintained high standards and followed the law. The wholesale industry responded with legal action against bootleggers, and many were forced out of business. However, bootleggers were not eradicated until the general economic conditions improved and consumers could afford premium ice cream again.[14]

A Quick Lick

In 1904, the ice cream cone quickly moved from fad to classic, boosting sales and giving ice cream lovers more freedom because it was an edible container that could be taken almost anywhere. No longer did patrons have to eat their ice cream at the soda fountain or near the hokey-pokey man. Moreover, a cone was neat, inexpensive, and fun to eat. Retailers liked it, too, because it reduced the number of dishes that had to be washed and the turnover was fast since patrons did not have to eat in the shop.

Not surprisingly, many claimants rushed, or at least sauntered, forward to tell how they had invented the new sensation. In fact, one industry executive stated that every major cone manufacturer from Boston to San Francisco swore that he had been the first to make ice cream cones in the United States. Nevertheless, the list of those with reasonable claims can be limited to a handful.[15]

As with other ice cream controversies, there is no physical evidence or reliable documentation to determine who invented the ice cream cone. Various types of cones were popular in Europe before they were introduced in the United States, but the American cone does not seem to have been imported from Europe. It seems to have originated independently, although at least one of the claimants acknowledged that he had seen cones in Europe.

Most of the legends about the first American ice cream cone state that it was created at the 1904 World's Fair in St. Louis. A prominent ice cream manufacturer from Baltimore remembered that he had seen his first cone at the fair. Since ice cream was this man's business and he would have been especially interested in a serving innovation the first time he saw it, his report lends credence to the theory that the cone was invented, or at least popularized, at the St. Louis fair.[16]

Version No. 1: Ernest A. Hamwi, a Syrian immigrant, was certainly a major contender for the honor of inventing the American ice cream cone. At the St. Louis fair, he operated a concession making zalabia, or waffles, in a section of the midway called Constantinople-on-the-Pike. According to Hamwi's own published recollections, his booth was located beside an ice cream concession. Since many customers bought his waffles and then went next door to purchase ice cream to eat with them, the workers in Hamwi's concession thought it would be a good idea to combine the two foods. Accordingly, they came up with several ideas that were promising but not quite right.[17]

Then Hamwi suggested rolling the zalabia into a funnel shape and filling it with ice cream. The workers tried it and liked it. Soon, Hamwi was selling waffles to ice cream concessions all over the fairgrounds, and the World's Fair cornucopia was born. Fairgoers loved the new treat because it was portable and they could eat it as they walked along the pike, looking at the curiosities, such as large plastic dioramas of Civil War battles, Gentleman Jim the Equine Millionaire, and 24 premature infants living in incubators—at least until an epidemic killed half of the babies.[18]

Immediately after the fair closed, Hamwi sold his waffle oven to J.P. Heckle, who started the Cornucopia Waffle Oven Company, manufacturing waffle machines in St. Louis. Then Hamwi went to work for Heckle, promoting the cornucopia in Georgia, Florida, Texas, and South Carolina. To introduce the new treat to the masses, he gave away thousands of free ice cream cones at county fairs and other public events.[19]

In 1910, Hamwi started the Missouri Cone Company in St. Louis. One of Hamwi's nephews later stated that his uncle had become a millionaire in the cone business. "My uncle designed his machines, and my aunt handled the money," the nephew told a newspaper reporter. "Then she died young, and my uncle went berserk. He took off for Europe, just disappeared for five years. A sister tried to run the company while he was gone. Finally, he came back with a Syrian wife and went back to the cone business."[20]

A trade magazine reported that the widowed Hamwi had returned to his homeland, had fallen in love, and had married a young Syrian girl, a Damascus merchant's daughter who "had many desirable suitors." However, the chronology in the article indicated that Hamwi was a widower for only about one year and there was no mention of a lengthy stay in Europe.[21]

The nephew also told the reporter, "He engineered and built all kinds of cone machines, but eventually he was broken by patent infringements, and his company was taken over. The cone business in those days was a dirty, vicious business."[22]

When Hamwi died in 1943, the newspaper obituary stated that he was the owner of the Western Company, which manufactured cones, and was survived by his widow and stepson, president of the Missouri Cone Company. The paper did not mention any business problems or bankruptcy, and Hamwi's original cone company was obviously still in the family.[23]

Stephen H. Sullivan, who was also in the cone business, claimed that he had seen Hamwi invent the cornucopia at the World's Fair. However, his eyewitness account varied somewhat from Hamwi's because Sullivan claimed that the inspiration had come when an ice cream vendor ran out of dishes and the Syrian, reacting quickly, handed him a rolled waffle to hold the ice cream. Yet another variation stated that the ice cream vendor, Arnold Fornachou, had suggested rolling up the waffle. In 1928, a trade magazine lent credibility to Hamwi's claim by publishing an article about him. In 1954, a group representing the International Association of Ice Cream Manufacturers evaluated various claims and decided that Hamwi had indeed created the treat.[24]

Version No. 2: During the day, Abe Doumar, an immigrant from Lebanon, worked in the Ancient City of Jerusalem exhibit at the World's Fair, selling River Jordan paperweights. At night, when the exhibit was closed, he passed the time by watching the hootchy-kootchy girls and hanging around a waffle stand. In some accounts, he was patronizing Hamwi's booth.[25]

Doumar was familiar with the Lebanese custom of rolling a piece of pita bread into a cone and spooning jam into it. After observing business at the waffle stand, he decided that the baker could make more money if he made cones from his waffles and filled them with ice cream. He suggested this to the concessionaire, who thought it was a great idea and asked Doumar to moonlight at the waffle booth. The cones were a big hit, and the grateful concessionaire gave Doumar one of his waffle ovens after the fair closed. Doumar devised some improvements in the oven design and hired a machinist in Hoboken, New Jersey, to build a new iron-and-brass oven for him.[26]

Doumar went into business with three partners, peddling cones at Coney Island near Steeplechase Park. When the cones did not sell, they hired pretty girls to stroll along the boardwalk eating the novelty. After one partner bought out the others, Doumar took his machine south, working at state fairs and amusement parks.[27]

During his wanderings, Doumar, who had a dozen siblings, established several family-run ice cream stands. One of his brothers settled in Norfolk, Virginia, and in the 1930s built a successful drive-in restaurant, selling barbecue as well as ice cream cones. When McDonald's opened in Norfolk in the late 1950s, the local barbecue restaurants lost most of their clientele to the newcomer. To compete, Doumar's nephew Al decided it was time to make something old new again. So he brought the cone oven out of storage and set it up in front of his shop, where it proved to be a conversation piece and crowd pleaser. Ninety years after the St. Louis World's Fair, Abe Doumar's descendants were still making waffle cones in his oven.[28]

Version No. 3: Nick Kabbaz, another Syrian immigrant, sold confectionery at the World's Fair. The details of his story are obscure, but his family claimed that he and his brother Albert were "the originators of the cone." Since Hamwi acknowledged that he had solicited ideas from his employees, it is intriguing to think that Kabbaz and/or his brother may have worked in Hamwi's booth. In fact, in one published interview, Hamwi stated that he and "two others hit on the idea first of folding . . . cakes to insert ice cream and then of making them in the cone shape." Newspapers reported that Kabbaz, who was president of the St. Louis Ice Cream Cone Company, made a fortune as a pioneer in ice cream cone manufacturing in the early 1900s.[29]

Version No. 4: While working at the World's Fair, Turkish immigrant David Avayou noticed that many fairgoers did not buy ice cream because they did not want to take the time to stop and eat it from a plate. He had seen people eating ice cream in paper cones in France, which led him to a better idea—an edible cone. "I spent three weeks and used hundreds of pounds of flour and eggs before I got it right, but finally I found the right combination," Avayou later recalled.

After the fair, Avayou went to work in a Philadelphia department store, making and selling ice cream cones. His confections sold so well that the store management told him to take a well-deserved vacation. When he returned, the store had appropriated his recipe and his concession. He left Philadelphia and moved to Atlantic City, New Jersey, where he sold ice cream on the Boardwalk until his retirement.[30]

Version No. 5: George F. Robinson did not claim to be the inventor of the ice cream cone but rather one of the first individuals to eat one. Robinson enjoyed strolling along the pike at the St. Louis fair, inhaling the tempting aromas and sampling the exotic cuisines. His favorite treat was rose kuchen, a sort of waffle that was fried in deep fat and then cooled in a mold that shaped it into a "toasted rose." The fairgoer could carry his rose kuchen with him as he saw the sights, periodically breaking off a few petals and eating them like popcorn.

One afternoon, just as Robinson walked into a stall to order a rose kuchen, another customer was leaving with one. Apparently on a whim, this man walked into the booth next door and asked the vendor to put some ice cream on his rose kuchen. When the ice cream seller stared blankly at the customer, he repeated his request. Somewhat reluctantly, the vendor complied.

"It was exactly at that moment that the ice cream cone was born, because the man had not walked ten feet before someone else got the idea that kuchen and ice cream could be combined in one article. And within three minutes, there was a line of men and women, buying kuchens and stepping next door to get some ice cream on them," remembered Robinson, who was the third person in line for the new delicacy.[31]

Robinson never knew the name of the customer who deserves the veneration of junk-food lovers everywhere for first combining ice cream and cone. When compared to the other stories, his anecdote has a refreshing modesty to it since he did not profess to be the inventor.

Version No. 6: Frank and Charles Menches of Canton, Ohio, were successful snack concessionaires who employed more than a hundred people and traveled from fair to fair in three railroad cars. At the St. Louis fair, they erected a large tent where they sold sausage sandwiches, raw oysters, pickled herring, hot cider, coffee, ice cream, hand-rolled cigars, and hamburgers, which they claimed to have invented at an earlier fair.

One busy day the Menches' operation had a shortage of ice-cream plates. A female employee took a waffle cookie from the booth next door, rolled it around her finger, and tried to fill it with ice cream, but it leaked. The next day, Charles was working around the tent, using a fid, a tapered wooden pin for separating the strands in a rope for splicing. Inspiration struck. He hurried next door for a couple of warm wafers, wrapped them around the fid, and created the waffle cone.

Charles quickly bought two waffle irons from the neighboring concessionaire and started selling ice cream cones. After leaving St. Louis, the Mencheses sold cones at other fairs and discovered that there was an enormous market for the new treat. An Akron foundry fabricated more waffle irons for them, and they employed more than 50 women to make cones at their Premium Cone and Candy Company.[32]

Charles Menches also played a prominent role in yet another tale about the first ice cream cone. In this anecdote, he was escorting a young lady around the fairgrounds. Evidently he was anxious to impress her because he bought her a bouquet of violets and an ice cream sandwich. The ambidextrous woman rolled one of the wafers from the sandwich into a vase for the flowers and the other into a container for the ice cream. Exactly how she accomplished this is unknown, but it must have been a messy maneuver. *Why* she wanted to do it is also a mystery![33]

This legend was discredited by a cone manufacturer who noted that the woman's ice cream sandwich would have been made of crisp wafers. Unless the wafers were hot from the waffle iron, they would have been brittle and would have cracked when she tried to roll them. Since the wafers in her sandwich had cooled enough not to melt the ice cream, they certainly would have broken into pieces when she bent them.[34]

Version No. 7: Italo Marchiony was the only claimant who actually had a patent that proved his story—or did he? An Italian immigrant, Marchiony peddled hokey-pokey from a pushcart on Wall Street and also owned a restaurant. Washing ice-cream dishes was a nuisance, and replacing broken ones reduced his profits. He was probably familiar with the paper cones used in Europe, because he tried that option first but found that the paper litter was a nuisance. Frustrated, he searched for a solution and decided that an edible container for ice cream would be ideal.[35]

Circa 1896, Marchiony began making edible ice cream containers for his own business. Then in 1903 he applied for a patent on a mold for shaping dough into "ice cream cups and the like" and was granted his patent several months before the St. Louis fair opened. Marchiony later pointed to his patent as proof that he had invented the ice cream cone. However, the patent drawing plainly shows a mold for shaping small cups, complete with tiny handles—not a cone. Even if Marchiony also had a cone-shaped mold, it would have produced a molded container rather than a rolled waffle like the World's Fair cornucopia.[36]

At some point, Marchiony established a factory in Hoboken for making cones and waffles. The time frame is unclear, but his family said that it was after he had received his patent. When cones became popular, Marchiony attempted to protect his patent through legal channels but failed.

When he died, a newspaper obituary stated, "The cone patent issue, a subject of much litigation and controversy, never was entirely resolved."[37]

An interview given by Max Goldberg, chairman of the board of the Illinois Baking Corporation, seemed to shed welcome light on the cone controversy. Goldberg, another pioneer in the industry, told a reporter that he had first sold cones in 1903 and had purchased them from a Brooklyn firm. Unfortunately, Goldberg's memory was not perfect. In another interview three years earlier, he had stated that the cone originated at the St. Louis World's Fair "sired by a genius whose name has been lost to time."[38]

Regardless of who sold the first World's Fair cornucopia, the idea was not new. Both paper and metal cones were used in France; custard-style ice cream was sold in cornets in England; and edible waffle cones were popular in Germany before the turn of the century. In the United States, Charles Ranhofer's 1893 cookbook contained recipes for rolled waffle-cornets filled with flavored whipped cream. He instructed the reader to make a batter and cook it in a waffle iron to form thin round wafers. Then the cook was directed to "roll them around some tin cornet forms and leave till cold." When they had cooled sufficiently, they were ready to be filled. Since nearly everything Ranhofer served was widely imitated, more than one upscale restaurant undoubtedly sold elegant waffle cornets filled with whipped cream. From there, it would have been a short step to a rolled waffle cone filled with ice cream.[39]

In an area murky with controversy, at least one fact is certain: after the St. Louis World's Fair, both manufacturers of cone ovens and cone sellers proliferated. Heckle's Cornucopia Waffle Oven Company produced ovens that heated three waffle irons simultaneously. Even though the waffles had to be rolled by hand while they were still hot, one person working steadily could produce about 1,500 cones per day using one of Heckle's ovens. Many wholesale cone manufacturers employed young women, who were paid 20 to 35 cents per hundred cones. Since the waffle cones were very brittle, they could not be shipped long distances without significant loss due to breakage. Therefore, many ice cream retailers preferred to make their own cones.[40]

Heckle's ovens were more or less typical because they produced waffle cones similar to the World's Fair cornucopia, but machines that molded cones were also marketed. Thomas Mills & Brother of Philadelphia, who manufactured a variety of tools for the bakery and confectionery trades, advertised models "embracing many valuable and wonderful improvements, making them not only entirely different from all other cone ovens, but absolutely the cheapest and best on the market."

For a mere $21.75, Mills sold a machine that molded and cooked three cones simultaneously. If the purchaser wanted two of these machines, the second was even cheaper. A complete outfit, consisting of a mold holding six penny-cones and a gasoline stove, went for the bargain price of $29. Mills's top-of-the-line machine, which made nine cones simultaneously, cost only $51. Since getting started in the cone business required so little capital and promised so much profit, it is not surprising that many small businessmen rushed to get in on the ground floor.[41]

By the late 1920s, the business of manufacturing cones had changed dramatically. Modern machines baked 64 to 240 cones simultaneously, and most of the manual labor had been removed from the process. The batter was mixed by machinery, squirted into the molds by machinery, baked, and packed into cases without ever being touched by human hands. Not surprisingly, the cost of getting started in the business had also risen dramatically, requiring an outlay of approximately $100,000 to open a large, mechanized plant.[42]

Many industry leaders believed that the cone would substantially expand ice cream sales because it appealed to children and taught consumers to eat the treat at a young age. "The first idea is to teach children to eat ice cream once a week, twice, or three times a week. When he grows up, he is going to want ice cream in his family," reasoned one industry executive, who presumably knew more about marketing than about pronouns and antecedents. The rising consumption of ice cream validated this argument as sales climbed from 50 million gallons in 1904 to 80 million five years later.[43]

As the cone industry matured, manufacturers experimented with various recipes and designs. Many of the design improvements were intended to prevent dripping or to make a scoop of ice cream look larger. Like automobile manufacturers, the large cone companies regularly introduced new models. One of the most innovative designs was the National Biscuit Company's Jack and Jill cone, which held two scoops side-by-side. The pointed-bottom cone dominated the industry until the late 1940s, when Joseph Shapiro of the Maryland Cup Corporation developed a flat-bottomed cone for Dairy Queen operators, who found it convenient to stand cones on the counter while they were filling large orders.[44]

Cones proved to be especially popular at places where people walked a lot, such as fairs, amusement parks, and the beach. In 1915 the National Ice Cream Company erected cone stands, ice cream parlors, and soda fountains at the Panama-Pacific International Exposition. None of the parlors sold enough ice cream to pay the waiters, and the soda fountains sold more ice cream in cones than in dishes. Accordingly, the company converted the parlors into cone stands by removing the tables and chairs. "People would buy cones and walk around seeing the sights, but they would take no time to sit down to eat a dish of ice cream," explained the company's sales manager.[45]

The universal popularity of the ice cream cone was acknowledged by a spokesman for the Texas State Bottlers Association who declared, "In but a few years the increase in sales of ice cream cones has been many times greater than the increase in the sale of popular-priced beverages during their best days. Formerly it may have been considered effeminate for men to eat ice cream in public, but now the ice cream cone is a serious rival to the always manly pop bottle."[46]

If there were any lingering doubts about the masculinity of ice cream, World War I removed them. American soliders at home and abroad ate ice cream with gusto. As a symbol of Main Street USA, ice cream played a role as a propaganda tool and morale-builder. When asked about American involvement in the war, a German officer replied, "We do not fear that nation of ice cream eaters." After his comment was printed in American newspapers, at least one editorial responded with a patriotic defense of the frozen treat. Recognizing the importance of ice cream, the Red Cross volunteered to supply it as often as possible to the troops in Europe. In a press release, the organization said, "They used to tell us that ice cream was undermining the constitution of the American people. If so, it is a bit like the brand of whiskey General Grant used to imbibe."[47]

Wherever American soldiers were stationed, they sought out sources of ice cream, even though it was usually very expensive. In France, the government had outlawed ice cream due to a severe sugar shortage. Nevertheless, enterprising Frenchmen operated blind-pigs (speak-easies) especially for American troops. A doughboy who knew the password could gain entrance and eat ice cream behind the locked doors of these illegal joints. Some blind-pigs served excellent ice cream while others sold an inferior product at inflated prices.[48]

As the war progressed, American troops went to great lengths for a creamy taste of home. For example, the 491st Air Squadron stationed near Paris improvised an ice cream freezer using old barrels, a pump, and gears from abandoned airplanes. Each day an airman who had worked in an ice cream plant before the war made enough for his own squadron and nearby units using cream purchased from neighboring farms.[49]

The Red Cross treated returning soldiers to ice cream at ports and train stations. At Pier Four in Hoboken, for example, the Red Cross fed each man who stepped off the ship two hot dogs, liberty cabbage, pie, ice cream, coffee, and buns. The soldiers appreciated both the traditional American fare and the generous portions. A magazine described the Red Cross port kitchen as "a cafeteria par excellence, a quick-lunch joint de luxe, an ice cream counter that cheers the soul and pleases the palate of every boy who passes through the line."[50]

As important as ice cream was to healthy soldiers, it was even more important to the wounded. Recognizing this need, the Red Cross supplied ice cream freezers to many military hospitals overseas. "The first thing returned wounded soldiers demand when they get off a ship is ice cream. . . . We use it by the gallon in every ward," reported an army nurse in a debarkation hospital. After the war, President and Mrs. Warren G. Harding hosted a garden party for thousands of wounded veterans and Red Cross nurses on the White House lawn. One of the special treats was a big dish of ice cream for each guest.[51]

Like all wars, World War I created shortages, but the ice cream industry fared better than many businesses. In 1918, the United States Food Administration classified ice cream, but not sherbets or water ices, as an essential food, allowing manufacturers to purchase as much sugar as they needed. Later that same year, when the sugar shortage became more acute, the food administration asked ice cream manufacturers to reduce their sugar usage to 75 percent of the previous year's consumption by utilizing alternatives, such as corn syrup, whenever possible.[52]

Eating ice cream was promoted as a patriotic alternative to consuming meat and wheat because the country had a surplus of dairy products but shortfalls of the other two commodities. The wheat shortage was a problem for cone manufacturers, who were forced to curtail production and look for alternatives to wheat flour. In Philadelphia, for example, some manufacturers used crushed, sweetened popcorn to make cones. The scarcity of wheat flour was especially hard on street vendors, who relied heavily on sales of ice cream cones.[53]

As American men went off to war, a general labor shortage was created. Somewhat reluctantly, the dairy industry began to hire women to perform many jobs formerly reserved for males. *The Ice Cream Trade Journal* reassuringly reported, "There are many jobs in the plant that can be handled nearly as well by women as by men." Moreover, the journal stated that women had proven to be especially adept at washing milk cans. Purdue University offered a special course to prepare women for jobs in dairies and ice cream plants. According to the university's press release, "It has been found that women scientifically trained are well able to cope with the difficulties of this highly important profession."[54]

In addition to pursuing new careers, women were becoming more involved in politics. Candidates eager to woo the newly enfranchised female voters realized that their traditional electioneering tactic, passing out cigars, was inappropriate. Many decided to tempt the feminine electorate with ice cream, giving away cones or bricks at the polls on election day.[55]

With the advent of the ice cream bar, politicians finally found the perfect inexpensive bribe. A trade journal predicted that "those candidates for office who look for something besides—or instead of—good looks and a persuasive manner to win feminine favor for them will be large-quantity buyers of ice cream bars." A newspaper agreed, saying that the ice cream bar would take its place along with cigars and stationery on the campaign expense report.[56]

Politicians seemed to enjoy eating ice cream as much as kissing babies. In the 1928 presidential election campaign, for example, both Herbert Hoover and Al Smith confessed that they ate ice cream. Hoover fearlessly proclaimed that his favorite foods were ham and eggs, corn bread, and chocolate ice cream. Smith, not wanting to alienate the vanilla vote, stated that he liked all flavors equally. Mrs. Smith backed him up, saying, "He likes all flavors. I've never seen him favor one kind more than another. I serve it frequently at home. He eats whatever kind I have and just as much of one kind as another." She also went on record that her husband had "always liked to treat the children to ice cream."[57]

Like his predecessor in the Oval Office, President Franklin D. Roosevelt preferred chocolate ice cream. In the Roosevelt White House, ice cream was served often at both family and state dinners for everyone from children to world leaders, including King George, who liked maple and almond ice cream. One of Eleanor Roosevelt's favorite annual events was the children's Christmas party, where the oldest guests were only four years of age. The customary menu was cereal with milk, scrambled eggs, brown bread and butter, peas, ice cream, and cookies. Also during the Christmas holidays, the Roosevelts hosted a dance for their older children and schoolmates. The menu for the midnight supper at this party included creamed oysters on snowflake crackers, chicken salad, ice cream, candied grapefruit peel, coffee, and punch. Of course, ice cream was traditionally served at the family's Christmas dinner, too.[58]

In 1935, when shipping ice cream via airplane was still a novelty, both Roosevelt and Secretary of War George Dern received their Thanksgiving dessert via air. The Snelgrove Ice Cream Company of Salt Lake City air expressed enough ice cream for Roosevelt and his 375 dinner guests in Warm Springs, Georgia. Meanwhile, the China Clipper, a seaplane that traveled between California and Manila, delivered ice cream to Dern on Wake Island in the Pacific Ocean.[59]

Novel Temptations

From the advent of Prohibition to the beginning of World War II, the headlines in the ice cream industry focused on novelties—Eskimo Pie, Good Humor, Popsicle, Ice Cream Omelette, Ice Pole, Polar Egg, Cremo Wafer, Chillie Bar, Honeymoon Pie, Dixie Cup, Sweetie Sundae, Big Bertha, Brown Cow, Strolling Sundae, Twistee Cup, and many more. Ice cream consumers loved them. Ice cream wholesalers learned to live with them.

It all began with Christian Nelson, who taught math, Latin, and psychology at Onawa High School in Onawa, Iowa. After school, he and a partner operated the Nelson-Mustard Cream Company, selling ice cream and candy. One spring day, a boy came into Nelson's confectionary and ordered a candy bar. Then, as children are wont to do, he changed his mind and asked for an ice cream sandwich. Then he decided that he really wanted a marshmallow-nut bar. Nelson had waited on indecisive youngsters before, but this time he was inspired: someone should combine chocolate and ice cream in a small bar for customers who had trouble choosing between ice cream and candy bars.[60]

Nelson spent several months trying to coat a slab of cold ice cream with warm chocolate, but the chocolate did not adhere well. Then a bonbon salesman told him that candy manufacturers added cocoa butter to chocolate to improve its adhesiveness. After more experiments, Nelson decided that dipping solid ice cream into a coating of chocolate heated to 80–90 degrees and then immediately placing it in a freezer would produce just the right bar. His new confection, which he called the Temptation I-Scream Bar, sold well at his shop and at the Onawa Firemen's Tournament, where his entire stock of 500 bars quickly vanished. Nelson even wrote a catchy advertising slogan for his new product: "I scream, you scream, we all scream for the I-Scream Bar."[61]

In the summer of 1921, Nelson went to Omaha, Nebraska, to consult an attorney about obtaining a patent for his bar. While he was there, he met Russell Stover, who was the superintendent of a local ice cream plant. Stover saw great potential in Nelson's idea, while Nelson was impressed by Stover's knowledge of the ice cream business. Before their first meeting had ended, they had signed a handwritten contract forming a partnership.

Stover, who thought Nelson's bar needed a better name, sent his sister and his new partner to the Omaha Public Library to compile a list of words pertaining to cold. At a dinner party, the guests reviewed the choices and Stover decided that "Eskimo" was best. He coupled it with "pie" because that was a familiar, popular dessert. Soon thereafter, Stover moved to Chicago and began to license ice cream manufacturers to make Eskimo Pies.[62]

The first licensees were overwhelmed by the demand, and within one year more than 1,500 licenses had been issued. One of the first licensees wrote, "We are making 600 or 700 dozen a day and have not been able to supply the trade." Demand for the Eskimo Pie was so great that within a few months of its introduction it had rescued the international cocoa market from a major depression. Equipment manufacturers rushed to provide licensees with chocolate warmers, dipping tables, bar formers and cutters, wrappers, and everything else needed to make the new treat.[63]

In January 1922, Christian Nelson received a patent for his confection. In the spring of that year, sales averaged 1 million pies per day. Stover and Nelson should have been getting rich, but they were not. In fact, the company was having severe financial difficulties due to litigation and problems collecting royalties from the licensees. Some licensees were paying only a portion of their royalties or none at all. Moreover, imitation Eskimo Pies were popping up everywhere, and it was necessary to pursue expensive lawsuits to try to stop them. Discouraged, Stover sold his share of the business and moved to Denver, where he opened the first Russell Stover Candy Store.

Nelson and some new partners formed the Eskimo Pie Corporation and searched for additional capital, but the company was broke by the end of 1923. With Eskimo Pie threatening to fold, R.S. Reynolds Sr. of U.S. Foil Company (later Reynolds Aluminum) purchased 80 percent of the stock. Because his company had made millions selling Eskimo Pie wrappers to licensees, Reynolds knew that he was making a good investment. Nelson withdrew from management but continued to receive royalties and became a licensee. Then he retired for a while. However, he longed to be active and, after a few years, rejoined the company, staying on until retirement. He invented an extruder and the Eskimo Pie Jug, a portable insulated container cooled by dry ice that allowed the bars to be sold almost anywhere.[64]

Although the courts declared Nelson's patent to be "invalid for lack of invention" because confectioners had long dipped ice cream balls (e.g., *plombierres)* in chocolate, Reynolds still owned the Eskimo Pie trademark. Since Eskimo Pie was well established, Reynolds was able to maintain a significant share of the market, even though the ruling opened the floodgates for imitators. The Klondike Bar, which Samuel Isaly introduced in Pittsburgh in 1928, proved to be one of the most enduring competitors.[65]

In 1927, Eskimo Pie became the first ice cream bar to be sold in nickel slot machines, the predecessor of today's vending machines. Reynolds's New York subsidiary built a plant in Brooklyn to manufacture the bars, provide storage for 5 million of them, and deliver up to 1 million per day for sale in the vending machines. To purchase a bar, the customer dropped in a nickel and turned a handle. The machine was refrigerated by a small electric compressor and plugged into an ordinary power line. It was leased to the retailer, who kept whatever was left after paying for the pies and the rental.[66]

The Eskimo Pie's phenomenal success was instrumental in the creation of the next big novelty sensation—Good Humor. In 1910, Harry B. Burt, Sr., had introduced the Good Humor sucker on a wooden stick, choosing the name because he believed that the humors of the palate influenced a person's state of mind. Burt of Youngstown, Ohio, also manufactured ice cream on a small scale in his basement and was one of the first dealers to use an automobile to make deliveries. His son, Harry B. Burt, Jr., joined the business at a young age, turning the crank on the ice cream freezer.

When the Eskimo Pie burst on the scene, the Burts began experimenting and soon developed their own chocolate-covered ice cream bar, using cocoa butter and coconut oil to improve the adhesiveness of chocolate. The elder Burt's daughter liked the taste but complained that the bar was too messy, sending the men back to the drawing board. In order to keep the consumer's hands clean, they decided to provide a handle for holding the bar. They experimented with softening the ice cream and inserting a stick, like the one used in their suckers. After the soft ice cream on a stick was dipped in the chocolate coating, the bars were packed in brine to harden. They adhered to the sticks, and the Good Humor Ice Cream Sucker was born.[67]

In January 1922, the elder Burt applied for two patents—one for the process of making the bar and the other for an apparatus for making it. Although several sources state that Burt waited three years for his patents, the *Official Gazette* shows that both applications were approved on October 9, 1923. According to legend, patent officials acted only after the younger Burt took a five-gallon container filled with Good Humor bars to Washington and "literally forced the evidence" down the throat of patent officials.[68]

While the patent application was still pending, the Burts began marketing the bars. To launch the new product, the elder Burt painted one of his delivery trucks white and equipped it with the bells from the family bobsled. Soon a fleet of a dozen trucks, driven by men in white uniforms and loaded with Good Humor bars packed in ice, jingled along the streets of Youngstown. Brisk sales encouraged the Burts to expand, and the son moved to Miami, Florida, to open operations there. In 1926, a hurricane buried most of the Florida fleet under tons of sand, but the employees extricated the trucks and had them back in working order within a month. That same year, Harry B. Burt, Sr., died. A group of Cleveland businessmen bought the patent rights, formed the Good Humor Corporation of America, and began selling franchises for a down payment of $100. In 1928, Harry B. Burt, Jr., sold his share of the Miami operations and established Burt's Good Humor Ice Cream Company in Tulsa, Oklahoma, where he made and distributed Good Humor products under a franchise arrangement.[69]

Another early Good Humor franchisee was Tom Brimer, who first opened a business in Detroit and then moved to Chicago, where mobsters warned him that his trucks would be blown up if he failed to pay protection money. After refusing to pay, Brimer took the precaution of increasing his legitimate insurance. True to their word, the gangsters destroyed eight of Brimer's trucks. When the explosions made headlines, Good Humor received free, front-page publicity in newspapers across the country and gained a reputation for honesty and decency.[70]

When Brimer needed additional capital, his father-in-law approached an old friend, Wall Street financier Michael J. Meehan, who bought some stock more or less as a favor. Meehan did not think much about the deal until the stock market crashed. While many other investments were suddenly worthless, his Good Humor stock paid handsome dividends. So Meehan decided to purchase control of the Good Humor Corporation.[71]

Meehan was very much a product of the 1920s, when a little expertise and a lot of daring could make speculators fabulously rich. He began his career as a messenger and gradually accumulated the funds to buy a seat on the New York Stock Exchange, where he specialized in radio stocks. In 1928, he became famous when newspapers reported that his behind-the-scenes manipulations had sent the stock of Radio Corporation of America (RCA) skyrocketing. Experts estimated that his personal profit from this stock manipulation was at least $5 million. Since this was an era when get-rich-quick schemes were rampant, he was widely admired for his savvy and boldness. A few years later, as the United States climbed out of the Depression, his personal fortune was again greatly enhanced because he owned a large portion of the preferred stock of Radio-Keith-Orpheum (RKO), which doubled in value due to the popularity of Fred Astaire–Ginger Rogers movies.[72]

In 1937, Meehan was in the news for a different reason. He became the first broker expelled from the New York Stock Exchange, the New York Curb Exchange, and the Board of Trade in Chicago under the new Securities Act. He had been involved in manipulating Bellanca Aircraft stock, just like the old days. Only times had changed. The stock market crash and the Depression had generated cries for reform. The old rules no longer applied. As one newspaper noted, "The transactions in Bellanca stock for which he was prosecuted by the SEC were the kind which made him the toast of trading circles in the Coolidge era."[73]

At the time Meehan was expelled, his wife and Mrs. John J. Raskob—wife of a vice president of the General Motors Corporation—were listed as the owners of the controlling share of Good Humor Corporation. Four years later, Meehan's son Joseph became president of the company, which owned several plants and franchised others to produce the Good Humor ice cream that was sold in 16 states by an army of men in white uniforms navigating trucks, tricycles, and pushcarts along city streets. (The company had a strict policy against hiring female vendors, except in California.)[74]

For decades, Good Humor trucks rolled through America's cities, a familiar and welcome sight, jingling bells or playing music to announce their arrival. To insure high standards of service, the drivers received several weeks of training in hygiene, etiquette, traffic safety, and sales before they hit the streets. Each day began at the district office where vendors dressed in their crisp, clean uniforms and were reminded to shine their shoes, clean their fingernails, and so forth. Then each man received a route sheet with the stops and lengths of stay specified in minute detail. Regular customers looked forward to their daily ice-cream fix from the polite fellow who always tipped his cap to ladies, saluted his male patrons, and helped youngsters cross the street safely.[75]

Good Humor men worked on a commission, and many found it to be quite lucrative. Like the Fuller Brush men, Good Humor vendors were fixtures in urban neighborhoods, where regular customers knew their names and treated them like friends. Because special patience was required when dealing with children, the company preferred to hire fathers or grandfathers. Vendors were trained to deal with small customers who tried to pay with play money, demanded change when none was needed, or used rare coins from Dad's collection to pay for a treat. A surprising number of vendors claimed dogs among their regular patrons. Indulgent pet owners happily bought treats for dogs who perked up their ears, wagged their tails, and sprinted down the street whenever they heard the familiar bells—shades of Pavlov![76]

Fueled by the company's publicity program, the Good Humor man's fame spread. Newspapers reported the good deeds of heroic Good Humor men who rescued mothers and children from burning houses, rushed accident victims to the hospital, and even helped police break up a counterfeiting ring on Long Island. The Good Humor man appeared in magazines, comic strips, radio shows, Broadway plays, and motion pictures. He moved from bit player to top billing when he became the title role in a movie starring Jack Carson. He was also the subject of jokes, including the following: Ripley knows a cannibal chief with a sweet tooth; for dessert he always eats a Good Humor man.[77]

For many years, Good Humor featured a special flavor each week from April 1 to September 30. Each new flavor was taste-tested by a panel of children, who had the good sense to reject prune, licorice, and chili-con-carne ice cream among others. Recipes were stored in a heavily guarded safe, and each week's flavor was kept secret until the last possible minute. The radio commercials were sent out in code, and a company executive called the stations to unscramble them on the day they were scheduled for broadcast.[78]

In 1961, the Meehan family sold Good Humor to Thomas J. Lipton, Inc. The familiar Good Humor trucks stayed on the road until the mid-1970s, when the company changed its marketing strategy. By 1978, the fleet of 1,200 vehicles had been reduced by more than 50 percent. At that time, Baltimore was one of the few major cities where the trucks still rolled. They had already vanished from New York City, Chicago, Philadelphia, Detroit, Hartford, New Haven, and many other locations. The company attributed the cutbacks to the high costs of gasoline, insurance, and maintenance along with a change in consumer buying habits. Some of the trucks were replaced by pushcarts, which did well in business districts and heavily populated areas. However, the new marketing emphasis was on selling Good Humor in grocery stores.[79]

During Prohibition and the Depression, while ice cream manufacturers with Eskimo Pie or Good Humor franchises were profiting from the novelties craze, many other wholesalers were disgruntled. Customers, especially youngsters and frugal housewives, were buying novelties rather than bulk packages. In some locations, the manufacturers formed associations and set standards for novelties in order to discourage what they saw as unfair competition. Others introduced new products, such as factory-filled cups, to compete for the nickels and dimes spent on novelties.[80]

For years, retailers had sold paper cups of ice cream hand-filled at the soda fountain or ice cream parlor. In the 1920s, wholesalers began to promote factory-filled cups. One of the very first was the Arctic Sweet-heart, a factory-packaged sundae. According to legend, the Arctic Sweetheart was invented by a woman who worked for a lithographer in Chicago. First, a long strip of paper was lithographed with an attractive design and was rolled into a tube. After one end of the tube had been covered and sealed, the container was partially filled with ice cream. When it was properly frozen, a heart-shaped piece was cut from the center and filled with flavored syrup. Then the top was covered and the tube was returned to the hardening room.

Because demand for the Arctic Sweetheart was tremendous, automated production was obviously needed. However, the Castle Ice Cream Company of Newark, New Jersey—one of the wholesalers manufacturing the packaged sundae—was unable to procure the necessary equipment. As a substitute, Castle asked a company that made containers to supply four-ounce cups to be filled at the factory. The Arctic Sweetheart faded from the picture, but the factory-filled cup had more staying power.[81]

Another early wholesaler of factory-filled cups was Weed Ice Cream of Allentown, Pennsylvania, which supplied cups called Dixies or Dixie Sundaes to drugstores, soda fountains, and other outlets. The containers were manufactured by the Individual Drinking Cup Company, which had originally called them Health Kups but had changed the name when they did not sell. Dixie was chosen because it was the name of a popular doll.

A few years later, lithographer Elliott Brewer suggested printing photographs on the underside of Dixie cup lids as a sales gimmick. To protect the picture, a thin layer of semi-transparent waxed paper was used. Since the *Dixie Circus* radio program was popular at the time, the first photographs were a set of 24 animals. Children collected the lids and traded with their friends in order to assemble an entire set. Subsequent sets of movie star pictures proved to be popular with adults as well as children. Virtually every major film actor and actress appeared on the lids at one time or another. A cowboy series included such actors as William Boyd, Don Barry, John Mack Brown, Smiley Burnette, Buck Jones, and the Range Busters.

During World War II, pictures of tanks and battleships were used in a Defend America promotion. The success of this series led to three others: America's Fighting Forces, America Attacks, and United Nations at War. These lids featured such subjects as the USS *Saratoga*, the Infantry Ski Troops, the USS *Plunkett*, the Armored Force Motorcycle Troops, torpedo boats, the U.S. Navy Nurse Corps, and the U.S. Army Air Corps bombardment planes.[82]

Today, many older adults fondly remember collecting Dixie lids. Humorist Lewis Grizzard was speaking for many people when he said that he would rather eat ice cream from an old-fashioned cup than pay outrageous prices for the superpremium brands. He remembered that his boyhood friend Weyman C. Wannamaker, Jr., especially liked actress Dorothy Malone. Wannamaker once splurged on 15 Dixie cups and was rewarded with a Debra Paget, two Joseph Cottons, three Debbie Reynolds, four Victor Matures, and five Dorothy Malones—enough to make any young man happy.[83]

Although some manufacturers resisted the idea of factory-filled cups, many jumped on the bandwagon. Industry leaders pointed out that the small containers of ice cream were part of a general trend toward more packaging. American grocery stores had once sold unpackaged coffee, sugar, butter, and crackers. Now all those commodities came prepackaged, although not without some consternation; at least one trade journal lamented "this nightmare of packaged crackers." Moreover, the ice cream industry needed a packaged product to compete with other nickel novelties, such as chocolate bars, soda pop, and chewing gum. Ice cream manufacturers who looked on the bright side saw the cup as advertising paid for by the consumer, who might decide to buy a larger container after tasting the product.[84]

Like the Good Humor bar, the IcyPi was a novelty inspired by messy ice cream. It was created by Giacomo (James) Denaro, an Italian immigrant who owned the Automatic Cone Company in Cambridge, Massachusetts. Denaro arrived in the United States in 1903, started a cone business with his brothers, patented an automatic cone maker, and became a successful businessman. One hot summer day while strolling in Cambridge Square, Denaro's wife noticed that people eating ice cream sandwiches were left with messy, sticky fingers. She suggested that Denaro invent an ice cream sandwich that did not drip. The result was the IcyPi, a sort of rectangular cone, or pastry pocket, that was hand-filled with ice cream using a special dipper. The IcyPi enjoyed enormous popularity in the mid- to late-1920s. By the end of the decade, the Automatic Cone Company had to license other cone manufacturers to keep up with the demand. IcyPi production declined during the Depression, partly because the cost-conscious soda fountain operators objected that the IcyPi dipper compressed both the ice cream and the profits. After World War II, Denaro attempted to introduce the IcyPi to a new generation with limited success.[85]

Despite all the novelties competing for the consumer's money, the old-fashioned ice cream cone managed to hold its own. Nevertheless, it was only a matter of time until it, too, would be prepackaged. In 1930, a chocolate-nut sundae in a sugar cone, called the Drumstick, was created by I.C. Parker, advertising manager for Pangburn Candy and Ice Cream Company in Ft. Worth, Texas. The following year, Parker and some Pangburn executives formed the Frozen Drumstick Company. The first commercially produced Drumsticks were hand-filled with ice cream and then placed in the hardening room. After the cones were frozen, they were hand-dipped in chocolate syrup and then rolled in ground peanuts. Finally, they were carefully placed in glassine bags. As demand increased, the manufacturing process became more automated.[86]

Ice Cream Inspiration

Ice cream has been the source of inspiration for many a romance and more than a few inventions. In Ole Evinrude's case, ice cream helped him woo Bess Cary *and* was the impetus for the invention that made him rich.

One hot summer day shortly after the turn of the century, Evinrude and Cary were picnicking with a group of friends on a lake near Milwaukee. The heat made Cary yearn for ice cream, but her companions said she was crazy because going for ice cream meant rowing five miles across the lake and back. Eager to impress the attractive young woman, Evinrude braved the scorching sun and ignored his aching muscles to satisfy her whim. As he rowed, he thought that someone should invent a motor to power small boats. By the time he reached shore, he had decided that he would do it himself.

Soon thereafter, he began experimenting with different designs but encountered problems because his early motors were too large to clamp onto the stern of a rowboat. By 1909, he had invented the first portable outboard motor, which had an internal combustion engine and a fintail that moved the boat about five miles per hour. Witnesses to the first trial runs made fun of it, but Evinrude and Cary, who was now his wife, had faith in the invention.

Mrs. Evinrude wrote an advertising slogan for the new product— "Don't row! Throw your oars away! Use an outboard!" She also suggested that they place a small advertisement in a boating trade journal. The day after the ad was printed, they received several hundred inquiries about the outboard motor. Encouraged, they placed an ad in *The Saturday Evening Post*, which prompted so many responses that they had to hire six stenographers to answer the mail.

The Evinrudes were convinced that there was a market for the motor, but they had only half of the money needed to begin large-scale production. Several investors offered them the necessary capital in return for control of the company. However, they held out until they found a man who was willing to form an equal partnership. In 1910, Evinrude Motors was founded in Milwaukee and was immediately successful. In 1913, the Evinrudes sold their interest in the company for 60 times their original investment and agreed not to compete with it for five years.

During this period, Evinrude continued to experiment. In 1920, he formed the Elco Outboard Motor Company and used his own capital to begin production of a two-cylinder motor, which soon captured a significant share of the market. At the end of the decade, his company was manufacturing half of the nation's outboard motors and he had parlayed a trip for ice cream into a multi-million-dollar corporation.[87]

Medium Tech

Advances in technology dramatically transformed ice cream manufacturing in the period before World War II. In 1906, an engineering journal reported that "antiquated methods of manufacture exist everywhere" in the ice cream industry. Ordinary household ice cream freezers, with slight modifications, were still being used in many small plants. In larger plants, 40-quart freezers were the norm and were often belt-driven with power from a gas engine. Some plants had installed ammonia refrigerating equipment to produce their ice and brine, but few used mechanical refrigeration to actually freeze ice cream. By the beginning of World War II, there had been a major transformation in the industry due to revolutionary new freezers and improvements in other equipment.[88]

The first major improvement in manufacturing was the invention of the circulating brine freezer at the turn of the century. Although sources disagree about the exact date of this event, it was probably 1900. The I.X.L. Ice Cream Company of Warren, Pennsylvania, was experiencing a shortage of ice and faced the prospect of closing, at least temporarily. The company's mechanical superintendent, Burr Walker (who was also the son of the owner), heard that the local oil refinery was using brine cooled by an ammonia compressor and realized that this concept could be applied in his plant. So he rigged up a pump and valve system to supply brine to a slightly modified tub ice cream freezer. His system used an ammonia compressor to make ice for the brine, which was kept at five degrees below zero and circulated around the tub, freezing a 40-quart batch in only six to eight minutes.[89]

The Walkers were not the only ice cream manufacturers experimenting with circulating brine. Charles A. Martin, foreman of an ice cream plant in Connecticut, came up with a similar arrangement at about the same time and sucessfully used it in his operations. He read about the Walkers' freezer in an engineering journal and boarded a train to Pennsylvania the very next day. He found that his system very closely resembled the Walkers'. The concept of the circulating brine freezer spread so quickly that a plant in faraway Oklahoma City designed one and had it in operation in 1902. Two years later, Harvey Miller introduced the Miller Globe Horizontal Brine Freezer, which found a ready market.[90]

In 1905, Emery Thompson, manager of the soda fountain in the Seigel Cooper Company department store in New York City, invented a gravity-fed vertical batch freezer. Thompson, who made ice cream in the basement of the store, wanted to expand but had no room for additional tub freezers. So he designed a vertical freezer in which brine circulated between a double jacket, or inside and outside shell. The driving gear was keyed to a shaft with a clutch pulley, which controlled the operation of the freezer. The operator could tell when the cream was frozen by looking through a peephole in the cover. A sliding gate at the bottom of the freezer allowed the finished product to be drawn off into cans. A new batch of mix was poured into the freezer via a pan suspended over the top, allowing a minimal interruption between batches.[91]

Thompson's freezer was a major step toward a truly continuous freezer, which would produce ice cream in a constant stream without the need to stop the freezer to empty a batch and then restart it. One of the first efforts in this direction was the Disc Continuous Freezer marketed by the Creamery Package Manufacturing Company as early as 1907. In this box-shaped freezer, cold brine was forced through a series of hollow, revolving discs that both cooled and agitated the ice cream mix. By the time the mixture reached the outlet chute, it was frozen to the desired consistency. One side of the freezer was plate glass, enabling the operator to watch the freezing process and make adjustments, if necessary. Several hundred of these freezers went into commercial operation, but manufacturers complained that they produced coarse ice cream.[92]

In 1914, Crispin S. Miesenhelter of York, Pennsylvania, received a patent for a continuous freezer that incorporated several advanced features, such as freezing the mix under pressure. Although Meisenhelter's design worked reasonably well, it never gained wide acceptance among wholesale manufacturers. However, the Miesenhelter and a similar model, the Light freezer, were often used to make frozen custard at fairs and other outdoor events where the product was sold directly from the freezer.[93]

In 1929, Clarence Vogt of Louisville, Kentucky, was issued a patent for a continuous freezer that soon gained a significant share of the market because it yielded a high-quality product. Vogt was an ingenious engineer who also held numerous patents for air-injection processes used in the production of margarine, solid fats, and shortening. He served in the military in both world wars, and during World War II he invented a process for vulcanizing tires by the use of electronics, which required less time than other methods.[94]

In Vogt's original freezer design, ice cream mix was cooled and piped into a reservoir. From there, it traveled through a vacuum delivery pipe into the freezer and quickly reached the desired consistency as it passed between two revolving cylinders filled with cold brine. As the cylinders turned, knives with scalloped edges scraped the frozen cream off, allowing it to fall in a continuous stream onto a conveyor belt. In later models, ammonia replaced the brine.[95]

Even before Vogt received his patent, the Cherry-Burrell Corporation bought the rights and began marketing his freezer. By 1932, both brine and direct-expansion freezers capable of freezing ice cream in about five minutes were available. By 1940, at least one-half of the total United States ice cream output was being made in continuous freezers. Although these freezers had some disadvantages, such as exacting maintenance requirements, they improved quality and productivity because operating procedures were standardized and, to a certain extent, regulated automatically.[96]

During the interwar period, ice cream manufacturers modernized their distribution equipment as well as their freezers. At the beginning of the 20th century, the horse-drawn ice cream wagon was a potent symbol of the industry and a conspicuous advertisement as it rolled along city streets. Each spring, manufacturers traditionally staged a parade of ice cream wagons, often accompanied by a local band, to open the biggest ice cream season of the year. Young and old alike lined the streets to watch the procession and claim the freebies, such as fans and samples of the company's ice cream.[97]

But the horse-and-wagon days were limited. Although the conversion to trucks came slowly, it was inevitable. At first, ice cream manufacturers were reluctant to switch to trucks because they were considered unreliable and required a larger investment than a new horse and wagon. However, as a few adventurous companies made the switch, it became apparent that a truck could cover more territory than a horse in the same amount of time, thereby increasing the number of deliveries per day. The Hendler Company of Baltimore was among the first major manufacturers to abandon the horse and wagon. By 1912 Hendler was experimenting with trucks, and by 1918 it was operating a large fleet of gasoline-powered and electric trucks.[98]

At the beginning of World War II, the American ice cream factory was far removed from the labor-intensive, salt-and-ice operations of the 19th century. Improvements in freezers, packaging equipment, the hardening process, and distribution had propelled the industry into an era of more automation, greater efficiency, better sanitation, and smoother ice cream. In addition, the consumer could buy ice cream at more outlets and in a greater variety of flavors and packages than ever before.

6

From Soft Serve to Superpremium: 1940–1995

Worth Fighting For

In World War II, GIs knew what they were fighting for—democracy, Mom, Betty Grable, Coca-Cola, and ice cream—but not necessarily in that order. Wherever American soldiers were stationed, ice cream was in demand as a palate-pleaser and morale-booster. Stateside, mess sergeants served it regularly. Overseas, troops made their own, using Yankee know-how to improvise freezers if necessary.

At the beginning of the war, the top brass gave little thought to ice cream. However, as the scope of the war expanded, the value of ice cream, as a food and as a symbol, became widely recognized. Dietitians discovered that ice cream relieved the monotony of field rations and stimulated the appetites of soldiers who were losing weight because food had lost its appeal. In 1943 the United Press reported that Army procurement priorities rated ice cream, candy, soft drinks, chewing gum, and tobacco products as essential for maintaining troop morale. Even the enemy helped to solidify ice cream's position as an American symbol. In Italy, Mussolini banned ice cream outright, while the Emperor of Japan ordered vendors to lower the price of ice cream sodas and sundaes, making it unprofitable to sell them.[1]

Location did not affect the GI's demand for ice cream, which was eaten in the Arctic as well as the tropics. Soldiers in the Arctic mixed powdered milk, eggs, sugar, water, and vanilla in a dishpan. One man held the pan while another stirred. In the 40-below-zero temperature and strong winds, they could whip up a batch of ice cream in five minutes. Airmen based in Britain discovered another efficient way of freezing ice cream. They stowed large cans of liquid mix in the rear gunner's compartment of a bomber, where the combination of the plane's vibrations and high-altitude temperatures produced a smooth ice cream.[2]

Navy Seabees on a Pacific island fabricated an ice cream freezer with tubing from an airplane, gears from a Japanese engine, a Japanese airplane starter, shell cases, a small gasoline motor, and miscellaneous

141

vehicle parts machined to fit the purpose. In North Africa, another Seabee unit built a freezer using abandoned equipment, including a German motor, Italian gears, and American tractor parts. In New Hebrides, a Navy PX operator named Burton Baskin persuaded a supply officer on a visiting aircraft carrier to take a jeep in exchange for an ice cream freezer. In a portent of things to come, Baskin used local fruits and flavorings to concoct exotic combinations resembling those that would later make Baskin-Robbins famous.[3]

One marine unit on Guadalcanal Island, "the big green hell," was fortunate because its officers had the foresight to purchase a freezer with their own funds before they shipped out. The freezer was disassembled, boxed up, and carried wherever the unit went. Whenever there was time for making ice cream, the mess sergeant served it as a special treat. Another marine unit on Guadalcanal was not blessed with a freezer but decided to rig up its own. The leathernecks scavaged for parts and improvised a freezer powered by a gas motor. Since there was no refrigerator to keep the ice cream frozen, it had to be served quickly, but this was never a problem because homesick marines always ate every bite.[4]

Even sailors on a sinking ship enjoyed ice cream. The USS *Lexington,* the second largest aircraft carrier in the world, was repeatedly hit by Japanese bombs and torpedoes during the Battle of the Coral Sea. These hits started numerous fires below deck, causing the ship to list and lose speed. Despite desperate efforts to control the flames, there was an explosion and the conflagration spread to the hangar deck. Eventually, the captain had no choice but to order the sailors to abandon ship. While they waited on deck for other vessels to come to their rescue, the sailors calmly ate ice cream cones distributed by the ship's storekeeper. Some men even filled their helmets with ice cream and carried them over the side. Although heavy casualties had been sustained during the battle, no lives were lost in the rescue operation.[5]

Military doctors routinely prescribed ice cream to help soldiers recover from combat fatigue. At a medical conference, a Navy psychiatrist told his colleagues that shell-shocked soldiers, who looked like "very old men" and behaved like "terrified wild animals," needed showers, rest, fresh air, sunshine, and wholesome food, especially ice cream. Air Force mess sergeants reported that ice cream was often the only food that fliers with queasy stomachs could eat after returning from missions.[6]

One wounded veteran recalled, "The finest time I had was in the sick bay one day when a Marine obtained an ice cream freezer." Fortunately, he was on a Pacific island where the Marines had taken over a Japanese icehouse, and hospital personnel were able to find the ingredients for ice cream. "We mixed them all together in the freezer, and there were fellows so homesick they were almost crying. Everyone wanted to turn the freezer," he remembered. There were so many soldiers that each could have only one or two spoonsful of ice cream, "but it was the best thing we ate on the island."[7]

Recognizing the value of ice cream to the troops, the Quartermaster Corps of the U.S. Army decided to supply the machinery and ingredients for making approximately 80 million gallons annually. In 1943 the corps shipped 135 million pounds of dehydrated ice cream mix to bases around the world. The powder was formulated so that any soldier who followed the instructions could make passable vanilla ice cream, which could be flavored with canned fruits, crushed candy, or any other flavoring that was handy. In February 1945 the Quartermaster Corps announced that it would set up miniature ice cream plants near the frontlines and rush half-pint cartons "right to the foxholes."[8]

Secretary of the Navy James Forrestal gave the distribution of ice cream "highest priority" after an assistant reported, "Ice cream in my opinion has been the most neglected of all the important morale factors." The aide's report noted that seamen at Guadalcanal were served ice cream only twice a week, while an adjoining Army unit had an excellent snack bar where the soldiers could eat ice cream, popcorn, and candy whenever they wanted. In order to provide ice cream for more sailors, the Navy built a concrete barge with a floating ice cream parlor at a cost of $1million. It also commissioned refrigeration barges, commonly called ice cream ships, which were equipped with ice cream plants and storage rooms.[9]

In March 1942 the manufacture of soda fountain equipment, except for high priority items, was discontinued by government order. The following year, the government purchased all known stocks of fountain equipment for distribution to Army and Navy posts as needed. The Bureau of Ships, General Electric, and Bastian Blessing Company cooperated to design small soda fountains for battleships and aircraft carriers, which had limited space for such luxuries.[10]

Of course, the war complicated life for ice cream manufacturers, who had to cope with government rationing of sugar and a shortage of vanilla, due to the British blockade of Madagascar. In 1941 the U.S. government classified ice cream as a nonessential food. After intense lobbying by the International Association of Ice Cream Manufacturers and the National Dairy Council, the ruling was reversed and the frozen treat was placed on the official Basic Seven Foods Chart. Although industry associations complained about sugar allotments, many manufacturers were permitted to exceed the limit because they supplied ice cream to military bases or were located in war-boom areas. The availability of milk solids was limited to a government-specified percentage of a firm's production for an earlier period, usually the preceding year.[11]

Retailers also had to cope with ice cream shortages due to the war. As production was curtailed or diverted to military use, restaurants and soda fountains altered their menus to suit the situation. For example, the menu for a New York City restaurant offered "Ice Cream—whatever we have, whenever we have it." Some restaurants posted placards encouraging customers to order sherbet, which contained less butterfat and fewer solids than ice cream. Other retailers sold half-and-half sundaes, with one scoop of sherbet and one of ice cream.

One entrepreneur promoted the idea of substituting cottage cheese for ice cream in sundaes. After test-marketing his Cottage Cheese Sundae with poor results, he advised retailers, "Do not under any circumstances call it that because it just will not sell under that name." The Ice Cream Merchandising Institute initiated a more successful marketing campaign, promoting Victory Sundaes, with a dime from each sale going to buy a war stamp.[12]

America Goes Soft

In the immediate postwar period, the big news in ice cream was soft serve. In 1946 and 1947 conventional ice cream production soared to new heights and then in 1948 began to decline slightly. Meanwhile, rapidly moving up the charts came soft serve—a category including iced milk, frozen custard, milk sherbets, and chilled (not frozen) ice cream. In 1956 the U.S. Department of Agriculture reported that consumption of soft ice cream had jumped more than 25 percent every year since World War II. Customers were flocking to roadside ice cream stands, eager for the soft serve that flowed out of the freezer while they watched. Whether these stands were chains or independents, they were mostly mom-and-pop operations that embodied the American dream. As one popular magazine wrote, "Probably never before in the history of American enterprise have so many people, from so many unrelated walks of life, with so little money to invest, taken such meager business experience and made so much money with it."[13]

The soft serve phenomenon was epitomized by the growth of the Dairy Queen chain. While virtually all ice cream retailers suffered some disruptions due to World War II, the fledgling Dairy Queen chain, which was poised for major expansion when the United States entered the war, was left in limbo. When the Japanese bombed Pearl Harbor in 1941, there were only three Dairy Queen stores but they had proved to be exceptionally profitable and potential owners were clamoring to open more. Because of the war, the number of Dairy Queen outlets had climbed to only eight by late 1945. Then, peacetime brought rapid growth, from 100 stores in 1947 to 1,400 only three years later.[14]

The origins of the chain can be traced to J.F. "Grandpa" McCullough and his son, H.A. "Alex" McCullough, proprietors of the Homemade Ice Cream Company in Green River, Illinois. The McCulloughs liked the taste of ice cream as it oozed from the freezer in its semi-solid state, before it was taken to the hardening room and frozen. Ice cream was typically served at about 5 degrees Fahrenheit, but Grandpa McCullough thought that it was most flavorful at around 23 degrees because colder temperatures numbed the taste buds. He felt that the optimum product would be a semifrozen, thick ice cream that was not runny and messy.

Fair and carnival vendors sometimes sold frozen custard directly from the freezer, but there was nothing on the market that produced exactly what the McCulloughs envisioned. Although the younger McCullough enjoyed tinkering with machines, he lacked the expertise to invent the type of freezer they needed. Nevertheless, they decided to do some primitive market research and persuaded a retailer to let them supply soft ice cream for a special sale at his store in Kankakee, Illinois. Advertisements promising "all the ice cream you can eat for only 10 cents" drew a large crowd to the store on August 4, 1938. Using a batch freezer, the McCulloughs and the retailer made ice cream and hand-dipped it into large cups while it was still soft. The lines of eager consumers stretched around the block and spilled into the corner tavern, where the regulars liked the soft ice cream, too.

A couple of weeks later, the McCulloughs repeated this experiment at an ice cream shop in Moline, with heartening success. They had proved that soft ice cream would sell, if only they could find a freezer that would make it practical. Alex McCullough contacted two dairy equipment manufacturers about engineering a special continuous freezer that would dispense semifrozen cream into cones or cups. One company was not interested. The other—Stoelting Brothers Company in Kiel, Wisconsin—showed no particular enthusiasm but did not actually reject the idea.[15]

Without a freezer, the McCulloughs placed their idea on the back burner until one fortunate day when Grandpa, who was reading a Chicago newspaper, spotted an advertisement for a new continuous freezer that dispensed frozen custard. Eagerly, the McCulloughs made an appointment to meet the inventor, Harry M. Oltz, who owned a hamburger stand in Hammond, Indiana. On July 31, 1939, the three men signed an agreement, giving the McCulloughs manufacturing rights to the freezer and its exclusive use in Illinois, Wisconsin, and the states west of the Mississippi River. Oltz retained rights for the exclusive use of the freezer in the eastern United States plus royalties based on the number of gallons of mix processed in all freezers manufactured under his patent.[16]

Oltz built a prototype freezer and, shortly thereafter, moved to Florida to establish AR-TIK Systems, a company that would launch the new frozen treat in the East. Meanwhile, Alex McCullough searched for a manufacturer to mass produce the freezer and improve Oltz's design, which had a number of flaws. Although the freezer made delicious ice cream, it was crude and difficult to operate. A motor fastened to the floor turned the auger in the bowl of the freezer via a sprocket pulley and chain. Ice and salt were packed into a galvanized iron trough that surrounded the bowl. The freezer had to be placed next to a large walk-in cooler and ice crusher to provide a steady supply of ice. Two men were needed to carry ice from the cooler, up a ladder, and shovel it into the trough. This was back-breaking work since literally tons of ice were required to keep the freezer running all day. Clearly, the most urgent improvement was mechanical refrigeration.

In September 1939 Alex McCullough reached an agreement with Stoelting Brothers to perfect and manufacture the freezer. Although Oltz had supplied blueprints, many modifications were necessary as the work progressed. McCullough spent a great deal of time finding the right parts and materials because all the metal had to be chrome-plated or hot-dipped in tin for sanitation. After several months, the freezer was finally ready and the Stoelting employees gathered for a demonstration. It is easy to imagine McCullough's sickening disappointment when the first ice cream oozed from the freezer speckled with tiny black particles![17]

McCullough loaded the freezer onto his truck and carted it to Grandpa's house in Green River. After widening the door so the freezer could be moved into the basement, he spent months tinkering with it, in order to eliminate the offensive black specks. Meanwhile, Grandpa experimented with ice cream mixes, searching for just the right formula. The basement floor was often splattered with gooey mix and littered with freezer parts as the two plodded along, unwilling to give up their dream. .

After many test batches, Grandpa decided that soft ice cream tasted best with 5 to 6 percent butterfat and held its shape best when dispensed at 18 degrees Fahrenheit. He also chose a name, Dairy Queen, because soft serve would be the queen of dairy products. The younger

McCullough solved the major problems with the freezer and located suppliers for the new parts. Then he placed an order with Stoelting for four freezers built to his new specifications. On Decoration Day, 1940, the McCulloughs took delivery of two freezers while the others were shipped to Oltz in Florida.

On June 22, 1940, the first Dairy Queen opened on North Chicago Street in Joliet, Illinois, owned by a local retailer, Sherb Noble. The menu was simple: vanilla cones, pints, quarts, and sundaes. Triple-decker cones cost a nickel, while quintuple-deckers were a dime. At the end of the first season, the store had recouped most of the initial investment. Encouraged, the McCulloughs ordered more freezers and in 1941 built a store in Moline, Illinois, which incorporated many features that came to typify Dairy Queen. The free-standing facility, painted gleaming white, had two walk-up serving windows in front, large plate-glass windows on the sides, and a flat, overhanging roof.[18]

Unfortunately, as the lines of customers clamoring for soft serve grew longer, its availability began to shrink due to rationing and shortages. One early Dairy Queen operator later recalled, "We were closed at least a week out of every month. Many times we ran out of soft serve with two long lines of customers standing in front of us." Despite the public's healthy appetite for Dairy Queen, expansion became impossible when freezer manufacturing was halted because materials were needed for the war effort.

While the war raged, the McCulloughs made plans for future expansion, selling rights to use the Dairy Queen freezer and open stores in prescribed geographical territories. Since neither of them understood franchising, they shied away from the type of licensing and royalty arrangements that would later dominate the fast food industry. Instead they carved out territories to fit each individual investor's finances; some could afford only a portion of one county; others purchased the rights to an entire state. The McCulloughs chose cash over the prospect of future income, unaware that their lack of business expertise would later haunt the company. Their contracts were informal, scribbled on any handy piece of paper, and sealed with a handshake.[19]

Although the McCulloughs kept in touch with Dairy Queen operators and sold them mix made in the Green River plant, they did not understand the need for a corporate structure or control over the individual stores. One day, Harry Axene, sales manager for a farm equipment company, drove past the Dairy Queen store in Moline and was amazed by the long lines. After making inquiries, he traveled to Green River and found Grandpa McCullough relaxing on his front porch. In a surprisingly short time, the two men reached an agreement:

Axene would buy 50 percent of the mix plant plus the rights to Iowa and Illinois. Since Grandpa had decided to retire and live with his daughter, Axene moved his family into Grandpa's house. Axene and his wife worked hard at the mix plant and, after a year, bought the entire plant.

Now the stage was set for Axene to operate the business in a more efficient, aggressive manner and to expand as soon as the war ended. Accordingly, he invited a number of potential investors to a special meeting where he presented his scheme for selling territories based on a royalty system. Under his plan, an investor would pay him a low, upfront fee for a territory plus a continuing royalty charge for all soft serve mix processed in a Dairy Queen freezer. Returning veterans and others who had postponed their dream of owning a small business were eager for an opportunity that required so little capital and offered so much promise. The Dairy Queen explosion began in earnest.[20]

Despite the public's enthusiastic endorsement of soft serve, the fledgling chain did encounter obstacles, especially legal technicalities. In many states, the law specified that ice cream must have a minimum butterfat content, usually at least 10 percent, or be labeled appropriately. In Minnesota, where state law required 12 percent butterfat, a Dairy Queen franchisee was arrested for using a mix with less butterfat. In court, his lawyer argued that the product was sanitary, satisfied all the state health laws, and would be legal if it were packaged in a box labeled "ice milk." His client's only crime had been selling soft serve in a cone rather than a box. The judge agreed with the attorney and dismissed the case. In Iowa, low-butterfat products had to be labeled "ice milk" or "imitation ice cream." Dairy Queen operators complied by slipping a paper doily stamped "ice milk" over the cone or by purchasing cones with "ice milk" embossed on them. In some states, including Pennsylvania, Dairy Queen owners complied with government regulations, dispensing a high-butterfat product until they could persuade their legislators to change the law.[21]

In 1948 a group of territory and store owners formed the Dairy Queen National Trade Association to insure uniformity and develop standardized products for the chain. Seven years later this trade association became the Dairy Queen National Development Company, a for-profit corporation owned by territory operators. In the early 1960s, disagreements among territory owners led to the formation of a new corporation, International Dairy Queen. The new company bought up territories to bring them under the corporate umbrella and purchased the McCulloughs' remaining interest, which now belonged to Alex's son Hugh. It established clear ownership of the Dairy Queen name, initiated an integrated national advertising and marketing program, renegotiated contracts, enhanced product uniformity, adopted the Brazier food program and started a national training school. However, management's efforts to diversify failed, leading to the need for new investors by 1970. An infusion of capital saved the company and by July 4, 1971, it was profitable again.[22]

In response to competition and consumer requests, new products were gradually added to the Diary Queen menu. Malts and shakes appeared in 1949. Banana splits followed two years later. Then the Stripenizer gave colorful stripes to soft serve as it curled out of the machine. In 1955, two Dairy Queen territory owners developed the Dilly bar, a chocolate-dipped, soft-serve bar on a stick. When the chain's regular suppliers ran short of sticks for the Dilly, company executives thought they might have to discontinue the bar. Then someone suggested buying tongue depressors from medical supply houses, and "Dairy Queen wound up almost controlling the market for doctors' tongue depressors."[23]

The Dilly's success prompted Dairy Queen to market more novelties, including the DQ Sandwich, Mr. Maltie, the Buster Bar, and Mr. Misty. In the 1950s, Dairy Queen replaced its small wooden spoons with plastic ones, which proved to be very popular, producing a virtual tidal wave of plastic sundae dishes and colorful containers. Competition from fast food chains motivated many Dairy Queen owners to add hamburgers, hot dogs, french fries, and so forth to their menus. This played havoc with the chain's national identity as Dairy Queens promoted various food systems—including A-Burger, Queen's Choice, Sizzle Kitchen, and Texas Country Foods—in different regions. In 1958, the Brazier system, featuring broiled hamburgers and hot dogs, was introduced in Georgia and was later adopted nationwide to standardize Dairy Queen menus.[24]

One of Dairy Queen's most recent innovations, the Blizzard, has become one of its biggest all-time hits. It was inspired by a concoction with the unappetizing name Concrete, which originated in St. Louis at an independent custard stand that had survived the onslaught of the big chains. Concrete was simply a blend of soft serve and fruit juice, but customers couldn't get enough of it. The sight of people waiting in long lines to buy Concrete apparently inspired the owner of another local outlet to one-upmanship: he mixed crushed candy and cookies into the blend.

Sam Temperato, a Dairy Queen territory owner, heard about Concrete and checked it out. Immediately, he knew it was right for Dairy Queen. He became even more excited when he learned that another

Dairy Queen owner was developing a high-powered mixer that would be perfect for making the thick blend. He was shocked when his first efforts to sell the idea to the company failed, but the corporate Concept Committee agreed to visit St. Louis and taste Concrete at the local stands. One visit to the stands convinced the committee, and the very next day it approved the product and the name Blizzard. It was briefly test marketed during the winter of 1984–85 and officially launched in the spring. The first year, Dairy Queen sold a remarkable 100 million Blizzards.[25]

Although Dairy Queen had the largest number of retail ice cream outlets, it was not the only roadside operation that boomed in the postwar era. While thousands of independents and dozens of chains competed for the consumer's loose change, Tastee Freez and Carvel Dari-Freeze emerged as Dairy Queen's major rivals. Like Dairy Queen, Tastee Freez was built around a freezer. Leo S. Maranz, a mechanical engineer, designed an automatic, continuous ice cream freezer that he thought would be perfect for Dairy Queen. He presented his concept to Axene, who agreed, because Maranz's freezer was both substantially smaller than the Oltz freezer and much easier to operate. However, when Axene proposed that Dairy Queen switch freezers, the board of directors empathically rejected the idea because the company was in the throes of a major effort to standardize operations and changing freezers would complicate that process.[26]

Axene left his brother in charge of the Dairy Queen mix plant in Green River and severed his other ties with the chain. Then he and Maranz formed the Harlee Manufacturing Company to produce the new freezer for a chain that Mrs. Axene named Tastee Freez. Due to differing business philosophies, the partnership lasted only two years. When it was dissolved, Axene retained the rights to Oregon, Washington, and California while Maranz controlled the rest of the United States. Tastee Freez, which was headquartered in Chicago, had 600 outlets in 1953 and more than 1,500 only three years later.[27]

In 1934 Thomas Carvel was struggling to make a living as a door-to-door radio salesman. He hated ringing doorbells, but he liked to take long drives in the country with his girlfriend. One Sunday, he and his girlfriend (later Mrs. Carvel) hitched a home-built trailer to his old Graham, loaded it with a big freezer of ice cream, and headed north from New York City until a flat tire interrupted their journey in Hartsdale, forcing them to sell their cargo on the spot. They liked Hartsdale and decided to rent a small store there for the summer. For the next five years, they ran an ice cream shop during the summer and worked at other jobs in the off-season.

Carvel used his savings and profits from the store to perfect an electric freezer that produced soft ice cream. By 1939, he had applied for a patent, had built several freezers, and was operating three ice cream stores. During World War II, he placed his freezers in PXs and lived off the royalties. When peace returned, he resumed production of his freezers, selling them to roadside stands. Although sales were good, he nearly went bankrupt because many of the people who bought the freezers lacked business experience and fell behind on their payments. To avoid a financial disaster, he formed two companies, Carvel Corporation and Carvel Dari-Freeze Stores, and sold stock. Then he began to build a chain by personally operating some stores and franchising others.[28]

The Carvel chain boasted 200 outlets by 1952 and more than 500 in 1956. The flagship was "the world's first ice-cream supermarket" in Hartsdale, which sold 53 flavors of soft ice cream and more than 200 items ranging from a dime cone to a $500 ice cream wedding cake. A chef with two assistants delivered and served the cake, which was more than seven feet tall.[29]

Many reasons have been advanced for the phenomenal growth of roadside ice cream stands after World War II. Not least, of course, was the taste of soft serve. But other factors were also at work. In the postwar era, gasoline and rubber were no longer rationed. Americans could afford to drive their cars again, and they had a love affair with automobiles. Even a ride to the local Dairy Queen was a special occasion. Moreover, most Americans had neither televisions nor air conditioning in their homes. A drive or a stroll to the Dairy Queen was a pleasant diversion—an evening's entertainment before Milton Berle, Ed Sullivan, and all the others came into the living room. Above all, ice cream stands were informal, family places. Children did not have to sit still, and no one cared if they made a little noise.

As the chains evolved, management gained expertise about why outlets failed or succeeded, until opening a new unit became almost a science. The most important factor was location. Carvel's ideal location was along a secondary highway with free-flowing traffic moving 25 miles per hour or less. It was important that the area have enough permanent residents to provide a nucleus of repeat customers. Both superhighways and bumper-to-bumper traffic were undesirable because drivers were reluctant to pull off the road if the traffic was moving too fast or too slow. If Carvel was unsure about a prospective site, the company's "location engineers" used counters to determine how much automotive and pedestrian traffic passed by.[30]

The next requirement for a successful stand was eye appeal. In the typical outlet, large windows on both the front and the sides created an open, welcoming atmosphere. High visibility was important since the driver had to prepare to stop. Therefore, large signs that were immediately recognizable were essential, and at night the shops had to be flooded with light. One architectural historian has described the style as utilitarian, vernacular design with "the straightforward construction characteristic of ordinary people, functional and unself-conscious, dictated by the need for economy rather than by sophisticated cultural aspirations."[31]

When the McCulloughs were handing out the blueprints for the first Dairy Queens, they would probably have been surprised at the deep meaning attributed to the design in the following architectural critique:

Dairy Queen's low, flat roof—probably attributable to the limited finances of the franchisees—gave the building a calm, soothing profile and in general a feeling of modesty, which could offer a welcome respite from an aggressively commercial landscape. Yet the attractiveness of the Dairy Queen stand was not entirely artless.

There were just enough features—the rounded overhangs, the brick base under the windows, the consistent absence of clutter on the concrete-block walls—to indicate that the building was consciously intended to project an image. These simple decorative touches made the stand just gracious enough to avoid looking pinched and severe.[32]

Low overhead and hard work were extremely important to a stand's success. A Department of Commerce study reported that, on average, soft-serve retailers spent 30 cents to generate a $1 sale, while retailers of other products spent 67 cents. A stand owner was both manufacturer and retailer, which eliminated the middleman. Stands did not need large inventories because most served only one flavor, and they were strictly a cash-and-carry business, eliminating the need for charge accounts or collections.

Despite the simplicity of the operation, selling soft serve was not for the weak or the faint-hearted. Even though stands were seasonal, operating only seven or eight months each year, the owners routinely worked 12 to 15 hours per day seven days a week during the summer. Even slack hours, like dinnertime, were no rest periods because this time was used for filling take-home containers and making novelties, like ice cream cakes or pies. Most stands were family businesses, and the large chains advised against hiring outsiders because employees had less to gain from a successful store. By the mid-1950s, Carvel was refusing to sell a franchise to anyone who did not intend to run the store personally. Although few franchisees became rich, an ice cream stand was the route to independence and a steady income for those with stamina and determination.[33]

Frozen Sin

After World War II, it seemed that the dire predictions about selling ice cream in grocery stores had come true. Many manufacturers had lowered their standards in order to produce cheaper ice cream for the mass market. The products in the grocer's freezer, especially the store or private labels, contained such ingredients as dextrose, lactose, fructose, calcium hydroxide, alginate, polysorbate 65, propylene glycol, gum acacia, carboxymethylcellulose, plastic cream, imitation flavors, antioxidants, neutralizers, buffers, bactericides, surfactants, artificial colors, stabilizers, and emulsifiers. Moreover, a typical supermarket brand had 75 to 100 percent overrun, meaning that a great deal of air had been whipped into it to produce a fluffy texture.

Not surprisingly, many consumers eschewed this bland, airy, synthetic-tasting supermarket ice cream and longed for the dimly remembered pleasure of archetypal ice cream with rich, pure, natural flavors—the kind they had tasted at a church picnic or a family reunion years ago, when it was made from scratch and frozen in a hand-cranked freezer. There was a market waiting for entrepreneurs daring enough and creative enough to satisfy America's jaded tastebuds. The world was ready for Baskin-Robbins, Ben and Jerry's, Häagen-Dazs, and the cyrogenic euphoria of exotic flavors with quirky names. It was time to make ice cream fun again.

Burton Baskin and Irvine Robbins, brothers-in-law who served in the military during World War II, were in the vanguard of the campaign to reinvent America's favorite treat. After being discharged from the armed forces, both decided to settle in California. Robbins, who had grown up in Washington where his father was in the dairy business, planned to open an ice cream store in the San Francisco area. However, because there was a shortage of commercial real estate in the area, he was unable to find a suitable location. Then, on a trip to Los Angeles, he discovered an empty shop in Glendale, immediately rented it, and opened the Snowbird Ice Cream Store.

Baskin, who had operated a haberdashery in Chicago's Palmer House Hotel before the war, planned to open a men's store in Beverly Hills. But Robbins convinced him that ice cream would be more fun and more lucrative. On the advice of Robbins's father, the two young men did not immediately become partners but decided to operate separately for a time, in order to try out their own ideas before they collaborated. So, Baskin opened his own ice cream parlor, Burton's. After about five years, they merged their businesses to form Baskin-Robbins, which soon expanded to several shops. Because they could not personally supervise each location, they decided to franchise stores. By 1994, their venture had grown to more than 3,500 franchises in 47 countries and a rotating roster of over 650 flavors.[34]

Unlike soda fountains and old-fashioned ice cream parlors, Baskin-Robbins did not encourage customers to eat in its dipping stores, as they were known in the trade. The company did not want courting couples ordering one soda and monopolizing a table for the entire evening. Nor did it want teenagers hanging out, littering and annoying the other customers. Each store was furnished with a dozen not-very-comfortable chairs, but most patrons took their ice cream with them.[35]

Baskin-Robbins ice cream, which contained up to 20 percent butterfat, was made with fresh cream and no preservatives. As a marketing gimmick, the chain decided to feature 31 flavors each month—one for each day. Steady sellers, or stock flavors, stayed on the menu indefinitely while others, such as Pumpkin and Quarterback Crunch, were seasonal. Ideally, each month's menu included a balance of sherbets and ice creams in a variety of colors and flavors, including chocolates, ribboned products, and seasonal or holiday specialties.

New flavors were often created to commemorate special events, such as Lunar Cheesecake when Apollo 11 landed on the moon or Beatle Nut when Beatlemania hit the United States. Creating Beatle Nut was a panic situation because Baskin and Robbins were not tuned into the rock music scene and were unaware of the Beatles' tour until a few days before the Mop Tops arrived. Nevertheless, they managed to improvise a flavor and have it in the stores in time. For the American Bicentennial, Baskin-Robbins celebrated with Concord Grape, Yankee Doodle Strudel (cherries and strudel crumbs), Valley Forge Fudge (chocolate ice cream with brownie bits), and Minute Man Mint (green peppermint ice cream with peppermint candy and marshmallow ribbons).

Baskin-Robbins' most popular specialty flavor, Pralines 'n' Cream, was inspired by a trip to New Orleans. While visiting the Big Easy, Robbins ate some toffee-coated pecans and immediately knew that they would make a great ice cream flavoring. After some experimentation, Baskin-Robbins found the right combination: candied nuts in vanilla ice cream with a buttery caramel ribbon. Within two months of its introduction, Pralines 'n' Cream was outselling vanilla in the dipping stores.

Robbins claimed that the chain had suffered only one major marketing disaster: Goody-Goody Gum Drop ice cream. The gumdrops froze so hard that consumers risked dental damage with each bite. Many other flavors, such as lox-and-bagel, were the beneficiaries of euthanasia before they reached the consumer. In honor of a friend who ate ketchup on everything, Baskin and Robbins featured ketchup ice cream at the opening of their store in Encino, California. But no one, not even the ketchup freak, liked it.[36]

In 1960, Häagen-Dazs, the creation of Reuben Mattus, went after the highest niche at the upper end of the ice cream market. As a young boy, Mattus had immigrated to New York with his mother and sister from Poland, after his father had been killed in World War I. The family survived by making lemon ice, which young Mattus delivered around the Bronx in a horse-drawn cart. Later, the family decided to make ice cream, too. The small business prospered until the major corporations began to squeeze the little manufacturers out of the New York market. Large companies like Breyers and Borden could make and sell ice cream more cheaply. Moreover, they often made deals with the supermarket chains that denied freezer space to smaller brands.[37]

Mattus later explained his decision to make a superpremium ice cream, saying, "I realized I couldn't keep up and maintain any kind of quality. I thought maybe if I made the very best ice cream, people would be willing to pay for it."[38]

Mattus believed that he could appeal to the "Danish modern" segment of the market: consumers willing to pay extra for high-quality, gourmet, status-symbol ice cream made of natural ingredients with no additives, preservatives, or stabilizers. Moreover, he felt that Denmark was a country with a favorable public image. While some ethnic groups suffered from hateful stereotypes and prejudice, Americans generally had a favorable impression of the Danes. His wife, Rose, conjured up the name Häagen-Dazs, which sounded reasonably Danish, even though there's no umlaut in the language. In keeping with the Danish modern-motif, a map of Scandinavia and an arrow pointing toward Copenhagen were printed on the ice cream carton.[39]

In the beginning, Mattus marketed only three flavors (vanilla, chocolate, coffee) and sold his entire output through small shops in Manhattan. To emphasize quality over quantity, Häagen-Dazs was packaged in pints rather than the familiar economy-size cartons found in the grocer's freezer. Even though it cost twice as much as the supermarket brands, demand grew steadily. Gradually, the supermarket chains started to stock Mattus's ice cream, usually beginning with one or two stores in affluent neighborhoods. Sixteen new flavors were added, and Häagen-Dazs decided to open its own retail outlets. By 1981, it had licensed more than 90 scoop shops and was selling 6 million gallons per year nationwide.[40]

The success of Häagen-Dazs spawned a number of upscale clones. Richie Smith, an ice cream manufacturer and distributor, produced several brands, including Dolly Madison. He created Frusen Gladje, meaning "frozen delight" in Swedish. To create an aura of authenticity, Smith established a shell corporation in Sweden and put a Stockholm address on the carton, which featured the requisite map of Scandinavia. As an extra touch, most of the information on the package was printed in both Swedish and English, even though the ice cream was made at a plant in Utica, New York. After Frusen Gladje had been on the market for a short time, a court ordered Smith to remove the Swedish address and identify the product as being made in the United States. Later, Smith sold the brand to Kraft.[41]

Abe Kroll of Gold Seal Riviera Ice Cream created Alpen Zauber, meaning "Alpine magic," which was made in Brooklyn but was "inspired by the Swiss commitment to excellence." Other clones vying for the superpremium market included Tres Chocolat, Perche No!, Ja, Le Glace de Paris, Gelare, Godiva, and Strasels. All slavishly copied the Häagen-Dazs formula: high butterfat, low overrun, and a glossy, snobbish image.[42]

Superpremium, status-symbol ice cream fit neatly into the Reagan era of conspicuous consumption. It was a deliciously sinful treat for yuppies who wanted aerobics-toned hard bodies but felt they had the right to indulge themselves, too. After all, everyone needed occasional relief from the fad diets hyped by the professional dieters on TV talk shows. Many baby boomers shared the enthusiasm of food critic Gael Greene, who wrote, "For me, it's not the least bit excessive to rank the quality ice cream explosion with the sexual revolution, the women's movement, and peace for our time. Great ice cream is sacred and brave, an eternal verity."[43]

By the time Pillsbury bought Häagen-Dazs in 1983, a superpremium with a different image had emerged in Vermont. Ben Cohen and Jerry Greenfield were two young men who had been high school friends on Long Island and wanted to go into business together. At the time they decided to take the plunge, Cohen was a college dropout teaching pottery-making while Greenfield was a medical school reject, working as a lab technician. Their first plan was to open the United Bagel Service (UBS), delivering bagels and the *New York Times* on Sunday mornings. However, this scheme had two flaws: they were stymied on what to do the other six days of the week and they couldn't afford the bagel-making equipment. So, they decided to sell homemade ice cream.[44]

After completing Penn State's correspondence course in ice-cream-making, they chose Saratoga Springs, New York, as the site of their ice cream parlor and moved there. However, before they could find the right location for their shop, someone else opened a homemade ice cream parlor. Sensing that the Saratoga Springs market would not support two parlors, they looked for an alternative. This time they chose Burlington, Vermont, which had both advantages and disadvantages for ice cream entrepreneurs. Approximately 20 percent of Vermont's entire population lived within a 10-mile radius of Burlington, and it was the site of a large university. On the other hand, Vermont's cold climate and short summers reduced the demand for ice cream, making it the only state without a single Baskin-Robbins franchise.[45]

The two men moved to Burlington, bought a used White Mountain salt-and-ice freezer, and rented half of an abandoned gas station near the University of Vermont. When bankers expressed misgivings about the profitability of an ice cream parlor in Vermont, Cohen and Greenfield added hot soup and crepes to their menu in order to procure the necessary financing. They bought used restaurant equipment at auctions and worked virtually around the clock, even sleeping at the gas station, to complete the necessary renovations. At the same time, they experimented with making ice cream "unencumbered by experience." Due to Cohen's sinus problems, he was unable to taste subtle flavors and found it necessary to increase the amount of flavorings normally used in ice cream recipes. This led to the decision to utilize lots of chunky add-ins in their product.[46]

Although add-ins, or mix-ins, were a comparatively new idea, they did not originate with Ben and Jerry's. Credit for introducing mix-ins is given to Steve Herrell, a Boston cab driver and sometime high school teacher, who also owned an ice cream shop in Somerville, Massachusetts. Herrell perfected a technique in which the scooper, using two spades, mixed add-ins into the frozen ice cream immediately before it was served. Cohen and Greenfield experimented with using Herrell's technique but decided that it was better to add the chunks while the ice cream was still in the freezer. [47]

Ben and Jerry's Homemade opened on May 5, 1978, even though the renovations were not quite complete. The fresh, rich ice cream with natural flavors and candy mix-ins was an immediate hit with the campus crowd. The shop offered up to 12 "orgasmic flavors" each day, and Oreo Mint was the best-selling item in the beginning. A pianist, who worked at the local IBM plant and loved ice cream, entertained the customers in exchange for free food.

As an added attraction, Cohen and Greenfield decided to screen free movies on the outside wall of an adjacent building during the summer. In order to do so, they needed to turn off the street lights outside the shop, which required the approval of Burlington's board of aldermen. They were surprised when the board emphatically rejected their proposal. One alderman even declared, "There'll be free movies in Burlington over my dead body." Undeterred, Cohen and Greenfield circulated a petition among other local businesses and ultimately persuaded the board of aldermen that the movies were a good idea.[48]

While their ice cream was a definite success and the demand for their soups was encouraging, the crepes never sold well. Therefore, during the slow winter months, Cohen and Greenfield decided to package their ice cream and wholesale it to restaurants to stay solvent. Even though this trade was sporadic and largely dependent on the weather at the nearby ski resorts, they needed more manufacturing capacity. So, they leased additional space for an ice cream plant and bought another used freezer. When the restaurant sales failed to increase as quickly as they expected, they decided to package their ice cream in pint containers and sell it to grocery stores in the area. They were amazed when their supermarket trade quickly soared from 35 accounts to more than 200.[49]

Buoyed by the success of their pints, they found distributors to wholesale their ice cream in neighboring states and decided to franchise scoop shops. As sales continued to grow, the company struggled to meet the demand and find the financing for more manufacturing capacity. Ignoring the advice of experts, Cohen decided to fund the company's expansion by selling stock to small investors in Vermont only. Although stockbrokers warned him that he could not raise enough cash from small investors, the stock offering was successful.[50]

Ben and Jerry's Homemade Ice Cream was prospering beyond the founders' wildest expectations. Then, in 1984, two of the company's largest distributors told Cohen that Häagen-Dazs had issued an ultimatum: in order to keep the Häagen-Dazs account, they had to drop Ben and Jerry's. It was, as Yogi Berra reportedly said, "*deja vu* all over again." Only Mattus's former upstart, now owned by Pillsbury, was the major brand, while Ben and Jerry's pint was the new kid on the block.[51]

Ben and Jerry's fought back with a two-pronged attack—through conventional legal channels and an unorthodox public relations campaign, making the case a struggle of the little man against the corporate giant. Exploiting Pillsbury's well-known mascot, Ben and Jerry's printed the slogan "What's the Doughboy Afraid Of?" on bumper stickers, T-shirts, and ice cream cartons. The company also opened a Doughboy Hot Line and handed out protest letters to be mailed to Pillsbury. Meanwhile, Greenfield set up a one-man picket line in front of Pillsbury headquarters. As media coverage grew, Häagen-Dazs began to "look like the snobby spawn of an evil corporate giant." Throughout all this, the attorneys exchanged threats, filed complaints, negotiated, and finally reached a settlement. Pillsbury agreed to stop intimidating distributors, while Ben and Jerry's agreed to end its Doughboy campaign.[52]

In 1985, Richie Smith introduced Steve's superpremium, named for Steve Herrell and an obvious attempt to capitalize on the success of Ben and Jerry's with a look-alike product. This prompted the Vermont company to expand into several additional major markets, in order to be well established before Steve's arrived. It was also the motivation for the "two real guys" ad campaign because Cohen and Greenfield were pictured on their ice cream carton, while the photo on Steve's carton was not Herrell. The radio commercials featured the following jingle:

> There ain't no Häagen, there ain't no Dazs,
> There ain't no Frusen, there ain't no Gladj',
> There ain't nobody named Steve at Steve's,
> But there's two real guys at Ben and Jerry's.[53]

Whether it was the ad campaign or the aggressive marketing, Ben and Jerry's survived the assault from Steve's. In fact, the Vermonters continued to expand until their market share was 25 percent in 1989, compared to 62 percent for Häagen-Dazs, less than 10 percent for Frusen Gladje, and less than 3 percent for Steve's. Six years later, Ben and Jerry's claimed a 40 percent share of the market, almost equal to that of Häagen-Dazs. Nevertheless, Ben and Jerry's growth had begun to taper off due to the maturity of the superpremium market and consumer concern about the fat content of foods. In 1995, the company appointed a new CEO, Robert Holland, Jr., who promised that he would improve the bottom line by marketing Ben and Jerry's overseas.[54]

From the beginning, Cohen and Greenfield felt that their company had a responsibility to the local community and to society at large. In the early days at the garage, their limited resources restricted them to occasionally giving away free cones and sponsoring community events. Later, Cohen formed a nonprofit organization, One Percent for Peace, and the company manufactured Peace Pops, an ice cream bar with information about military spending printed on the wrapper. Subsequently, Cohen's group merged into the Business Partnership for Peace, and the Peace Pops wrapper described the Children's Defense Fund's Leave No Child Behind campaign.

In Ben and Jerry's Partnershops, groups with high unemployment rates, such as teenagers and the homeless, manage scoop shops and learn real-world skills, with the profits going to community projects, like homeless shelters and drug counseling centers. Ben and Jerry's Rainforest Crunch flavor, which is made with Brazil-nuts and cashews, supports efforts to stop world-wide deforestation. The company sometimes buys ingredients, such as fruits and add-ins, from alternative suppliers. Of the company's pre-tax profits, 7.5 percent are earmarked for social responsibility projects, and a great deal of free ice cream is given to community organizations and charities.[55]

High Tech

In the latter half of the 20th century, automated equipment accelerated the process of manufacturing ice cream, guaranteed a more uniform product, and improved sanitation in the plants. In 1960, H.P. Hood and Sons of Boston unveiled "the ice cream industry's first automated batching process" for blending raw ingredients into a finished mix. Electronic controls, taking their cues from IBM punch cards, opened the valves in pipes connecting raw ingredient storage tanks with blending tanks, portioned out the ingredients, and then closed the valves. The correct amount of each ingredient was determined by a single-purpose analog computer designed by the Brown Instruments Divison of Minneapolis-Honeywell Regulator Company. Thus, ice cream making entered the computer age.[56]

As new technology spawned newer technology in virtually every field, more automation and more computers were the inexorable trend in manufacturing. In 1982, Giant Food opened an ice cream plant with "the most modern equipment available in a completely automated, computer-controlled system." Texas Instruments programmable controllers slaved to a microcomputer directed all processing functions. The company claimed that the advanced automation ensured a consistent product, minimized operator error, produced less waste, required fewer employees, and accelerated cost recovery.[57]

In 1988, Carnation opened what was billed as "the world's largest ice cream plant" in Bakersfield, California. The $80 million facility was capable of producing 35 million gallons of ice cream and frozen novelties per year. The product mix included ice-cream and ice-milk bars, cups, cones, push-ups, and sandwiches as well as fruit-flavored water ices and several sizes of packaged ice cream, ranging from low-fat to premium grade. The plant was designed for straightforward product flow, continuous operation, production flexibility, excellent sanitation, and easy expansion. Computers controlled all operations from receiving to shipping, including batching, blending, freezing, packaging, hardening, storage, and retrieval.[58]

More Than a Dessert

The saga of ice cream in the United States has been one of growth and innovation. Consumption has spread from the elite to the masses. Production has expanded from small confectionaries to large industrial plants, from pot freezers to computerized production lines. The selection of flavors has grown from a handful to hundreds, with no end in sight. Early consumers sipped their ice cream from a cup or saucer. Today's ice cream aficionado chooses among cones, bars, sandwiches, cups, and cartons of low-fat to superpremium grades in scoop shops, supermarkets, restaurants, fast food outlets, and convenience stores.

In 1902 a newspaper reported, "America is the only country in the world where ice cream is a staple article of food."[59] Today, ice cream remains a staple of the American diet and is known around the world as an American food. It is a symbol of the United States because it is a national food—unlike Boston baked beans, Maryland crab cakes, or other regional dishes. It will continue to be an American symbol in the future as United States chains expand internationally, spreading the ice cream gospel around the globe.

Ice cream is a symbol of the American dream because so many entrepreneurs have built businesses, large and small, around it. The tiny, mom-and-pop stores have disappeared in many industries, but independent shops and small operators can still prosper in the ice cream industry. An individual can fulfill his or her dream of owning a business and being his or her own boss through an independent scoop shop or a franchise with one of the chains. Entrepreneurs built successful businesses around ice cream in the 19th century, and they continue to do so as the 21st century approaches.

However the industry develops in the future, ice cream seems destined to retain a special niche in American cuisine. It represents good times, birthday parties, picnics, days at the beach, noisy celebrations, and quiet summer evenings. It suggests special occasions, luxury, and self-indulgence. Not everyone can afford designer clothes, a Mediterranean cruise, or a Cadillac. But nearly everybody can afford a little pampering in the form of wickedly delicious butter pecan or almond fudge.

Ice cream is wholesome and sinful at the same time. It is smooth and creamy, soothing and comforting. More than nourishment, it is a sensual experience—the stuff ecstacy is made of. The best ice cream should be savored, eaten slowly with discriminating appreciation of both the flavor and the texture. The orgiastic delight of tasting a divine heavenly hash or fantastic rum raisin is one of the little pleasures that make life fun. In moderation, ice cream is good for the body and the soul. It is more than a dessert. It is an experience.

Notes

Abbreviations

ICTJ = *The Ice Cream Trade Journal*
ICR = *The Ice Cream Review*

1. An Elite Treat

1. "Philadelphia Version," *ICTJ*, September 1918: 35.

2. William Black, "Journal of William Black," *Pennsylvania Magazine of History and Biography* 1 (1877): 118–19.

3. *Ibid.*, 126.

4. Louise Conway Belden, *The Festive Tradition: Table Decoration and Desserts in America, 1650–1900* (New York: W.W. Norton, 1983), 145. *An Inventory of the Contents of the Governor's Palace Taken after the Death of Lord Botetourt*, October 24, 1770, Botetourt Papers, O.A. Hawkins Collection of Virginians, Virginia State Library.

5. William Fauquier, "An Account of an Extraordinary Storm of Hail in Virginia," *Philosophical Transactions, Giving Some Account of the Present Undertakings, Studies, and Labours of the Ingenious, in Many Considerable Parts of the World* 50, no. 2 (1759): 746.

6. Belden, *op. cit.,* 104. Joe Gray Taylor, *Eating, Drinking, and Visiting in the South: An Informal History* (Baton Rouge: Louisiana State University Press, 1962), 42.

7. Belden, *op. cit.* 104–07.

8. Sara Agnes Rice Pryor, *The Mother of Washington and Her Times* (New York: Macmillan, 1903), 200. William Maclay, *The Journal of William Maclay: United States Senator from Pennsylvania, 1789–1791* (New York: Albert and Charles Boni, 1927), 71–72.

9. Esther Singleton, *Social New York under the Georges, 1714–1776* (New York: Benjamin Blom, 1902), 366–67.

10. "First Ice Cream Advertising," *ICTJ*, July 1928, 39–41.

11. *Ibid.*

12. *Ibid.*, 40–42.

13. *Ibid.*

14. *Ibid.*, 41–42.

15. Belden, *op. cit.*, 146, 168. Jean Anthelme Brillat-Savarin, *The Physiology of Taste, or, Meditations on Transcendental Gastronomy* (New York: Heritage Press, 1949), 404.

16. *MacPherson's Directory for the City and Suburbs of Philadelphia* (Philadelphia: Francis Bailey, 1785). Sarah Lowrie and Mabel Stewart Ludlum, *The Sesqui-centennial High Street* (Philadelphia: J.B. Lippincott, 1926), 38.

17. Waverley Root and Richard de Rochemont, *Eating in America: A History* (New York: William Morrow, 1976), 426. Ralph Selitzer, *The Dairy Industry in America* (New York: Dairyfield and Books for Industry, 1976), 28. *The History of Ice Cream* (Washington, D.C.: International Association of Ice Cream Manufacturers, 1951), 11. *Inventory of the Contents of Mount Vernon, 1810* (Cambridge, Mass.: University Press, 1909), 42.

18. Root, *op. cit.*, 114–15. Mary A. Stephenson, *Foods, Entertainment, and Decorations for the Table: Fashionable in Virginia and the Southern Colonies in the 18th Century and Early 19th Century* (Williamsburg, Va.: Colonial Williamsburg Foundation, 1989), microfiche, 7. Rufus Wilmot Griswold, *The Republican Court, or American Society in the Days of Washington* (New York: D. Appleton, 1854), 157–58. Mrs. E.F. Ellet, *Court Circles of the Republic, or the Beauties and Celebrities of the Nation* (Philadelphia: Philadelphia Publishing, 1869), 19. Pryor, *op. cit.*, 199.

19. Stephenson, *op. cit.*, 7. Abigail Adams, *New Letters of Abigail Adams, 1788–1801* (Boston: Houghton Mifflin, 1947), 19, 55.

20. Ellet, *op. cit.*, 18–19. William Seale, *The President's House: A History,* vol. 1. (Washington, D.C.: White House Historical Association, 1986), 8. Benson J. Lossing, *The Home of Washington* (Hartford, Conn.: A.S. Hale, 1870), 224–25.

21. Maclay, *op. cit.*, 134–35.

22. Belden, *op. cit.*, 146–48, 150–52. Mary V. Thompson, "Background Information for Dairying Program" (Mount Vernon, Va.: Mount Vernon Ladies Association), 21–22. Several Anonymous Philadelphians, *Philadelphia Scrapple: Whimsical Bits Anent Eccentrics and the City's Oddities* (Richmond, Va.: Dietz Press, 1956), 224.

23. Singleton, *op. cit.*, 369. Michael and Ariane Batterberry, *On the Town in New York from 1776 to the Present* (New York: Charles Scribner's Sons, 1973), 27–28.

24. Batterberry, *op. cit.*, 28. Singleton, *op. cit.*, 369–70. Advertisement for Vauxhall Garden, *The Daily Advertiser*, July 18, 1798.

25. Batterberry, *op. cit.*, 27.

26. *Ibid.*, 28, 30. Abram C. Dayton, *Last Days of Knickerbocker Life in New York* (New York: G.P. Putnam's Sons, 1897), 184.

27. Batterberry, *op. cit.*, 30–31. Dayton, *op. cit.*, 183–85.

28. Dayton, *op. cit.,* 122. Charles H. Haswell, *Reminiscences of an Octogenarian, 1816–1860* (New York: Harper, 1896), 53.

29. Eliza S. Bowne, *A Girl's Life 80 Years Ago: Selections from the Letters of Eliza Southgate Bowne* (New York: Charles Scribner's Sons, 1887), 153–54, 167.

30. Dayton, *op cit.*, 304–05.

31. *Ibid.*, 305–06.

32. *Ibid.*, 306–07.

33. Batterberry, *op. cit.*, 31. Dayton, *op. cit.*, 159. Haswell, *op. cit.*, 59.

34. "The Funeral of John H. Contoit," *New York Times*, October 6, 1875, 8. Dayton, *op cit.*, 203. Belden, *op. cit.*, 168.

35. Batterberry, *op. cit.*, 31. Dayton, *op. cit.*, 159.

36. Dayton, *op. cit.,* 34.

37. Batterberry, *op. cit.*, 31.

38. Advertisement for Gray's Gardens, *Pennsylvania Packet and the General Advertiser*, July 1, 1790.

39. Advertisements for Joseph Delacroix, *Pennsylvania Packet and the General Advertiser*, July 15, 1784; July 19, 1791.

40. Edmund Hogan. *The Prospect of Philadelphia*. . . . (Philadelphia: Francis and Robert Bailey, 1795). *Stephen's Philadelphia Directory for 1796* (Phila-delphia: W. Woodward, 1796). Belden, *op cit.,* 167. M.L.E. Moreau de St. Mery, *American Journey, 1793–1798* (Garden City, N.Y.: Doubleday, 1947), 323.

41. Advertisement for Monsieur Collot, *Pennsylvania Packet,* May 13, 1795.

42. Moreau de St. Mery, *op. cit.,* 34, 42, 177–78, 274, 323.

43. *Ibid.*, 323.

44. Joseph Jackson, *Market Street, Philadelphia: The Most Historic Highway in America* (Philadelphia: Joseph Jackson, 1918), 141. Advertisement for Bossee, *Aurora Daily Advertiser*, July 19, 1800. Cecil K. Drinker, *Not So Long Ago: A Chronicle of Medicine and Doctors in Colonial Philadelphia* (New York: Oxford University Press, 1937), 17.

45. Belden, *op. cit.,* 83, 146.

46. Horace Mather Lippincott, *Philadelphia* (Philadelphia: Macrae Smith Co., 1926), 142–45. Mary Carolina Crawford, *Romantic Days in the Early Republic* (Boston: Little, Brown, 1912), 60–62.

47. Roger Lane, *William Dorsey's Philadelphia and Ours: On the Past and Future of the Black City in America* (Oxford: Oxford University Press, 1991), 115. *Desilver's Philadelphia Directory and Stranger's Guide* (Philadelphia: Robert Desilver, 1829), 104.

48. Mary Carolina Crawford, *Old Boston Days and Ways.* (Boston: Little, Brown 1909), 403.

49. *History of Ice Cream*, 11. Harry Emerson Wildes, *Anthony Wayne: Trouble Shooter of the American Revolution* (New York: Harcourt, Brace, 1941), 437.

50. Stephenson, *op. cit.*, 10. Eleazer Elizer, *A Directory for 1803* (Charleston, S.C.: W.P. Young, 1803). T. Michael Miller, *Artisans and Merchants of Alexandria, Virginia, 1784–1820* (Bowie, Md.: Heritage Books, 1991–92), vol. 1, 122; vol. 2, 152, 278. Advertisement for Jessop, *South Carolina Gazette*, August 23, 1799.

51. Barbara G. Carson, *Ambitious Appetites: Dining, Behavior, and Patterns of Consumption in Federal Washington* (Washington, D.C.: The American Institute of Architects Press, 1990), 83.

52. "The Beginnings of the Ice Cream Industry in Baltimore," *Baltimore*, June 1947, n.p.

53. *Ibid.*

54. *Ibid.*

55. Stephenson, *op. cit.*, 17.

56. Marie Kimball, *Thomas Jefferson's Cook Book* (Charlottesville, Va.: University Press of Virginia, 1976), 9–14, 19.

57. *Ibid.*, 2–3, 10, 35–36.

58. *Ibid.*, 10, 35–36. Barbara G. Carson, *op. cit.*, 196.

59. Jane Carson, *Colonial Virginia Cookery* (Charlottesville, Va.: University Press of Virginia, 1968), 181.

60. Barbara G. Carson, *op. cit.*, 158, 196.

61. Allen C. Clark, *Life and Letters of Dolly Madison* (Washington, D.C.: Press of W.F. Roberts, 1914), 50.

62. Barbara G. Carson, *op. cit.*, 153.

63. *Ibid.*, 158.

64. Josephine Seaton, *William Seaton of the "National Intelligencer": A Biographical Sketch* (Boston: James R. Osgood, 1871), 84–88.

65. *Ibid.*, 90–91.

66. *Ibid.*, 99.

67. *Ibid.*, 112–13.

68. Mary Boardman Crowninshield, *Letters of Mary Boardman Crowninshield, 1815–1816* (Cambridge, Mass.: Riverside Press, 1935), 25–26.

69. Selitzer, *op cit.*, 29.

70. Harriott Pinckney Horry, *A Colonial Plantation Cookbook: The Receipt Book of Harriott Pinckney Horry, 1770* (Columbia, S.C.: University of South Carolina Press, 1984), 12.

71. Henry Cogswell Knight, *Letters from the South and West* (Boston: Richardson and Lord, 1824), 71–73, 130–31.

72. E.A. Cooley, *A Description of the Etiquette at Washington City* (Philadelphia: L.B. Clark, 1829), 6.

73. *Ibid.,* 8–10. Ellet, *op cit.*, 133.

74. Una Pope-Hennessy, ed., *The Aristocratic Journey: Being the Outspoken Letters of Mrs. Basil Hall Written during a Fourteen Months' Sojourn in America, 1827–28* (New York: G.P. Putnam's Sons, 1931), 169.

75. *Ibid.,* 28.

76. *Ibid.,* 63–66.

77. *Ibid.,* 127, 130.

78. *Ibid., passim.*

79. Selitzer, *op cit.*, 30. Batterberry, *op cit.* 91.

80. Seale, *op. cit.,* 176.

81. *Ibid.,* 177.

82. Amy LaFollette Jensen, *The White House and Its Thirty-two Families* (New York: McGraw-Hill, 1958), 47.

83. *Ibid.,* 47. Seale, op cit., 177–79.

84. Ellet, *op. cit.,* 250–51, 260–61.

85. Crawford, *Romantic Days in the Early Republic,* 231.

86. Root, *op. cit.,* 426. Harriet Martineau, *Retrospect of Western Travel* (London: Saunders and Otley, 1838), 272.

87. Root, *op. cit.,* 121.

88. Taylor, *op. cit.,* 57–58.

89. Stephenson, *op. cit.,* 10–11.

90. Taylor, *op. cit.,* 56–57.

91. Anna Wells Rutledge, ed., *The Carolina Housewife by Sarah Rutledge, A Facsimile of the 1847 Edition* . . . (Columbia, S.C.: University of South Carolina Press, 1979), xxiv.

92. Richard Henry Dana, Jr., *Two Years before the Mast: A Personal Narrative of Life at Sea* (Los Angeles: Ward Ritchie Press, 1964), vol. 2, 292.

93. E.C. Wines, *A Trip to Boston, in a Series of Letters to the Editor of the United States Gazette* (Boston: Little, Brown, 1838), 51–53, 208–09.

94. Richard J. Hooker, *Food and Drink in America: A History* (Indianapolis, Ind: Bobbs-Merrill, 1981), 125. Frederick Marryat, *Diary in America* (Bloomington: Indiana University Press, 1960), 254. Paton Yoder, *Taverns and Travelers: Inns of the Early Midwest* (Bloomington: Indiana University Press, 1969), 145.

95. "Restaurant Patron Criticizes Ice Cream: From the St. Louis *Missouri Argus,* July 19, 1839," *Missouri Historical Review* 27 (July 1933): 379–80.

96. "Directions for Making Ice Cream: From the City of Jefferson *Metropolitan,* June 22, 1847," *Missouri Historical Review* 36 (October 1941): 121–22.

97. Bessie Louise Pierce, *A History of Chicago* (New York: Alfred A. Knopf, 1937), vol. 1, 200–01.

98. Ben Perley Poore, *Perley's Reminiscences of Sixty Years in the National Metropolis* (Philadelphia: Hubbard Brothers, 1886), vol. 1, 297–98.

99. Susan Williams, *Savory Suppers and Fashionable Feasts: Dining in Victorian America* (New York: Pantheon Books, 1985), 145.

100. Ellet, *op. cit.,* 345–46.

101. Ralph Waldo Emerson, *The Complete Works of Ralph Waldo Emerson* (Boston: Houghton Mifflin, 1883), vol. 1, 244.

102. Catherine Beecher, *A Treatise on Domestic Economy* (New York: Schocken Books, 1977), 81.

103. Carol Callahan, *Prairie Avenue Cookbook: Recipes and Recollections from Prominent 19th-Century Chicago Families* (Carbondale, Ill.: Southern Illinois University Press, 1993), 196. Adams, *op. cit.,* 98.

104. Meade Minnigerode, *The Fabulous Forties, 1840–1850* (Garden City, N.Y.: Garden City Publishing, 1924), 99.

105. Sarah Mytton Maury, *An Englishwoman in America* (London: Thomas Richardson and Son, 1848), 197–98.

106. Ellet, *op. cit.,* 394–95.

107. Catherine Elizabeth Havens, *Dairy of a Little Girl in Old New York, 1849–1850* (New York: Henry Collins Brown, 1920), 60–61.

108. *Ibid.,* 116–17.

109. Root, *op. cit.,* 129–30, 133.

110. Root, *op cit.,* 130–31. Jensen, *op cit.,* 71. Louis Auchincloss, ed., *The Hone and Strong Diaries of Old Manhattan* (New York: Abbeville Press, 1989), 25.

111. Root, *op cit.,* 132. Edwin Tunis, *The Young United States, 1783–1830* (New York: World Publishing, 1969), 109–10.

112. Root, *op. cit.,* 96, 145. Eugene L. Schwaab, ed., *Travels in the Old South Selected from Periodicals of the Time* (Lexington, Ky.: University Press of Kentucky, 1973), vol. 2, 413.

113. Root *op. cit.,* 133.

114. Barbara G. Carson, *op. cit.,* 108.

2. Homemade and Hand-cranked

1. Grover Dean Turnbow, Paul Hubert Tracy, and Lloyd Andrew Raffetto, *The Ice Cream Industry* (New York: John Wiley and Sons, 1947), 1–2.

2. Elizabeth David, *An Omelette and a Glass of Wine* (New York: Elisabeth Sifton Books, Viking, 1985), 240.

3. Raymond Sokolov, "Between Rock and a Soft Place," *Natural History* 102, no. 8 (1993), 70.

4. David, *op. cit.,* 240.

5. Eric Quayle, *Old Cook Books: An Illustrated History* (New York: E.P. Dutton, 1978), 190–91.

6. Richard Briggs, *The English Art of Cookery, According to the Present Practice; Being a Complete Guide to All Housekeepers on a Plan Entirely New* . . . (London: G.G.J. and J. Robinson, 1788). Richard Briggs, *The New Art of Cookery, According to the Present Practice, Being a Complete Guide to All Housekeepers, on a Plan Entirely New* . . . (Philadelphia: W. Spotwood, R. Campbell, and D. Johnson, 1792).

7. Quayle, *op. cit.*, 127–28. Frederic Nutt, *The Complete Confectioner, or, the Whole Art of Confectionery Made Easy* (New York: Richard Scott, 1807).

8. Quayle, *op. cit.*, 133. Amelia Simmons, *American Cookery; or, the Art of Dressing Viands, Fish, Poultry and Vegetables* . . . (Hartford, Conn.: Hudson and Goodwin, 1796), *passim.*

9. A Society of Gentlemen in New York, *The Universal Receipt Book, or, Complete Family Directory* . . . (New York: Riley, 1814), 154–55.

10. Mary Randolph, *The Virginia House-wife* (Columbia, S.C.: University of South Carolina Press, 1984), 174–79.

11. Patrick Dunne and Charles L. Mackie, "Philadelphia Story," *Historic Preservation* 46, no. 4 (1994), 72.

12. Dunne and Mackie, *op. cit.*, 74. Miss [Eliza] Leslie, *Directions for Cookery: Being a System of the Art in Its Various Branches* (Philadelphia: E.L. Cary and A. Hart, 1837), 322.

13. Miss [Eliza] Leslie, *New Receipts for Cooking* (Philadelphia: T.B. Peterson, 1854), 205–06.

14. Lettice Bryan, *The Kentucky Housewife* (Columbia, S.C.: University of South Carolina Press, 1991), 338–45.

15. William Woys Weaver, ed., *A Quaker Woman's Cookbook: The Domestic Cookery of Elizabeth Ellicott Lea* (Philadelphia: University of Pennsylvania Press, 1982), xiii, lxiii–lxiv, 108–09.

16. Rutledge, *op. cit.*, 153–56. Dunne and Makie, *op. cit.*, 72.

17. "Directions for Making Ice Cream: From the City of Jefferson *Metropolitan*, June 22, 1847," *Missouri Historical Review* 36 (October 1941), 121–22.

18. *Inquire Within for Anything You Want to Know* (New York: Garrett, Dick, and Fitzgerald, 1857), 82.

19. U.S. Patent #3254.

20. *Ibid.*

21. Autumn Stanley, *Mothers and Daughters of Invention: Notes for a Revised History of Technology* (Metuchen, N.J.: Scarecrow Press, 1993), 76. William A. Walsh, *A Handy Book of Curious Information* (Philadelphia: J.B. Lippincott, 1913), 403. *McElroy's Philadelphia Directory for 1842* (Philadelphia: Orrin Rogers, 1842). U.S. Patent #3254.

22. McElroy's, *op. cit.* National Archives, Patent and Patent Assignment Files for Nancy M. Johnson, Record Group 214, Liber R, 365.

23. Anna L. MacDonald, *Feminine Ingenuity: Women and Invention in America* (New York: Ballantine Books, 1992), 8–10. "Research Study Traces the History of the Ice Cream Freezer," *ICTJ*, August 1932, 21. National Archives, Patent and Patent Assignment Files for Nancy M. Johnson, Record Group 214, Liber R, 365.

24. *O'Brien's Philadelphia Wholesale Directory* (Philadelphia: J.G. O'Brien, 1843–1850), 1845, 74–75; 1850, 84–85, 88–89.

25. U.S. Patent #5601.

26. U.S. Patent #5960. H.B. Masser, *Directions, Recipes, and History of Masser's Patent Five-Minute Freezer* (Sunbury, Pa.: n.p., 1865), 3.

27. Masser, *op. cit.*, 4–10.

28. *Ibid.*, 16–18. "Modern Ice Cream and the Philosophy of Its Manufacture," *Godey's Lady's Book* 60 (1860): 460–61.

29. Masser, *op. cit.*, 23–24.

30. Elizabeth Prentiss, *The Life and Letters of Elizabeth Prentiss* (New York: Anson D.F. Randolph, 1882), 350.

31. *Catalogue of Hardware Specialties Manufactured by American Machine Company, with Recipes* (n.p., n.d.), 24–25. Kate Edna Negley, *The Negley Cook Book* (Pittsburgh, Pa.: Index Press, 1898), 181.

32. *Montgomery Ward and Company Catalogue No. 57* (n.p., 1895), 396. *Sears, Roebuck and Company Catalogue Spring-Summer* (n.p., 1934), 620. *Descriptive Catalogue and Price List of Sands' Patent Triple Motion White Mountain Freezers* (n.p., n.d.), 1–2.

33. Mrs. S.T. Rorer, *Dainty Dishes for All the Year Round* (Philadelphia: n.p., 1903), 1. *Sears, Roebuck and Company Catalogue No. 104* (n.p., 1897), 103; *No. 110* (n.p., 1900), 806.

34. *Catalogue of Yankee Tools and Ice Cream Freezers* (Philadelphia: n.p., 1912), 65.

35. *Blatchley's Horizontal Ice Cream Freezer, Tingley's Patent* (catalog) (n.p., n.d.), 1–4. John W. Miller, "Reminiscences of a Veteran," *ICTJ*, April 1929, 53.

36. Walter Buehr, *Home Sweet Home in the Nineteenth Century* (New York: Thomas Y. Crowell, 1965), 44–45. *Catalogue of Yankee Tools and Ice Cream Freezers* (Philadelphia, n.p., 1912), 66.

37. Advertisement for Easy Freezer, *Ladies Home Journal*, June 1899.

38. Paul Richard, *Paul Richards' Pastry Book* (Chicago: Hotel Monthly Press, 1907), 80. Harriet Beecher Stowe and Catherine E. Beecher, *The American Woman's Home* (New York: J.B. Ford, 1869), 189.

39. Mary Cornelius, *The Young House Keeper's Friend* (Boston: Taggard and Thompson, 1864), 96.

40. Marion Cabell Tyree, *Housekeeping in Old Virginia* (Louisville, Ky.: John P. Morton, 1879), 430.

41. *ICTJ*, September 1930.

42. Clementine Paddleford, *How America Eats* (New York: Charles Scribner's Sons, 1960), 291–92.

43. Joseph C. Jones, *America's Icemen: An Illustrative History of the United States Natural Ice Industry, 1665–1925* (Humble, Tex.: Jobeco Books, 1984), 14, 74–75.

44. A.F.M. Willich and Thomas Cooper, *The Domestic Encyclopedia: Or, a Dictionary of Facts and Useful Knowledge Chiefly Applicable to Rural and Domestic Economy* (Philadelphia: n.p., 1826), 371.

45. Jones, *op. cit.,* 75–78.

46. Ibid., 79. Richard O. Cummings, *The American Ice Harvests: A Historical Study in Technology, 1800–1918* (Berkeley and Los Angeles: University of California Press, 1949), 2.

47. Cummings, *op. cit.,* 2–3. Jones, *op. cit.,* 108.

48. J.P. Brissot de Warville, *New Travels in the United States of America* (Cambridge, Mass.: Belknap Press, 1964), 279–80. Charles H. Sherrill, *French Memoirs of Eighteenth-Century America* (New York: Charles Scribner's Sons, 1915), 80. J.C. Furnas, *The Americans: A Social History of the United States, 1587–1914* (New York: G.P. Putnam's Sons, 1969), 457.

49. Isaac Weld, *Travels through the States of North America and the Provinces of Upper and Lower Canada during the Years 1795, 1796, and 1797* (London: John Stockdale, 1807), vol. 1, 253.

50. Cummings, *op. cit.*, 6. Miller, *op. cit.*, vol. 1, 129.

51. A.J. Morrison, ed., *Travels in Virginia in Revolutionary Times* (Lynchburg, Va.: J.P. Bell, 1922), 128. Elizabeth Donaghy, *At Home: The American Family, 1750–1870* (New York: Harry N. Abrams, 1990), 204.

52. Jones, *op. cit.,* 108. Cummings, *op. cit.,* 2–3.

53. Jones, *op. cit.*, 109. Selitzer, *op. cit.,* 29.

54. Thomas Moore, *An Essay on the Most Eligible Construction of Icehouses, Also, a Description of the Newly Invented Machine Called the Refrigerator* (Baltimore: Bonsal and Niles, 1803).

55. Horry, *op. cit.*, 11–12.

56. Elizabeth K. Langhorne, K. Edward Lay, and William D. Rieley, *A Virginia Family and Its Plantation Houses* (Charlottesville, Va.: University of Virginia Press, 1987), 101.

57. Maury, *op. cit.*, 200–01. Marryat, *op. cit.,* 262.

58. Cummings, *op. cit.,* 9. Stewart H. Holbrook, "Yankee Ice King," *American Mercury* 61, no. 260 (August 1954), 179.

59. Holbrook, *op. cit.,* 180. Selitzer, *op. cit.,* 29.

60. Holbrook, *op. cit.,* 181.

61. *Ibid.* Cummings, *op. cit.*, 11.

62. Holbrook, *op. cit.*, 181–82.

63. *Ibid.,* 182, 184. H. Greenley, *The Great Industries of the United States* (Hartford, Conn.: J.B. Bun and Hyde, 1872), 156.

64. Holbrook, *op. cit.*, 182. Cummings, *op. cit.*, 8.

65. Jones, *op. cit.,* 94–114.

66. Greenley, *op. cit.*, 157. Jones, *op. cit.*, 115–20. Fred L. Holmes, *Side Roads*: *Excursions into Wisconsin's Past* (Madison, Wis.: The State Historical Society of Wisconsin, 1949), 81–84. A.T. Andreas, *History of Chicago from the Earliest Period to the Present Time* (Chicago: A.T. Andreas, 1886), vol. 3, 337.

67. Jones, op. cit., 122. Arthur Ribbel, "Good Times Cometh as City Warms Up to the Ice Age," *San Diego Union*, September 26, 1982.

68. "Ice History," *Transit Readers' Digest*, May 4, 1970.

69. Greenley, *op. cit.,* 156.

70. Jones, *op. cit.*, 20–24, 42–43, 57–58. Henry Hall, *The Ice Industry of the United States with a Brief Sketch of Its History and Estimates of Production in the Different States* (n.p., n.d.), 6–17.

71. Jones, op. cit., 15. Chauncey M. Depew, ed., *One Hundred Years of American Commerce* (New York: D.O. Haynes, 1895), vol. 2, 466–68.

72. Depew, *op. cit.,* vol. 2, 469.

73. Selitzer, *op. cit.,* 239.

74. "A Large Philadelphia Ice Making Plant," *Scientific American* 70 (February 10, 1894), 85. "Harvesting Ice," *Scientific American Supplement* 2069 (August 28, 1915), 132. Artemas Ward, *The Grocer's Encyclopedia* (New York: Artemas Ward, 1911), 310.

3. Wholesalers and Heavyweights

1. "Jacob Fussell: Industry Founder," *ICR,* June 1951, 43, 65.

2. *Ibid.* Joel H. Ross, *What I Saw in New York or a Bird's Eye View of City Life* (Auburn, N.Y.: Derby and Miller, 1857), 239–47. Irene M. Franck and David M. Brownstone, *Restaurateurs and Innkeepers* (New York: Facts on File, 1989), 71–73.

3. "What Five Years Taught the Industry," *ICTJ*, May 1925, 44. Ross, *op. cit.* 243–45.

4. Selitzer, *op. cit.,* 101. "What Five Years Taught," 44.

5. "What Five Years Taught," 44. "The First Ice Cream," *New York Times,* February 17, 1929, Section 9, 17.

6. "What Five Years Taught," 44. Armand Gladfelter, "Ice Cream: First Commercial Production Began in Seven Valleys," *York (Pa.) Sunday News,* October 9, 1994: C, 1–2.

7. "What Five Years Taught," 44. Gladfelter, *op. cit.*, 2.

8. Gladfelter, *op. cit.,* 1–2.

9. "What Five Years Taught," 44.

10. "Jacob Fussell," 43.

11. *Ibid.,* 66.

12. "What Five Years Taught," 44–45. Samuel Eliot Morison, *The Maritime History of Massachusetts, 1783–1860* (Boston: Houghton Mifflin, 1921), 280.

13. Selitzer, *op. cit.,* 102–03. *King's Handbook of New York* (Boston: Moses King, 1893), 984.

14. Selitzer, *op. cit.*, 103. King, *op. cit.,* 984. "Ice Cream for Ocean Voyagers," *New York Daily Tribune*, November 22, 1896: Section 3, 4.

15. "State Makes Claim on Fussell Fortune," *New York Times* (June 1, 1914), 4.

16. Turnbow, *op. cit.,* 6.

17. "What Five Years Taught," 45–46.

18. "Breyers Ice Cream: Marking a Milestone," *Dairy Dialogue* 7, no. 4 (June 1991): 5–9.

19. "Kansan Made Ice Cream in '66," *ICTJ* (July 1924), 62. Other pioneers and the approximate dates they entered the wholesale ice cream business were John R. Clauson, Salt Lake City, Utah, 1860; J.T. Rausley, Cincinnati, Ohio, 1862; The Coon Ice Cream Company, Burlington, Vermont, 1873; The Tinkelpaugh Ice Cream Company, Minneapolis, Minnesota, 1874; George Cuscaden, Louisville, Kentucky, 1875; Roszell Company, Peoria, Illinois, 1876; G.G. Carlson, Denver, Colorado, 1880; Jacob Huber, Bridgeport, and John Semon, New Haven, Connecticut, 1880; Collins Ice Cream Company, Huntington, Indiana, 1880; Bloc Brothers, Chicago, Illinois, 1885; Reid and Union Dairy Company, Brooklyn, New York, 1886; Carter Brothers, Napa, California, 1886; Sidwell Dairy Co., Iowa City, Iowa, 1887; Ives Ice Cream Company, Minneapolis, Minnesota, 1888; F.D. Hutchinson, Iowa, 1890; J.E. Mathews, Albuquerque, New Mexico, 1894; G.L. Boedecker, Dallas, Texas, 1897; Little Rock Dairy Company, Little Rock, Arkansas, 1900; George Pirie Company, Fargo, North Dakota, 1900; Ward-Owsley Company, Aberdeen, South Dakota, 1903; and Henry Chism, Nevada, 1908.

20. "Dairy Pioneers Recall the Early Industry," *ICTJ*, July 1934, 18.

21. Selitzer, *op. cit.,* 99.

22. Selitzer, *op. cit.,* 109.

23. "When This Industry Was Young in Iowa," *ICTJ*, March 1935, 24.

24. "A Steam Ice Cream Manufactory," *Scientific American*, July 21, 1894, 40.

25. "When We Were Very Young," *ICTJ*, May 1935, 27.

26. Hyatt A. Verrill, *Foods America Gave the World* (Boston: L.C. Page, 1937), 138–39. Kenneth T. Farrell, *Spices, Condiments, and Seasonings* (New York: Van Nostrand Reinhold, 1990), 206–07.

27. Verrill, *op. cit.,* 140–42.

28. *Ibid.,* 139–43. Farrell, *op. cit.,* 206–07.

29. Artemas Ward, *The Grocer's Hand-book and Directory* (Philadelphia: Philadelphia Grocer Publishing, 1886), 270.

30. Bernard W. Minifie, *Chocolate, Cocoa, and Confectionery: Science and Technology* (New York: Van Nostrand Reinhold, 1989), 4–5. Tom Stobart, *Herbs, Spices, and Flavorings* (Woodstock, N.Y.: Overlook Press, 1982), 79–81.

31. Moreau, *op. cit.*, 361. Advertisement for Michael Jeanes, *South Carolina Gazette*, November 23, 1747. Advertisement for Isaac Navarro, *Maryland Gazette*, January 4, 1749. *The Arts and Crafts in New York, 1726–1776: Advertisements and News Items from New York City Newspapers* (New York: New York Historical Society, 1938), 295. Advertisement for Chocolate Mill, *Pennsylvania Packet and General Advertiser*, May 18, 1772, 1.

32. Minifie, *op. cit.*, 4–5. Edward Winslow Martin, *The Secrets of the Great City: A Work Descriptive of the Virtues and the Vices, the Mysteries, Miseries, and Crimes of New York City* (Philadelphia: Jones Brothers, 1868), 506. *The Chocolate-Plant (Theobrama Cocao) and Its Products* (Dorchester, Mass.: Walter Baker, 1891), 28–29.

33. Selitzer, *op. cit.*, 109.

34. *Ibid.* "Obituary: Thomas W. Dunn," *ICTJ*, April 1919, 68.

35. Richard Match, "The World's Milkman," *Reader's Digest* 63 (September 1953): 82–86.

36. John W. Miller, *op. cit.*, 53.

37. *Ibid.*

38. "Young in Iowa," 24.

39. *Blatchley's*, 1–3. *Catalogue of Yankee Tools*, 60–73.

40. *Descriptive Catalogue*, 1–9. Selitzer, *op. cit.*, 104–09.

41. *Descriptive Catalogue*, 3.

42. Selitzer, *op. cit.*, 106.

43. "When We Were Very Young," 27.

44. Selitzer, *op. cit.*, 105.

45. "Early Pioneers Recall," 18.

46. Selitzer, *op. cit.*, 106. Richards, *op. cit.*, 79.

47. Selitzer, *op. cit.*, 108. "Young in Iowa," 24.

48. Selitzer, *op. cit.*, 106.

49. Ward, *Encyclopedia*, 38. "Recall Development of Butterfat Test at Babcock Anniversary Celebration," *ICR*, October 1943, 56.

50. "When We Were Very Young," 27. "Recall Development," 56.

51. John W. Miller, *op. cit.*, 53.

52. Richards, *op. cit.*, 79. John W. Miller, *op. cit.*, 54. *Pewter in American Life* (Providence, R.I.: Pewter Collectors Club of America, 1984), 134. "Phases of Ice Cream," *New York Daily Tribune*, July 13, 1902, Section 2, 6.

53. Richards, *op. cit.*, 97.

54. John W. Miller, *op. cit.*, 53–54.

55. *Ibid.*, 54.

56. *Ibid.* Selitzer, *op. cit.*, 106.

57. "Steam Ice Cream Manufactory," 40.

58. John W. Miller, *op. cit.*, 54. M.M. Mathews, *A Dictionary of Americanisms* (Chicago: University of Chicago Press, 1951), vol. 2, 1758. J.F. Mariani, *The Dictionary of American Food and Drink* (New Haven, Conn.: Ticknor and Fields, 1983), 420. Henry B. Allen, *The Useful Companion and Artificer's Assistant* (St. Louis: Scammell, 1878), 285.

59. Root, *op. cit.*, 322–33. Lewis A. Erenberg, *Steppin' Out: New York Nightlife and the Transformation of American Culture, 1890–1930* (Westport, Conn.: Greenwood Press, 1981).

60. Charles Ranhofer, *The Epicurean: A Complete Treatise of Analytical and Practical Studies of the Culinary Art* (New York: Dover Publications, 1971), 977–89.

61. *Ibid.*, 1007. Mary Henderson, *Practical Cooking and Dinner Giving* (New York: Harper, 1876), 306.

62. Ranhofer, *op. cit.*, 1016–17, 1007–11.

63. Ranhofer, *op. cit.*, 1017, 1019, 1021.

64. Root, *op. cit.*, 331–32. Ward McAllister, *Society As I Have Found It* (New York: Caswell Publishing, 1890), 187–88.

65. McAllister, *op. cit.*, 188. A.B. Marshall, *Ices Plain and Fancy* (New York: Metropolian Museum of Art), *x*.

66. Ranhofer, *op. cit.*, 1007.

67. *The American Heritage Cookbook* (New York: American Heritage Press, 1969), 161.

68. Mariani, *op. cit.*, 23.

69. Erenberg, *op. cit.*, 48–49.

70. Albert Stevens Crockett, *Peacocks on Parade: A Narrative of a Unique Period in American Society History and Its Most Colorful Figures* (New York: Sears Publishing, 1931), 66–68.

71. Hooker, *op. cit.*, 250.

72. Leon H. Grandjean, *Crayon Reproductions of Leon J. Fremaux's New Orleans Characters and Additional Sketches* (New Orleans: Alfred F. Bayhi, 1949), n.p. Schwaab, *op. cit.*, vol. 2, 419.

73. Selitzer, *op. cit.*, 30.

74. Rorer, *op. cit.*, 15.

75. A. Barrere and C.G. Leland, *A Dictionary of Slang, Jargon, and Cant* (Detroit: Gale Research, 1967), vol. 1, 468. *A New English Dictionary on Historical Principles* (Oxford: Clarendon Press, 1919), vol. 5, 330. Eric Partridge, *Origins: A Short Etymological Dictionary of Modern English* (London: Routledge and Kegan Paul, 1958), 323.

76. *New English Dictionary.* Herman Hueg, *The Practical Confectioner and Cake Baker* (New York: Gibbs Brothers and Moran, 1892), 52.

77. Eric Partridge, *A Dictionary of Slang and Unconventional English* (New York: Macmillan, 1984), 559.

78. Roger D. Abrahams, ed., *Jump-Rope Rhymes: A Dictionary* (Austin, Tex.: University of Texas Press, 1969), 65. *One Hundred Years in Philadelphia: "The Evening Bulletin's" Anniversary Book* (Philadelphia: Bulletin Company, 1947), 21. Partridge, *Slang and Unconventional English*, 559.

79. *American Heritage Cookbook and Illustrated History of American Eating and Drinking* (New York: American Heritage Publishing, 1964), 245. Bruce Henstell, *Los Angeles: An Illustrated History* (New York: Alfred A. Knopf, 1980), 44–45.

80. Martin, *op. cit.,* 502–11.

81. Junius Henri Browne, *The Great Metropolis: A Mirror of New York* (Hartford, Conn.: American Publishing, 1869), 93–99.

82. *Harper's Weekly,* August 3, 1895, 725. Grace Mayer, *Once Upon a City* (New York: Macmillan, 1958), 79.

83. Selitzer, *op. cit.,* 244. Barbara Heggie, "Ice Woman," *The New Yorker* 17 (September 6, 1941), 23–24.

84. John Mullaly, *The Milk Trade in New York and Vicinity* (New York: Fowler and Wells, 1853), 100. "Poisoned by Ice Cream," *New York Daily Tribune,* July 7, 1884, 8.

85. John W. Miller, *op. cit.,* 53. "Modern Ice Cream and the Philosophy of Its Manufacture," *Godey's Lady's Book* 60 (1860), 460.

86. Selitzer, *op. cit.,* 30. Edwin Wolf, *Philadelphia: Portrait of an American City* (Harrisburg, Pa.: Stackpole Books, 1975), 201. Gideon Burton, *Reminiscences of Gideon Burton* (Cincinnati: Press of George P. Houston, 1895), 115.

87. Mariani, *op. cit.,* 205.

88. Selitzer, *op. cit.,* 107.

89. Carl D. Lane, *American Paddle Steamboats* (New York: Coward-McCann, 1943), 15. Francis Pulszky and Theresa Pulszky, *White, Red, Black: Sketches of American Society in the United States during the Visit of Their Guests* (New York: Redfield, 1853), vol. 2, 4.

90. Root, *op. cit.,* 318–19.

91. Will Anderson, *Mid-Atlantic Roadside Delights: Roadside Architecture of Yesterday and Today in New York, New Jersey, and Pennsylvania* (Portland, Maine: Anderson and Sons Publishing, 1991), 43. Leslie Dorsey and Janice Devine, *Fare Thee Well: A Backward Look at Two Centuries of Historic American Hostelries, Fashionable Spas, and Seaside Resorts* (New York: Crown Publishers, 1964), 91.

92. Anne O'Hagan, "A Summer Evening in New York," *Munsey's Magazine* 21 (1899), 854.

93. Williams, *op. cit.,* 67, 89. Mary A. Taft, "Woman and Her Spoons," *Harper's Bazaar* 34 (November 1901), 778.

94. *Our Drummer* (catalog) (n.p., 1894), 82. *Montgomery Ward and Company Catalogue No. 57* (n.p., 1895), 533.

95. "Masser's Self-acting Patent Ice Cream Freezer and Beater," *Godey's Magazine and Lady's Book* 41 (July 1850), 124. Mrs. John A. Logan, *The Home Manual: Everybody's Guide in Social, Domestic, and Business Life* (Philadelphia: H.J. Smith, 1889), 7. Alessandro Filippini, *The Table: How to Buy Food, How to Cook It, and How to Serve It* (New York: Merriam, 1899), 23.

96. C. Vann Woodward, ed., *Mary Chestnut's Civil War* (New Haven, Conn.: Yale University Press, 1981), 600. Dorsey and Devine, *op. cit.,* 200.

97. Samuel Eliot Morison, *One Boy's Boston, 1887–1901* (Boston: Houghton Mifflin, 1962), 49–57.

98. Esther Singleton, *The Story of the White House* (New York: McClure, 1907), vol. 2, 42. Ethel Lewis, *The White House: An Informal History of Its Architecture, Interiors, and Gardens* (New York: Dodd, Mead, 1937), 208. Edna M. Colman, *White House Gossip from Andrew Jackson to Calvin Coolidge* (Garden City, N.Y.: Doubleday, 1927), 77, 80–81.

99. Seale, *op. cit.,* 482.

100. Poore, *op. cit.,* 516–22.

101. Ellen Maury Slayden, *Washington Wife: Journal of Ellen Maury Slayden from 1897 to 1919* (New York: Harper, 1962), 12, 153.

102. Catherine Bigham Brode, *Life in Chatsworth, 1865–1885* (Santa Monica, Calif.: Howard S. Brode, 1946), 72.

103. *American Heritage Cookbook and Illustrated History,* 196–97.

104. Harriet Ross Colquitt, ed., *The Savannah Cookbook: A Collection of Old-fashioned Recipes from Colonial Kitchens* (New York: Farrar and Rinehart, 1933), 174.

105. Everett Dick, *The Sod-house Frontier* (Lincoln: University of Nebraska Press, 1979), 199.

106. *Jordan (Mont.)Tribune,* January 12, 1933, 1.

107. John L. Sullivan, *I Can Lick Any Sonofabitch in the House* (New York: Proteus Publishing, 1980), 225–26.

108. *Ibid.,* 225–236. James J. Corbett, *The Roar of the Crowd: The True Tale of the Rise and Fall of a Champion* (New York: Garden City Publishing, 1926), 203.

109. Corbett, *op. cit.,* 179, 268–69.

110. "Ice Cream Plays a Part in the Fight Story," *ICTJ,* November 1926, 76.

4. Sodas, Sundaes, and Other Innovations

1. Thomas Chester, *Carbonated Beverages: The Art of Making, Dispensing, and Bottling Soda Water, Mineral Waters, Ginger Ale, and Sparkling Liquors* (New York: n.p., 1882), 3.

2. *Ibid.,* 3–4. Depew, *op. cit.,* vol. 2, 470.

3. Chester, *op. cit.,* 4.

4. *Ibid.,* 4. Depew, *op. cit.,* 470. Morrison, *op. cit.,* 10. Root, *op. cit.,* 419. M.D. Leggett, *Subject-matter Index of Patents for Inventions Issued by the United States Patent Office from 1790 to 1873, Inclusive* (Washington, D.C.: Government Printing Office, 1874), 1377–78.

5. Carl J. Palmer, *History of the Soda Fountain Industry* (Washington, D.C.: Soda Fountain Manufacturers Association, 1947), 5.

6. Chester, *op. cit.,* 5–7.

7. Morrison, A.J., *op. cit.,* 10–11. Furnas, *op. cit.,* 459. Eleanor Alexander, "A Uniquely American Watering Hole: The Drug Store Soda Fountain at the Turn of the Twentieth Century," (master's thesis, University of Delaware, 1986), 5, 7.

8. Alexander, *op. cit.,* 3–4.

9. Chester, *op. cit.,* 4.

10. Morrison, Joseph L., *op. cit.,* 11.

11. Depew, *op. cit.,* vol. 2, 470. Morrison, Joseph L., *op. cit.,* 11.

12. Morrison, Joseph L., *op. cit.,* 11.

13. *Ibid.* Frederick Stansbury, "The Evolution of the Soda Water Industry in New York City," *Pharmaceutical Era* 7 (May 15, 1892), 332.

14. Joseph F. Barker, "History of Boston's Soda Fountain Trade," *Pharmaceutical Era* 7 (May 1, 1892), 289.

15. Alexander, *op. cit.,* 15–18.

16. Baker, *op. cit.,* 289.

17. Alexander, *op. cit.,* 19–22. Stansbury, *op. cit.,* 330–33.

18. Palmer, *op. cit.,* 6.

19. *One Hundred Years in Philadelphia,* 109. Root, *op. cit.,* 420.

20. Stansbury, *op. cit.,* 330.

21. Depew, *op. cit.,* Vol. 2, 470–71.

22. "Soda Water in Chicago," *Pharmaceutical Era* 7 (June 15, 1892), 409–10.

23. Dick, *op. cit.,* 63, 384.

24. Depew, *op. cit.,* vol. 2, 471.

25. Barker, *op. cit.,* 290–19.

26. Depew, *op. cit.,* vol. 2, 471. "The Soda Fountain Business of St. Louis," *Pharmaceutical Era* 7 (June 1, 1892), 369.

27. Depew, *op. cit.,* vol. 2, 471. Barker, *op. cit.,* 90–291.

28. Barker, *op. cit.,* 290.

29. "Soda Water in Chicago," 410. Charlotte Gale and David M. Gale, "The Drugstore Soda Fountain: A Study and Catalog of Nineteenth-Century Soda Tokens," *The Numismatist*, January 1983, 13–18.

30. Depew, *op. cit.,* vol. 2, 471.

31. *Ibid.,* 471–72. Barker, *op. cit.,* 294.

32. Barker, *op. cit.,* 292. Depew, *op. cit.,* 471.

33. Barker, *op. cit.,* 292.

34. "Soda Water in Chicago," 410–11.

35. Barker, *op. cit.,* 291.

36. *Ibid.,* 291–92.

37. Root, *op. cit.,* 419. Depew, *op. cit.,* vol. 2, 472.

38. Depew, *op. cit.,* 472. Morrison, Joseph L., *op. cit.,* 12.

39. Depew, *op. cit.,* Vol. 2, 471. "Soda Fountain Business of St. Louis," 369.

40. Alexander, *op. cit.,* 30. Morrison, Joseph L., *op. cit.,* 11–12. *Catalogue of Puffer's Frigid Soda and Mineral Water Apparatus* (n.p., 1878), *passim. James W. Tufts, Patentee and Manufacturer of Arctic Soda Water Apparatus* (n.p, 1887), *passim.*

41. "Soda Water in Chicago," 411.

42. *James W. Tufts,* 3. *Catalogue of Puffer's,* 102. "Soda Water in Chicago," 414.

43. Mariani, *op. cit.,* 372. J.S. Ingram, *The Centennial Exposition, Described and Illustrated . . .* (Philadelphia: Hubbard Brothers, 1876), 287–91.

44. Depew, *op. cit.,* vol. 2, 472. "Soda Fountain Business of St. Louis," 370.

45. John Leng, *America in 1876: Pencillings during a Tour in the Centennial Year, with a Chapter on the Aspects of American Life* (Dundee, England: Dundee Advertiser Office, 1877), 22.

46. "Soda Fountain Business of St. Louis," 370.

47. Barker, *op. cit.,* 292–93. Stansbury, *op. cit.,* 334.

48. Depew, *op. cit.,* vol. 2, 473–74. Root, *op. cit.,* 420.

49. "Soda Fountain Business of St. Louis," 372.

50. Depew, *op. cit.,* vol. 2, 474. Barker, *op. cit.,* 293.

51. Stansbury, *op. cit.,* 329–30, 333.

52. *Ibid.,* 334–35.

53. "Soda Water in Chicago," 414.

54. *Ibid.* Barker, *op. cit.,* 294.

55. Stansbury, *op. cit.,* 329, 335–36.

56. Alexander, *op. cit.,* 84. Batterberry, *op. cit.,* 152–55.

57. Alexander, *op. cit.,* 84–85. "Don'ts for the Soda Fountain," *Pharmaceutical Era* 7 (May 1, 1892), 294.

58. Batterberry, *op. cit.,* 153–54.

59. *Ibid.,* 153. Alexander, *op. cit.,* 85–86. "Soda Water in Chicago," 412.

60. Alexander, *op. cit.,* 87. Stansbury, *op. cit.,* 335.

61. Mathews, *op. cit.,* 1021. "Soda Water in Chicago," 413.

62. "Soda Water in Chicago," 412.

63. Barker, *op. cit.,* 289.

64. *Ibid.,* 289–90.

65. Palmer, *op. cit.,* 20.

66. *Ibid.,* 20–21.

67. J.T. Swager, "Story of Ice Cream as Told to West Virginians," *ICTJ,* December 1923, 70.

68. "Stop Me If You've Heard This One Before," *ICTJ,* July 1927, 68.

69. *New English Dictionary,* 365. "Ice Cream Sodas Praised in Newspaper Editorial," *ICTJ,* January 1934, 28.

70. Alexander, *op. cit.,* 75. "Ice Cream Sodas Praised," 28.

71. "Too Many Sodas Wins Divorce" *ICTJ,* December 1933, 18. "Ice Cream Term," *ICTJ,* December 1921, 54.

72. *A Standard Dictionary of the English Language* (New York: Funk and Wagnalls, 1893). E.F. White, "How to Run a Small Fountain Right," *Supply World* 13 (June 1900), 18.

73. *American Soda Book of Receipts and Suggestions* (Boston: American Soda Fountain Company, n.d.), 15, 19, 52.

74. Palmer, *op. cit.*

75. Holmes, *op. cit.,* 77–79. H.L. Mencken, *The American Language: An Inquiry into the Development of English in the United States* (New York: Alfred A. Knopf, 1963), Supplement 1, 376–77. Thomas Pyles, *Words and Ways of American English* (New York: Random House, 1952), 170–73.

76. Mencken, *op. cit.,* 109–91.

77. "Is Ice Cream Food or Medicine?" *ICTJ,* September 1916, 50.

78. Mencken, *op. cit.,* Supplement 1, 377. Gilbert M. Tucker, *American English* (New York: Alfred A. Knopf, 1921), 306.

79. "Stop Me If You've Heard This One Before," 68.

80. William Lyon Phelps, *Autobiography with Letters* (New York: Oxford University Press, 1939), 919–20. Clyde D. Foster, *Evanston's Yesterdays* (Evanston, Ill.: n.p., 1956), 26, 90–91.

81. Foster, *op. cit.,* 89–90.

82. Mencken, *op. cit.,* Supplement 1, 377.

83. "Story of Ice Cream as Told to West Virginians," 70.

84. Selitzer, *op. cit.,* 245. "Phases of Ice Cream," 6.

85. Josephine Grenier, "Afternoon Tea," *Harper's Bazaar* 37 (February 1903), 176. *American Soda Book,* 188.

86. Funk and Wagnalls (1890, 1893), 1124. Holmes, *op. cit.,* 80.

87. E.F. White, "A Chat about Soda Water," *The Supply World* 13 (April 1900), 18–19. *American Soda Book*, 132.

88. "Soda Water in Chicago," 412.

89. Wayne Smith, *Ice Cream Dippers: An Illustrated History and Collector's Guide to Early Ice Cream Dippers* (Walkersville, Md.: Wayne Smith, 1986), 28.

90. *Ibid.,* 66.

91. *Ibid.,* 26, 31.

92. *Ibid.,* 33–34, 94.

93. *Ibid.,* 37–40.

94. *Ibid.,* 39–42. Malcolm Stogo, *Frozen Desserts: A Complete Retailer's Guide* (New York: Van Nostrand Reinhold, 1991), 99.

95. Smith, *op. cit.,* 171.

96. "Missouri Concentrates on Ice Cream Cones," *ICTJ,* June 1934, 21.

97. Smith, *op. cit.,* 115.

98. Thomas P. Jones, *Ice Cream World of Baskin-Robbins* (New York: Pinnacle Books, 1975), 54–57.

5. Flappers, Doughboys, Blind-Pigs, and Eskimo Pies

1. John A. Jakle, *The American Small Town: 20th-Century Place Images* (Hamden, Conn.: Archon Books, 1982), 135. "Mike Sits In," *ICTJ,* October 1918, 55.

2. Selitzer, *op. cit.,* 247.

3. "The Ice Cream Sales Index for 1931 Shows Decrease of 11.82 Percent," *ICTJ,* April 1932, 40–44. "Estimate 244 Million Gallons Output for 1921," *ICTJ,* June 1922, 37–38. "Estimate 263,520,000 Gallons Output in 1922," *ICTJ,* June 1923, 47–48. "Production Estimate Close to 300 Million Gallons," *ICTJ,* June 1924, 47–48. "Ice Cream Consumption in U.S. Shows Continued Rise," *Food Industries,* September 1930, 424. "Gallonage Estimate for 1931 Is 300,818,000; Per Capita 2.42," *ICTJ,* December 1932, 40. "The Ice Cream Sales Index for 1932 Shows Decrease of 24.35 Percent," *ICTJ,* May 1933, 29–34. "Ice Cream in the 1933 Census," *ICTJ,* December 1934, 35. "Dairy Products Manufactured 1933: As Reported to Bureau of Agricultural Economics," *ICTJ,* October 1934, 32. "1934 Sales Index Shows Increase of 16.35 Percent over 1933," *ICTJ,* May 1935, 19–20.

4. "How Glorified Ice Cream Stands Advertise and Sell the Product," *ICTJ,* May 1928, 47–48. "Uplifting the Roadside Stand," *ICTJ,* January 1929, 55–56.

5. "How Glorified Ice Cream Stands Advertise and Sell the Product," 47. "Chain Stores as Profitable Outlets for California Manufacturers," *ICTJ,* November 1929, 43.

6. "Chain Stores as Profitable Outlets for California Manufacturers," 44–45.

7. *Howard Johnson's Presents Old Time Ice Cream Soda Fountain Recipes or How to Make a Soda Fountain Pay* (New York: Winter House, 1971), 16–19.

8. Philip Langdon, *Orange Roofs, Golden Arches: The Architecture of American Chain Restaurants* (New York: Alfred A. Knopf, 1986), 46–50. "Twenty-eight Flavors Head West," *Life* 25 (September 6, 1948), 71.

9. Langdon, *op. cit.*, 47. *Howard Johnson's*, 18–19. Phil Patton, *Open Road: A Celebration of the American Highway* (New York: Simon and Schuster, 1986), 196.

10. Rudi Volti, "How We Got Frozen Food," *Invention and Technology* 9, no. 4 (Spring 1994), 50, 53. "Mechanical Refrigerators," *Consumers' Digest* 1, no. 1 (January 1937), 9–10. Selitzer, *op. cit.*, 286.

11. "New York Firm Develops Home Trade with Grocery Stores as Outlets," *ICTJ*, July 1930, 33–35.

12. "Detroit Grocery Stores Sell Ice Cream," *ICTJ*, June 1930, 38.

13. "Grocery Stores Develop as Outlets for the Ice Cream Industry," *ICTJ*, August 1932, 15–16.

14. George L. Boedeker, "Problems Facing the Industry," *ICTJ*, November 1932, 23.

15. L.J. Schumaker, "How the Rising Generation Learns to Eat Ice Cream," *ICTJ*, January 1920, 59.

16. *Ibid.*

17. "How They Met the Cone in St. Louis," *ICTJ*, May 1928, 78. Joseph Gustaitis, "Who Invented the Ice Cream Cone?" *American History Illustrated* 23, no. 4 (Summer 1988), 42.

18. "How They Met the Cone," 78.

19. *Ibid.*

20. *Ibid.* Elaine Viets, "Melting Claims on First Ice Cream Cone," *St. Louis (Mo.) Post-Dispatch*, June 4, 1978, 30.

21. "How They Met the Cone," 78.

22. "Melting Claims," 30.

23. "Originator of Ice Cream Cone Dies," *St. Louis (Mo.) Globe-Democrat*, April 28, 1943.

24. "Melting Claims," 30. "How They Met the Cone," 78. Charles Panati, *Panati's Extraordinary Origins of Everyday Things* (New York: Harper, 1987), 421.

25. "Melting Claims," 31. Gustaitis, *op. cit.*, 43.

26. "Melting Claims," 31. Richard F. Snow, "King Cone," *Invention and Technology* 9, no. 2 (Fall 1993), 5. Gustaitis, *op. cit.*, 43.

27. Snow, *op. cit.*, 5.

28. *Ibid.*

29. "Ice Cream Cone Originator Dies," *St. Louis (Mo.) Post-Dispatch,* November 23, 1950. "Nick Kabbaz, Ice Cream Cone Manufacturer, Is Buried," *St. Louis Post-Dispatch,* November 24, 1950.

30. "David Avayou, Made Ice Cream Cone in '04," *New York Times,* February 12, 1965, 30.

31. "St. Louis Is the Birthplace of the Ice Cream Cone," *St. Louis Globe-Democrat,* March 27, 1927.

32. "Double-dip of Cone History," Janet Beighle French, *Cleveland Plain Dealer,* July 17, 1993.

33. Stanley, *op. cit.,* 103–104.

34. "Melting Claims," 30.

35. "Italo Marchiony, 86, Made Ice Cream Cone," *New York Times* (July 29, 1954), 23. Gail Damerow, *Ice Cream: The Whole Scoop* (Macomb, Ill.: Glenbridge Publishing, 1991), 231.

36. Damerow, *op cit.,* 231. U.S. Patent #746971.

37. "Italo Marchiony," 23.

38. Selitzer, *op. cit.,* 242. "Early Development of Ice Cream Cone Revealed in Newspaper Interview," ICR (April 1944), 44.

39. "Melting Claims," 31. Selitzer, *op. cit.,* 242. Ranhofer, *op. cit.,* 913, 929.

40. "How They Met the Cone," 78. "Industry's Veteran Hails Cone's Anniversary," *ICTJ,* November 1929, 46.

41. *The King of All Confections: 1908 Automatic Parisian Ice Cream Cone Ovens* (n.p., 1908), 1–4.

42. "St. Louis Is the Birthplace of the Ice Cream Cone," *St. Louis Globe-Democrat,* March 27, 1927.

43. Schumaker, 59.

44. *The Cone with the Curl on Top: Celebrating Fifty Years, 1940–1990* (Minneapolis: International Dairy Queen, 1990), 32.

45. "Industry's Veteran Hails Cone's Anniversary," 46.

46. "Ice Cream Cone Cited as Bottlers' Competitor," *ICTJ,* March 1933, 26.

47. "Ice Cream Eaters," *ICTJ,* April 1919, 48. "Fighting on Ice Cream," *ICTJ,* November 1918, 54.

48. "Ice Cream Blind-Pig," *ICTJ,* June 1918, 52.

49. "Fliers Made Ice Cream," *ICTJ,* May 1919, 40.

50. "Returning Soldiers Enjoy Ice Cream," *ICTJ,* November 1919, 57.

51. "They Missed It," *ICTJ,* May 1919, 52. Francis Parkinson Keyes, *Letters from a Senator's Wife* (New York: D. Appleton, 1924), 232.

52. "The Sugar Situation for Ice Cream Makers," *ICTJ,* July 1918, 27–28. "Sugar Released for Ice Cream," *ICTJ,* May 1918, 45.

53. "Eat Ice Cream," *ICTJ*, June 1918, 32. "New Cone," *ICTJ*, August 1918, 53.

54. "The Labor Problem," *ICTJ*, January 1919, 49. "Women Ice Cream Makers," *ICTJ*, March 1918, 49.

55. "Ice Cream Politics," *ICTJ*, September 1918, 52–53.

56. "Votes for Ice Cream Bars," *ICTJ*, September 1922, 74.

57. "Hoover and Smith Like to Eat Ice Cream," *ICTJ*, October 1928, 70.

58. Henrietta Nesbitt, *White House Diary* (Garden City, N.Y.: Doubleday, 1948), 48, 70, 107–08, 156, 200, 239–40.

59. "We See Where," *ICTJ*, December 1935, 42.

60. Selitzer, *op. cit.*, 263. Carolyn Wyman, *I'm a Spam Fan* (Stamford, Conn.: Longmeadow Press, 1993), 35. "Christian Kent Nelson: The Inventor of Eskimo Pie," Good Humor-Breyers Ice Cream Co. (Photocopy), 1.

61. Selitzer, *op. cit.*, 263. Wyman, *op. cit.*, 35.

62. "Christian Kent Nelson," 1. Wyman, *op. cit.*, 35–36.

63. Selitzer, *op. cit.*, 263. "Christian Kent Nelson," 1. "Eskimo Pie and Export Trade," *ICTJ*, March 1922, 46.

64. "Christian Kent Nelson," 2–4. Selitzer, *op. cit.*, 263–64.

65. "Another Court Decision on Eskimo Pie Patent," *ICTJ*, April 1928, 74. "Eskimo Pie Corporation Loses Patent Appeal Suit," *ICTJ*, November 1929, 95. "Christian Kent Nelson," 4.

66. "Ice Cream in Slot Machines," *ICTJ*, May 1927, 64–65.

67. Selitzer, *op. cit.*, 264–65.

68. U.S. Patent #1,470,524 and #1,470,525. Selitzer, *op. cit.*, 265.

69. Selitzer, *op. cit.*, 265. Eleanor Harris, "The Pied Pipers of Ice Cream," *Saturday Evening Post* 222 (August 20, 1949), 37, 93.

70. Harris, *op. cit.*, 93.

71. *Ibid.*

72. L.B.N. Gnaedinger, "Radio Has Made a New Millionaire," *New York Times*, March 18, 1928, Section 10, 3.

73. "SEC Expels Meehan on Rigging Charge," *New York Times*, August 3, 1937, Section L, 27. "Meehan Rose with Radio," *New York Times*, August 3, 1937, Section L, 31.

74. "M.J. Meehan Died; Once Stockbroker," *New York Times*, January 3, 1948, Section K, 13. Harris, *op. cit.*, 93–94. Don Wharton, "That Good Humor Man," *Readers' Digest* 60 (June 1952), 68.

75. Selitzer, *op. cit.*, 266. Harris, *op. cit.*, 94, 96.

76. Harris, *op. cit.*, 36–37. Wharton, *op. cit.*, 67–68.

77. Selitzer, *op. cit.*, 266. Harris, *op. cit.*, 37.

78. "Cold Secrets," *The New Yorker* 37 (June 24, 1961), 18–19.

79. "Frozen Assets," *Newsweek* 57 (May 8, 1961), 74. Ted Shelsby, "Good Humor Trucks Dwindle," *Baltimore Sun*, September 21, 1979.

80. "How Southern California Put a Stop to All that Novelty Nonsense," *ICTJ*, December 1934, 17–18. J.E. McGiffert, "The Case for Five-Cent Cups," *ICTJ*, March 1934, 33–34.

81. Selitzer, *op. cit.*, 268–69.

82. *Ibid.* Steve Leone, "Dixie War Lids," *The Ice Screamer* 66 (May 1995), 4–5.

83. Lewis Grizzard, *Won't You Come Home, Billy Bob Bailey?* (Atlanta: Peachtree Publishers, 1980), 56–58.

84. McGiffert, *op. cit.*, 33–34.

85. Wayne Smith, *op. cit.*, 34.

86. Selitzer, *op. cit.*, 269.

87. "Ole Evinrude Dies; Inventor of Motor," *New York Times*, July 13, 1934, 17.

88. Joseph H. Hart, "The Application of Mechanical Refrigeration to Ice Cream Manufacture," *Journal of the Franklin Institute* 162 (November 1906), 397–403.

89. "Ice Cream's Centennial Year," *ICR*, June 1951, 122. Selitzer, *op. cit.*, 235.

90. "This Was the Industry Thirty-five Years Ago," *ICTJ*, April 1943, 31. D.F. Solliday, "We Had No Experts to Advise Us When We Opened a Plant in 1902," *ICTJ*, August 1935, 23. "Obituary: Harvey H. Miller," *ICTJ*, August 1935, 39.

91. Selitzer, *op. cit.*, 236.

92. Turnbow, *op. cit.*, 212. *Ice Cream Makers' Apparatus and Supplies, Catalog No. 302* (N.p., 1911), 4–9.

93. U.S. Patent #1,113,807. Turnbow, *op. cit.*, 212.

94. "Clarence Vogt, Engineer, Dies in Florida," *Louisville Times*, July 2, 1973.

95. U.S. Patent #1,733,740. Turnbow, *op. cit.*, 212.

96. *A Century of Innovation for Industry* (N.p.: Cherry-Burrell Corporation, 1979), 23–25.

97. Selitzer, *op. cit.*, 248.

98. "Fifty Years of Achievement in Ice Cream," *Baltimore*, June 1955.

6. From Soft Serve to Superpremium

1. "Ice Cream Regarded as Essential by Army," *ICR*, April 1943, 64. "Ice Cream for Fighting Marines," *ICR*, February 1944, 26. Selitzer, *op. cit.*, 339.

2. Paul Dickson, *The Great American Ice Cream Book* (New York: Atheneum, 1972), 48. "Value of Ice Cream Recognized by Armed Forces," *ICR*, January 1944, 38.

3. Dickson, *op. cit.*, 48. "The Freeze that Pleases," *Time* 97 (June 21, 1971), 76.

4. "Ice Cream for Fighting Marines," 26. "Marines Make Their Own Ice Cream on Guadalcanal," *ICR,* October 1943, 72. "Ice Cream in the War News," *ICR,* July 1943, 42.

5. "U.S.S. Lexington: Carrier Upholds Our Fighting Tradition," *Yank: The Army Newspaper* 1, no. 2 (June 24, 1942), 4–5.

6. "Ice Cream: Favorite Food of Our Fighting Men," *ICR,* June 1943, 18. "Vanilla, Please," *Newsweek* 25, no. 10 (March 5, 1945), 72.

7. "Ice Cream in the War News," *ICR,* May 1943, 57.

8. "Vanilla, Please," 72. Selitzer, *op. cit.,* 338.

9. Robert Goralski, *World War II Almanac* (New York: G.P. Putnam's Sons, 1981), 382. Selitzer, *op. cit.,* 337.

10. Palmer, *op. cit.,* 128. "So You'll Eat Better," *American Mercury* 61, no. 260 (August 1945), 128.

11. Selitzer, *op. cit.,* 339. "Ice Cream Outcry," *Business Week,* June 13, 1942, 56–57. "Ice Cream Doubts," *Business Week,* June 19, 1943, 37–38.

12. "Ice Cream Outcry," 56–57. "Sundae without Ice Cream!" *ICR,* July 1943, 44. Jennie S. Wilmot and Margaret Q. Batzer, *Food for the Family* (Philadelphia: J.B. Lippincott, 1944), 473.

13. "Ice Cream at the Melting Point," *Business Week*, August 4, 1951, 46, 48. A. Lansing, "Cold Licks and Hot Profits: Soft Ice Cream," *Collier's* 138 (August 3, 1956), 31.

14. *The Cone with the Curl on Top: Celebrating Fifty Years, 1940–1990* (Minneapolis: International Dairy Queen, 1990), 25, 30, 36.

15. *Ibid.,* 11–12.

16. *Ibid.,* 13, 19.

17. *Ibid.,* 14, 22.

18. *Ibid.,* 23–25.

19. *Ibid.,* 26–27.

20. *Ibid.,* 28–29.

21. *Ibid.,* 33, 77.

22. *Ibid.,* 35, 51, 94, 97.

23. *Ibid.,* 47–50. Lansing, *op. cit.,* 34.

24. *Cone with the Curl,* 47–50.

25. *Ibid.,* 183–139.

26. *Ibid.,* 39. Langdon, *op. cit.,* 68.

27. *Cone with the Curl,* 39. Lansing, *op. cit.,* 34. Langdon, *op. cit.,* 68–69.

28. "Ice-cream Parlay," *Fortune* 48 (July 1953), 166.

29. Langdon, *op. cit.,* 69. Lansing, *op. cit.,* 32, 34.

30. Lansing, *op. cit.,* 32, 34.

31. *Ibid.* Langdon, *op. cit.,* 68.

32. Langdon, *op. cit.,* 68.

33. Lansing, *op. cit.* 32, 34.

34. Linda Francke and Sunde Smith, "Chip Chip Hooray!" *Newsweek* 87 (February 16, 1976), 71. "Freeze that Pleases," 76. "Thirty-one Flavors," *The New Yorker* 47 (July 10, 1971), 19–20. Selitzer, *op. cit.*, 349. Thomas P. Jones, *op. cit.*, 167–73. "Six Hundred Fifty Flavors Offer a Taste for Every Taste!" 1, 4.

35. "Thirty-one Flavors," 20.

36. Francke, *op. cit.*, 71. Thomas P. Jones, *op. cit.*, 71, 123–24. "Six Hundred Fifty Flavors Offer a Taste for Every Taste!" 2.

37. Jane Stern and Michael Stern, *Encyclopedia of Pop Culture* (New York: Harper Perennial, 1992), 203. Bobbie Stein, "Reuben Mattus Scooped the Competition with His Pricey and Nonsense-named Häagen-Dazs," *People Weekly* 16 (August 17, 1981), 15, 85.

38. Stein, *op. cit.*, 85.

39. Stern, *op. cit.*, 203. Fred Lager, *Ben and Jerry's: The Inside Scoop* (New York: Crown Publishers, 1994), 78.

40 Stein, *op. cit.*, 85. " John Skow, "They All Scream for It," *Time* 118, no. 6 (August 10, 1981): 55. Lager, *op. cit.*, 78–79.

41. Lager, *op. cit.*, 79, 135.

42. Stern, *op. cit.*, 204. Lager, *op. cit.*, 80.

43. Skow, *op. cit.*, 56.

44. Lager, *op. cit.*, 7, 12.

45. *Ibid.*, 13–14.

46. *Ibid.*, 17–23.

47. *Ibid.*, 134–35.

48. *Ibid.*, 25–26, 35.

49. *Ibid.*, 37–38.

50. *Ibid.*, 52, 95–96.

51. *Ibid.*, 106–08.

52. Stern, *op. cit.*, 205. Lager, *op. cit.*, 110–19.

53. Lager, *op. cit.*, 135, 153, 191–92.

54. *Ibid.*, 214–215. "A New CEO for Cherry Garcia's Creators," *Wall Street Journal*, February 2, 1995, B1, B11.

55. Lager, *op. cit.*, 125, 183–86, 224, 231–32.

56. "Mixing Ice Cream by Push Button," *Business Week*, July 23, 1960, 64, 67.

57. Bill Drennan, "Highly Automated Plant," *Food Engineering* 54, no. 7 (July 1982), 86–87.

58. Charles E. Morris, "World's Largest Ice-cream Plant," *Food Engineering* 61, no. 3 (March 1989), 85–92, 94, 96, 98, 100.

59. "Phases of Ice Cream," *New York Daily Tribune*, July 13, 1902, 2, 6.

Bibliography

Newspaper and Journal Series

Food Industries, 1929–1937.
Ice Cream Review, 1943–1951.
Ice Cream Trade Journal, 1916–1935.
Pennsylvania Journal/Weekly Advertiser, 1747–1796.
Pennsylvania Packet and General Advertiser, 1772–1795.
South Carolina and American General Gazette, 1772–1776.
South Carolina Gazette, 1799.
South Carolina Gazette and Country Journal, 1772.

Books

Abrahams, Roger D., ed. *Jump-Rope Rhymes: A Dictionary.* Austin, Tex.: University of Texas Press, 1969.
Adams, Abigail. *New Letters of Abigail Adams, 1788–1801.* Edited by Stewart Mitchell. Boston: Houghton Mifflin, 1947.
Adamson, Helen Lyon. *Grandmother in the Kitchen.* New York: Crown Publishers, 1965.
Alexander, Eleanor. "A Uniquely American Watering Hole: The Drug Store Soda Fountain at the Turn of the Twentieth Century." Master's thesis, University of Delaware, 1986.
Allen, Henry B. *The Useful Companion and Artificer's Assistant.* St. Louis: Scammell, 1878.
Alsop, Richard. *The Universal Receipt Book, or Complete Family Directory.* New York: Van Winkle and Wiley, 1814.
The American Heritage Cookbook. New York: American Heritage Press, 1969.
The American Heritage Cookbook and Illustrated History of American Eating and Drinking. New York: American Heritage Publishing, 1964.
American Soda Book of Receipts and Suggestions. Boston: American Soda Fountain Co., n.d.
Anderson, Will. *Mid-Atlantic Roadside Delights: Roadside Architecture of Yesterday and Today in New York, New Jersey, and Pennsylvania.* Portland, Maine: Anderson and Sons, 1991.
Andreas, A.T. *History of Chicago from the Earliest Period to the Present Time.* Vol. 3. Chicago: A.T. Andreas, 1886.
Armour, Richard. *Drug Store Days: My Youth among the Pills and Potions.* New York: McGraw-Hill, 1959.

The Arts and Crafts in New York, 1726–1776: Advertisements and News Items from New York City Newspapers. New York: New York Historical Society, 1938.

Auchincloss, Louis, ed. *The Hone and Strong Diaries of Old Manhattan.* New York: Abbeville Press, 1989.

Bailey, Nathaniel. *Dictionarium Domesticum, Being a New and Compleat Household Dictionary.* London: C. Hitch, 1736.

Barrere, A., and C.G. Leland. *A Dictionary of Slang, Jargon, and Cant Embracing English, American, and Anglo-Indian Slang, Pidgin English, Tinker's Jargon, and Other Irregular Phraseology.* 1889. Vol. 1. Reprint. Detroit: Gale Research, 1967.

Batterberry, Michael, and Ariane Batterberry. *On the Town in New York from 1776 to the Present.* New York: Charles Scribner's Sons, 1973.

Beecher, Catherine. *A Treatise on Domestic Economy.* New York: Marsh, Capen, Lyon, and Webb, 1841. Reprint. New York: Schocken Books, 1977.

Belden, Louise Conway. *The Festive Tradition: Table Decoration and Desserts in America, 1650–1900.* New York: W.W. Norton, 1983.

Bowne, Eliza S. *A Girl's Life 80 Years Ago: Selections from the Letters of Eliza Southgate Bowne.* New York: Charles Scribner's Sons, 1887.

Briggs, Richard. *The English Art of Cookery, According to the Present Practice; Being a Complete Guide to All Housekeepers, on a Plan Entirely New . . . of thirty-eight chapters.* London: G.G.J. and J. Robinson, 1788.

——. *The New Art of Cookery, According to the Present Practice, Being a Complete Guide to All Housekeepers, on a Plan Entirely New . . . of thirty-eight chapters.* Philadelphia: W. Spotswood, R. Campbell, and D. Johnson, 1792.

Brillat-Savarin, Jean Anthelme. *The Physiology of Taste, or, Meditations on Transcendental Gastronomy.* Translated by M.F.K. Fisher. New York: Heritage Press, 1949.

Brissot de Warville, J.P. *New Travels in the United States of America.* 1788. Reprint. Cambridge, Mass.: Belknap Press, 1964.

Brode, Catherine Bigham. *Life in Chatsworth, 1865–1885.* Santa Monica, Calif: Howard S. Brode, 1946.

Brown, Henry Collins. *Delmonico's: A Story of Old New York.* New York: Valentine's Manual, 1928.

Browne, Junius Henri. *The Great Metropolis: A Mirror of New York.* Hartford, Conn.: American Publishing, 1869.

Bryan, Lettice. *The Kentucky Housewife.* 1839. Reprint. Columbia, S.C.: University of South Carolina Press, 1991.

Buehr, Walter. *Home Sweet Home in the Nineteenth Century.* New York: Thomas Y. Crowell, 1965.

Burton, Gideon. *Reminiscences of Gideon Burton.* Cincinnati: Press of George P. Houston, 1895.

Calkins, Raymond. *Substitutes for the Saloon.* Boston, Mass.: Houghton Mifflin, 1901.

Callahan, Carol. *Prairie Avenue Cookbook: Recipes and Recollections from Prominent 19th-Century Chicago Families.* Carbondale, Ill.: Southern Illinois University Press, 1993.

Carson, Barbara G. *Ambitious Appetites: Dining, Behavior, and Patterns of Consumption in Federal Washington.* Washington, D.C.: American Institute of Architects Press, 1990.

Carson, Jane. *Colonial Virginia Cookery.* Charlottesville, Va.: University Press of Virginia, 1968.

A Century of Innovation for Industry. N.p.: Cherry-Burrell Corporation, 1979.

Chester, Thomas. *Carbonated Beverages: The Art of Making, Dispensing, and Bottling Soda Water, Mineral Waters, Ginger Ale, and Sparkling Liquors.* New York: n.p., 1882.

Child, L. Maria. *Letters from New York.* 2nd series. New York: C.S. Francis, 1845.

The Chocolate-plant (Theobrama Cacao) and Its Products. Dorchester, Mass.: Walter Baker, 1891.

Clark, Allen C. *Life and Letters of Dolly Madison.* Washington, D.C.: Press of W.F. Roberts, 1914.

Colman, Edna M. *White House Gossip from Andrew Jackson to Calvin Coolidge.* Garden City, N.Y.: Doubleday, Page, 1927.

Colquitt, Harriet Ross, ed. *The Savannah Cook Book: A Collection of Old-fashioned Recipes from Colonial Kitchens.* New York: Farrar and Rinehart, 1933.

The Combined Big Directory of New York City, Boston, Philadelphia, and Baltimore. New York: Austin Publishing, 1889.

The Cone with the Curl on Top: Celebrating Fifty Years, 1940–1990. Minneapolis: International Dairy Queen, 1990.

Cooley, E. *A Description of the Etiquette at Washington City.* Philadelphia: L.B. Clark, 1829.

Corbett, James J. *The Roar of the Crowd: The True Tale of the Rise and Fall of a Champion.* New York: Garden City Publishing, 1926.

Cornelius, Mary. *The Young House Keeper's Friend.* Boston: Taggard and Thompson, 1864.

A Corps of Experts. *Mackenzie's Ten Thousand Recipes in All the Useful and Domestic Arts.* Philadelphia: T. Ellwood Zell, 1867.

Crawford, Mary Caroline. *Old Boston Days and Ways.* Boston: Little, Brown, 1909.

——. *Romantic Days in the Early Republic.* Boston: Little, Brown, 1912.

Crockett, Albert Stevens. *Peacocks on Parade: A Narrative of a Unique Period in American Social History and Its Most Colorful Figures.* New York: Sears Publishing, 1931.

Crowninshield, Mary Boardman. *Letters of Mary Boardman Crowninshield, 1815–16.* Edited by Francis Boardman Crowninshield. Cambridge, Mass.: Riverside Press, 1935.

Cummings, Richard O. *The American Ice Harvests: A Historical Study in Technology, 1800–1918.* Berkeley and Los Angeles: University of California Press, 1949.

Dallas, Sandra. *No More than Five in a Bed: Colorado Hotels in the Old Days.* Norman, Okla.: University of Oklahoma Press, 1967.

Damerow, Gail. *Ice Cream: The Whole Scoop.* Macomb, Ill.: Glenbridge Publishing, 1991.

Dana, Richard Henry, Jr. *Two Years Before the Mast: A Personal Narrative of Life at Sea.* Vol. 2. Edited by John Haskell Kimble. Los Angeles: Ward Ritchie Press, 1964.

David, Elizabeth. *An Omelette and a Glass of Wine.* New York: Elisabeth Sifton Books-Viking, 1985.

Dayton, Abram C. *Last Days of Knickerbocker Life in New York.* New York: G.P. Putnam's Sons, 1897.

Depew, Chauncey M., ed. *One Hundred Years of American Commerce.* 2 vols. New York: D.O. Haynes, 1895.

Desilver's Philadelphia Directory and Stranger's Guide. Philadelphia: Robert Desilver, 1829, 1831.

Dick, Everett. *The Sod-house Frontier.* Lincoln, Nebr.: University of Nebraska Press, 1979.

Dickson, Paul. *The Great American Ice Cream Book.* New York: Atheneum, 1972.

Dorsey, Leslie, and Janice Devine. *Fare Thee Well: A Backward Look at Two Centuries of Historic American Hostelries, Fashionable Spas, and Seaside Resorts.* New York: Crown Publishers, 1964.

Drinker, Cecil K. *Not So Long Ago: A Chronicle of Medicine and Doctors in Colonial Philadelphia.* New York: Oxford University Press, 1937.

Earle, Alice Morse. *Home Life in Colonial Days.* New York: Macmillan, 1919.

Elizer, Eleazer. *A Directory for 1803.* Charleston, S.C.: W.P. Young, 1803.

Ellet, Mrs. E.F. *Court Circles of the Republic, or the Beauties and Celebrities of the Nation.* Philadelphia: Philadelphia Publishing, 1869.

Emerson, Ralph Waldo. *The Complete Works of Ralph Waldo Emerson.* Vol. 1. Boston: Houghton Mifflin, 1883.

Erenberg, Lewis A. *Steppin' Out: New York Nightlife and the Transformation of American Culture, 1890–1930.* Westport, Conn.: Greenwood Press, 1981.

Ervin, Janet Halliday. *The White House Cookbook.* Chicago: Follett Publishing, 1964.

Farrell, Kenneth T. *Spices, Condiments, and Seasonings.* New York: Van Nostrand Reinhold, 1990.

Fennelly, Catherine. *Life in an Old New England Country Village.* New York: Thomas Y. Crowell, 1969.

Filippini, Alessandro. *The Table: How to Buy Food, How to Cook It, and How to Serve It.* New York: Merriam, 1899.

Foster, Clyde D. *Evanston's Yesterdays.* Evanston, Ill.: n.p., 1956.

Franck, Irene M., and David M. Brownstone. *Restaurateurs and Innkeepers.* New York: Facts on File, 1989.

Furnas, J.C. *The Americans: A Social History of the United States, 1587–1914.* New York: G.P. Putnam's Sons, 1969.

Garrett, Elizabeth Donaghy. *At Home: The American Family, 1750–1870.* New York: Harry N. Abrams, 1990.

Goralski, Robert. *World War II Almanac.* New York: G.P. Putnam's Sons, 1981.

Grandjean, Leon H. *Crayon Reproductions of Leon J. Fremaux's New Orleans Characters and Additional Sketches.* New Orleans: Alfred F. Bayhi, 1949.

Greenley, H. *The Great Industries of the United States.* Hartford, Conn.: J.B. Bun and Hyde, 1872.

Greenstein, Lou. *A la Carte: A Tour of Dining History.* Glen Cove, N.Y.: PBC International, 1992.

Griswold, Rufus Wilmot. *The Republican Court, or American Society in the Days of Washington.* New York: D. Appleton, 1854.

Grizzard, Lewis. *Won't You Come Home, Billy Bob Bailey?* Atlanta: Peachtree Publishers, 1980.

Hall, Henry. *The Ice Industry of the United States with a Brief Sketch of Its History and Estimates of Production in the Different States.* Washington, D.C.: Government Printing Office, 1888.

Haswell, Charles H. *Reminiscences of an Octogenarian, 1816–1860.* New York: Harper and Brothers, 1896.

Havens, Catherine Elizabeth. *Diary of a Little Girl in Old New York, 1849–1850.* New York: Henry Collins Brown, 1920.

Henderson, Mary. *Practical Cooking and Dinner Giving.* New York: Harper and Brothers, 1876.

Henstell, Bruce. *Los Angeles: An Illustrated History.* New York: Alfred A. Knopf, 1980.

Hess, Karen, ed. *Martha Washington's Book of Cookery.* New York: Columbia University Press, 1981.

Hilliard, Sam Bowers. *Hog Meat and Hoecake: Food Supply in the Old South, 1840–1860.* Carbondale, Ill.: Southern Illinois University Press, 1972.

The History of Ice Cream (booklet). Washington, D.C.: International Association of Ice Cream Manufacturers, 1951.

Hogan, Edmund. *The Prospect of Philadelphia and Check on the Next Directory, Part I.* Philadelphia: Francis and Robert Bailey, 1795.

Holmes, Fred L. *Side Roads: Excursions into Wisconsin's Past.* Madison, Wis.: State Historical Society of Wisconsin, 1949.

Hooker, Richard J. *Food and Drink in America: A History.* Indianapolis, Ind.: Bobbs-Merrill, 1981.

Horry, Harriott Pinckney. *A Colonial Plantation Cookbook: The Receipt Book of Harriott Pinckney Horry, 1770.* Edited by Richard J. Hooker. Columbia, S.C.: University of South Carolina Press, 1984.

Howard Johnson's Presents Old Time Ice Cream Soda Fountain Recipes or How to Make a Soda Fountain Pay. New York: Winter House, 1971.

Hubbard, N.T. *Autobiography of N.T. Hubbard with Personal Reminiscences of New York City from 1789 to 1875.* New York: John F. Trow and Son, 1875.

Hueg, Herman. *The Practical Confectioner and Cake Baker.* New York: Gibbs Brothers and Moran, 1892.

Husband, Joseph. *The Story of the Pullman Car.* Chicago: A.C. McClurg, 1917.

Ingram, J.S. *The Centennial Exposition, Described and Illustrated, Being a Concise and Graphic Description . . . of the First Centennary of American Independence.* Philadelphia: Hubbard Brothers, 1876.

Inquire Within for Anything You Want to Know, Or, Over 3,700 Facts Worth Knowing . . . New York: Garrett, Dick, and Fitzgerald, 1857.

Inventory of the Contents of Mount Vernon, 1810. Cambridge, Mass.: University Press, 1909.

Jackson, Joseph. *Market Street, Philadelphia: The Most Historic Highway in America.* Philadelphia: Joseph Jackson, 1918.

Jakle, John A. *The American Small Town: 20th-Century Place Images.* Hamden, Conn.: Archon Books, 1982.

Jensen, Amy LaFollette. *The White House and Its Thirty-two Families.* New York: McGraw-Hill, 1958.

Jones, Joseph C. *America's Icemen: An Illustrative History of the United States Natural Ice Industry, 1665–1925.* Humble, Tex.: Jobeco Books, 1984.

Jones, Thomas P. *Ice Cream World of Baskin-Robbins.* New York: Pinnacle Books, 1975.

Kelley, Etna M. *Business Founding Date Directory.* Scarsdale, N.Y.: Morgan & Morgan, 1954.

Keyes, Frances Parkinson. *Letters from a Senator's Wife.* New York: D. Appleton, 1924.

Kimball, Marie. *Thomas Jefferson's Cook Book.* Charlottesville, Va.: University Press of Virginia, 1976.

King's Handbook of New York. Boston: Moses King, 1893.

Klinkowstrom, Axel Leonhard. *Baron Klinkowstrom's America, 1818–1820.* Translated by Franklin D. Scott. Evanston, Ill.: Northwestern University Press, 1952.

Knight, Henry Cogswell [Arthur Singleton, pseud.]. *Letters from the South and West.* Boston: Richardson and Lord, 1824.

Lager, Fred. *Ben and Jerry's: The Inside Scoop.* New York: Crown Publishers, 1994.

Lane, Carl D. *American Paddle Steamboats.* New York: Coward-McCann, 1943.

Lane, Roger. *William Dorsey's Philadelphia and Ours: On the Past and Future of the Black City in America.* Oxford: Oxford University Press, 1991.

Langdon, Philip. *Orange Roofs, Golden Arches: The Architecture of American Chain Restaurants.* New York: Alfred A. Knopf, 1986.

Langhorne, Elizabeth, K. Edward Lay, and William D. Rieley. *A Virginia Family and Its Plantation Houses.* Charlottesville, Va.: University of Virginia Press, 1987.

Leggett, M.D. *Subject-matter Index of Patents for Inventions Issued by the United States Patent Office from 1790 to 1783, Inclusive.* Washington, D.C.: Government Printing Office, 1874.

Leng, John. *America in 1876: Pencillings during a Tour in the Centennial Year, with a Chapter on the Aspects of American Life.* Dundee, England: Dundee Advertiser Office, 1877.

Leslie, Miss [Eliza]. *Directions for Cookery; Being a System of the Art in Its Various Branches.* Philadelphia: E.L. Cary and A. Hart, 1837.

——. *New Receipts for Cooking.* Philadelphia: T.B. Peterson, 1854.

Lewis, Ethel. *The White House: An Informal History of Its Architecture, Interiors, and Gardens.* New York: Dodd, Mead, 1937.

Lippincott, Horace Mather. *Philadelphia.* Philadelphia: Macrae Smith, 1926.

Logan, Mrs. John A. *The Home Manual: Everybody's Guide in Social, Domestic, and Business Life.* Philadelphia: H.J. Smith, 1889.

Longworth's American Almanac, New York Register, and City Directory for the 26th Year of American Independence. New York: Longworth, 1801.

Lossing, Benson J. *The Home of Washington.* Hartford, Conn.: A.S. Hale, 1870.

Lowrie, Sarah, and Mabel Stewart Ludlum. *The Sesqui-centennial High Street.* Philadelphia: J.B. Lippincott, 1926.

Lynes, Russell. *The Domesticated Americans.* New York: Harper and Row, 1957.

MacDonald, Anne L. *Feminine Ingenuity: Women and Invention in America.* New York: Ballantine Books, 1992.

Maclay, William. *The Journal of William Maclay: United States Senator from Pennsylvania, 1789–1791.* New York: Albert and Charles Boni, 1927.

MacPherson's Directory for the City and Suburbs of Philadelphia. Philadelphia: Francis Bailey, 1785.

Mariani, J.F. *The Dictionary of American Food and Drink.* New Haven, Conn.: Ticknor and Fields, 1983.

Marryat, Frederick. *Diary in America.* 1839. Reprint. Bloomington, Ind.: Indiana University Press, 1960.

Marshall, A.B. *Ices Plain and Fancy.* Reprint. Introduction by Barbara Ketcham Wheaton. New York: Metropolitan Museum of Art, 1976.

Martin, Edward Winslow. *The Secrets of the Great City: A Work Descriptive of the Virtues and the Vices, the Mysteries, Miseries, and Crimes of New York City.* Philadelphia: Jones Brothers, 1868.

Martineau, Harriet. *Retrospect of Western Travel.* London: Saunders and Otley, 1838.

Masser, H.B. *Directions, Recipes, and History of Masser's Patent Five-minute Freezer.* Sunbury, Pa.: n.p., 1865.

Matchett's Baltimore Directory for 1851. Baltimore: Richard J. Matchett, 1851.

Mathews, M.M. *A Dictionary of Americanisms.* Vol. 2. Chicago: University of Chicago Press, 1951.

Maury, Sarah Mytton. *An Englishwoman in America.* London: Thomas Richardson and Son, 1848.

Mayer, Grace. *Once Upon a City.* New York: Macmillan, 1958.

McAllister, Ward. *Society as I Have Found It.* New York: Cassell Publishing, 1890.

McCabe, James D. *A Collector's Reprint: The Illustrated History of the Centennial Exposition.* Philadelphia: National Publishing, 1975.

McElroy's Philadelphia Directory for 1842. Philadelphia: Orrin Rogers, 1842.

McKenzie, William A. *Dining Car to the Pacific.* St. Paul, Minn.: Minnesota Historical Society Press, 1990.

Mencken, H.L. *The American Language: An Inquiry into the Development of English in the United States . . . with Annotations and New Material.* New York: Alfred A. Knopf, 1963.

Michael, P. *Ices and Soda Drinks.* London: MacLaren and Sons, n.d.

Miller, T. Michael. *Artisans and Merchants of Alexandria, Virginia, 1784–1820.* 2 vols. Bowie, Md.: Heritage Books, 1991–92.

Miller, Val. *Thirty-six Years an Ice Cream Maker: Receipts and Pointers.* Davenport, Iowa: n.p., 1907.

Minifie, Bernard W. *Chocolate, Cocoa, and Confectionery: Science and Technology.* 3rd edition. New York: Van Nostrand Reinhold, 1989.

Minnigerode, Meade. *The Fabulous Forties, 1840–1850.* Garden City, N.Y.: Garden City Publishing, 1924.

Moore, Thomas. *An Essay on the Most Eligible Construction of Ice-houses, Also, a Description of the Newly Invented Machine Called the Refrigerator.* Baltimore: Bonsal and Niles, 1803.

Moreau de St. Mery, M.L.E. *American Journey, 1793–1798.* Translated by Kenneth and Anne M. Roberts. Garden City, N.Y.: Doubleday, 1947.

Morgan, George. *History of Philadelphia: The City of Firsts.* Philadelphia: Historical Publication Society, 1926.

Morison, Samuel Eliot. *The Maritime History of Massachusetts, 1783–1860.* Boston: Houghton Mifflin, 1921.

——. *One Boy's Boston, 1887–1901.* Boston: Houghton Mifflin, 1962.

Morrison, A.J., ed. *Travels in Virginia in Revolutionary Times.* Lynchburg, Va.: J.P. Bell, 1922.

Mullaly, John. *The Milk Trade in New York and Vicinity.* New York: Fowler and Wells, 1853.

Negley, Kate Edna. *The Negley Cook Book.* Pittsburgh, Pa.: Index Press, 1898.

Nesbitt, Henrietta. *White House Diary.* Garden City, N.Y.: Doubleday, 1948.

A New English Dictionary on Historical Principles. Oxford: Clarendon Press, 1919.

The New Trade Directory for Philadelphia Anno 1800. Philadelphia: Way and Groff, 1799.

Nutt, Frederic. *The Complete Confectioner, or, the Whole Art of Confectionery Made Easy.* 4th edition. New York: Richard Scott, 1807.

O'Brien's Philadelphia Wholesale Directory. Philadelphia: J.G. O'Brien, 1843–1850.

The Official Gazette of the United States Patent Office. Washington, D.C.: Government Printing Office, 1843–1930.

One Hundred Years in Philadelphia: "The Evening Bulletin's" Anniversary Book. Philadelphia: Bulletin Company, 1947.

Paddleford, Clementine. *How America Eats*. New York: Charles Scribner's Sons, 1960.

Palmer, Carl J. *History of the Soda Fountain Industry*. Washington, D.C.: Soda Fountain Manufacturers Association, 1947.

Partridge, Eric. *A Dictionary of Slang and Unconventional English*. 8th edition. New York: Macmillan, 1984.

———. *Origins: A Short Etymological Dictionary of Modern English*. London: Routledge and Kegan Paul, 1958.

Patton, Phil. *Open Road: A Celebration of the American Highway*. New York: Simon and Schuster, 1986.

Pewter in American Life. Providence, R.I.: Pewter Collectors Club of America, 1984.

Phelps, William Lyon. *Autobiography with Letters*. New York: Oxford University Press, 1939.

Pierce, Bessie Louise. *A History of Chicago*. 3 vols. New York: Alfred A. Knopf, 1937.

Poore, Ben Perley. *Perley's Reminiscences of Sixty Years in the National Metropolis*. 2 vols. Philadelphia: Hubbard Brothers, 1886.

Pope-Hennessy, Una, ed. *The Aristocratic Journey: Being the Outspoken Letters of Mrs. Basil Hall Written during a Fourteen Months' Sojourn in America, 1827–28*. New York: G.P. Putnam's Sons, 1931.

Prentiss, Elizabeth. *The Life and Letters of Elizabeth Prentiss*. New York: Anson D.F. Randolph, 1882.

Prowell, George R. *History of York County Pennsylvania*. Vol. 1. Chicago: J.H. Beers, 1907.

Pryor, Sara Agnes Rice. *The Mother of Washington and Her Times*. New York: Macmillan, 1903.

Pulszky, Francis, and Theresa Pulszky. *White, Red, Black: Sketches of American Society in the United States during the Visit of Their Guests*. Vol. 2. New York: Redfield, 1853.

Pyles, Thomas. *Words and Ways of American English*. New York: Random House, 1952.

Quayle, Eric. *Old Cook Books: An Illustrated History*. New York: E.P. Dutton, 1978.

Randolph, Mary. *The Virginia Housewife*. 1824. Reprint. Columbia, S.C.: University of South Carolina Press, 1984.

Ranhofer, Charles. *The Epicurean: A Complete Treatise of Analytical and Practical Studies of the Culinary Art*. 1893. Reprint. New York: Dover Publications, 1971.

Richards, Paul. *Paul Richards' Pastry Book*. Chicago: Hotel Monthly Press, 1907.

Robacker, Earl F. *Old Stuff in Up-country Pennsylvania*. New York: A.S. Barnes, 1973.

Root, Waverley, and Richard de Rochemont. *Eating in America: A History*. New York: William Morrow, 1976.

Rorer, Mrs. S.T. *Dainty Dishes for All the Year Round*. Philadelphia: n.p., 1903.

Ross, Joel H. *What I Saw in New York or a Bird's Eye View of City Life.* Auburn, N.Y.: Derby and Miller, 1857.

Rutledge, Anna Wells, ed. *The Carolina Housewife by Sarah Rutledge, A Facsimile of the 1847 Edition, with an Introduction and a Preliminary Checklist of South Carolina Cookbooks Published before 1935.* Columbia, S.C.: University of South Carolina Press, 1979.

Sanders, Walter R. *Selling Ice.* Chicago: Nickerson and Collins, 1922.

Schwaab, Eugene L., ed. *Travels in the Old South Selected from Periodicals of the Time.* Vol. 2. Lexington, Ky.: University Press of Kentucky, 1973.

Seale, William. *The President's House: A History.* Vol. 1. Washington, D.C.: White House Historical Association, 1986.

Seaton, Josephine. *William Winston Seaton of the "National Intelligencer": A Biographical Sketch.* Boston: James R. Osgood, 1871.

Selitzer, Ralph. *The Dairy Industry in America.* New York: Dairyfield & Books for Industry, 1976.

Several Anonymous Philadelphians. *Philadelphia Scrapple: Whimsical Bits Anent Eccentrics and the City's Oddities.* Richmond, Va.: Dietz Press, 1956.

Sherrill, Charles H. *French Memoirs of Eighteenth-Century America.* New York: Charles Scribner's Sons, 1915.

Simmons, Amelia. *American Cookery; or, the Art of Dressing Viands, Fish, Poultry and Vegetables, and the Best Modes of Making Pastes, Puffs, Pies, Tarts, Puddings, Custards and Preserves, and All Kinds of Cakes, from the Imperial Plumb to Plain Cake.* Hartford, Conn.: Hudson and Goodwin, 1796.

Singleton, Esther. *Social New York under the Georges, 1714–1776.* New York: Benjamin Blom, 1902.

——. *The Story of the White House.* Vol. 2. New York: McClure, 1907.

Slayden, Ellen Maury. *Washington Wife: Journal of Ellen Maury Slayden from 1897 to 1919.* New York: Harper and Row, 1962.

Smith, Marie. *Entertaining in the White House.* Washington, D.C.: Acropolis Books, 1967.

Smith, Wayne. *Ice Cream Dippers: An Illustrated History and Collector's Guide to Early Ice Cream Dippers.* Walkersville, Md.: Wayne Smith, 1986.

Snyder, Charles Fisher. *Sunbury, Pennsylvania: Two Hundred Years, 1772–1972.* East Stroudburg, Pa.: Sunbury Bicentennial, 1972.

A Society of Gentlemen in New York [Richard Alsop]. *The Universal Receipt Book, or, Complete Family Directory. Being a Repository of Useful Knowledge in the Several Branches of Domestic Economy: Containing Scarce, Curious, and Valuable Receipts, and Choice Secrets.* New York: Riley, 1814.

Stafford, Cornelius William. *The Philadelphia Directory for 1799.* Philadelphia: William W. Woodward, 1799.

A Standard Dictionary of the English Language. New York: Funk and Wagnalls, 1890.

Stanley, Autumn. *Mothers and Daughters of Invention: Notes for a Revised History of Technology.* Metuchen, N.J.: Scarecrow Press, 1993.

Stephen's Philadelphia Directory for 1796. Philadelphia: W. Woodward, 1796.

Stephenson, Mary A. *Foods, Entertainment, and Decorations for the Table: Fashionable in Virginia and the Southern Colonies in the 18th Century and Early 19th Century.* Typescript, 1948. Williamsburg, Va.: Colonial Williamsburg Foundation, 1989. Microfiche.

Stern, Jane, and Michael Stern. *Encyclopedia of Pop Culture.* New York: Harper-Perennial, 1992.

Stobart, Tom. *Herbs, Spices, and Flavorings.* Woodstock, N.Y.: Overlook Press, 1982.

Stogo, Malcolm. *Frozen Desserts: A Complete Retailer's Guide.* New York: Van Nostrand Reinhold, 1991.

Stowe, Harriet Beecher, and Catherine E. Beecher. *The American Woman's Home.* New York: J.B. Ford, 1869.

Sullivan, John L. *I Can Lick Any Sonofabitch in the House.* Edited by Gilbert Odd. New York: Proteus Publishing , 1980.

Tannahill, Reay. *Food in History.* New York: Crown Publishers, 1989.

Taylor, Joe Gray. *Eating, Drinking, and Visiting in the South: An Informal History.* Baton Rouge: Louisiana State University Press, 1962.

Tucker, Gilbert M. *American English.* New York: Alfred A. Knopf, 1921.

Tunis, Edwin. *The Young United States, 1783–1830.* New York: World Publishing, 1969.

Turnbow, Grover Dean, Paul Hubert Tracy, and Lloyd Andrew Raffetto. *The Ice Cream Industry.* New York: John Wiley and Sons, 1947.

Tyree, Marion Cabell. *Housekeeping in Old Virginia.* Louisville, Ky.: John P. Morton, 1879.

Verrill, A. Hyatt. *Foods America Gave the World.* Boston: L.C. Page, 1937.

Vollmer, William. *The United States Cook Book: A Complete Manual for Ladies, Housekeepers, and Cooks with Particular Reference to the Climate and Productions of the United States.* Translated by J.C. Oehlschlager. Philadelphia: John Weik, 1856.

Walsh, William S. *A Handy Book of Curious Information.* Philadelphia: J.B. Lippincott, 1913.

Ward, Artemas. *The Grocer's Hand-book and Directory.* Philadelphia: Philadelphia Grocer Publishing, 1886.

——. *The Grocer's Encyclopedia.* New York: Artemas Ward, 1911.

Weaver, William Woys, ed. *A Quaker Woman's Cookbook: The Domestic Cookery of Elizabeth Ellicott Lea.* Philadelphia: University of Pennsylvania Press, 1982.

Weld, Isaac. *Travels through the States of North America and the Provinces of Upper and Lower Canada during the Years 1795, 1796, and 1797.* Vol. 1. London: John Stockdale, 1807.

Wildes, Harry Emerson. *Anthony Wayne: Trouble Shooter of the American Revolution.* New York: Harcourt, Brace, 1941.

Williams, Susan. *Savory Suppers and Fashionable Feasts: Dining in Victorian America.* New York: Pantheon Books, 1985.

Willich, A.F.M., and Thomas Cooper. *The Domestic Encyclopedia: Or, a Dictionary of Facts and Useful Knowledge Chiefly Applicable to Rural and Domestic Economy.* 2nd edition. Philadelphia: n.p., 1826.

Wilmot, Jennie S., and Margaret Q. Batzer. *Food for the Family.* Philadelphia: J.B. Lippincott, 1944.

Wilson, Mrs. Henry Lumpkin. *Tested Recipe Cook Book.* Atlanta: Foote & Davies, 1895.

Wines, E.C. *A Trip to Boston, in a Series of Letters to the Editor of the United States Gazette.* Boston: Little, Brown, 1838.

Wolf, Edwin. *Philadelphia: Portrait of an American City.* Harrisburg, Pa.: Stackpole Books, 1975.

Women's Institute of Domestic Arts and Sciences. *Women's Institute of Cookery.* Scranton, Pa.: International Educational Publishing, 1919.

Woodward, C. Vann, ed. *Mary Chestnut's Civil War.* New Haven, Conn.: Yale University Press, 1981.

Wyman, Carolyn. *I'm a Spam Fan.* Stamford, Conn.: Longmeadow Press, 1993.

Yoder, Paton. *Taverns and Travelers: Inns of the Early Midwest.* Bloomington, Ind.: Indiana University Press, 1969.

Articles and Other Sources

Atkinson, A.S. "Different Types of Ice Houses." *Scientific American Supplement,* no. 1655 (1907): 188–89.

Attaran, Mohsen, and Carl E. Upthegrove. "Carnation Aims for Smooth and Creamy Process with State-of-the-Art Systems." *Industrial Engineering* 23, no. 9 (Sept 1991): 38–43.

—— "Integrating Automation in an Ice Cream Processing Plant." *Journal of Systems Management* 42, no. 5 (May 1991): 6–8, 30.

Baker, Joseph F. "History of Boston's Soda Fountain Trade." *Pharmaceutical Era* 7 (May 1, 1892): 289–94.

"The Beginnings of the Ice Cream Industry in Baltimore." *Baltimore* (January 1947): n.p.

Black, William. "Journal of William Black." Edited by R. Alonzo Brock. *Pennsylvania Magazine of History and Biography* 1, no. 2 (1877): 117–32.

Blatchley's Horizontal Ice Cream Freezer, Tingley's Patent (catalog), n.p., n.d.

"Breyers Ice Cream: Marking a Milestone." *Dairy Dialogue* 7, no. 4 (June 1991): 5–11.

"Can Franchises Keep Their Flavor?" *Business Week,* November 2, 1963: 62, 64.

Catalogue of the Alaska Line of Hand Ice Cream Freezers. N.p., 1923.

Catalogue of Hardware Specialties Manufactured by American Machine Company, with Recipes. N.p., n.d.

Catalogue of Puffer's Frigid Soda and Mineral Water Apparatus. N.p., 1878.

Catalogue of Yankee Tools and Ice Cream Freezers. Philadelphia: N.p., 1912.

"Cold Secrets." *New Yorker* 37 (June 24, 1961): 18–19.

Descriptive Catalogue and Price List of Sands' Patent Triple Motion White Mountain Freezers. Np., n.d.

"Directions for Making Ice Cream: From the City of Jefferson *Metropolitan,* June 22, 1847." *Missouri Historical Review* 36, no. 1 (October 1941): 121–22.

Drennan, Bill. "Highly Automated Plant." *Food Engineering* 54, no. 7 (1982): 86–87.

Dunne, Patrick, and Charles L. Mackie. "Philadelphia Story." *Historic Preservation* 46, no. 4 (1994): 72–75, 103.

Fauquier, William. "An Account of an Extraordinary Storm of Hail in Virginia." *Philosophical Transactions, Giving Some Account of the Present Undertakings, Studies, and Labours of the Ingenious, in Many Considerable Parts of the World* 50, no. 2 (1759): 746–47.

Francke, Linda, and Sunde Smith. "Chip Chip Hooray!" *Newsweek* 87 (February 16, 1976): 71.

"The Freeze that Pleases." *Time* 97 (June 21, 1971): 76, 78.

"Frozen Assets." *Newsweek* 57 (May 8, 1961): 74.

Gale, Charlotte, and David M. Gale. "The Drugstore Soda Fountain: A Study and Catalog of Nineteenth-Century Soda Tokens." *Numismatist,* January 1983: 13–19.

Gladfelter, Armand. "Ice Cream: First Commercial Production Began in Seven Valleys." *York (Pa.) Sunday News,* October 9, 1994, Section C, 1–2.

"Gold Bond–Good Humor Ice Cream" (typescript photocopy). Good Humor–Bryers Ice Cream Co. N.p., n.d.

Grenier, Josephine. "Afternoon Tea." *Harper's Bazaar* 37 (February 1903): 174–76.

Gustaitis, Joseph. ""Who Invented the Ice Cream Cone?" *American History Illustrated* 23 (Summer 1988): 42–44.

Harris, Eleanor. "The Pied Pipers of Ice Cream." *Saturday Evening Post* 222 (August 20, 1949): 36+.

Hart, Joseph H. "The Application of Mechanical Refrigeration to Ice Cream Manufacture." *Journal of the Franklin Institute* 162 (November 1906): 397–403.

Heggie, Barbara. "Ice Woman." *New Yorker* 17 (September 6, 1941): 23+.

Holbrook, Stewart H. "Yankee Ice King." *American Mercury* 61, no. 260 (August 1945): 179–85.

"Ice Cream at the Melting Point." *Business Week,* August 4, 1951: 46, 48.

"Ice Cream Doubts." *Business Week,* June 19, 1943: 37–38.

"Ice Cream for Ocean Voyagers." *New York Daily Tribune,* November 22, 1896: Section 3, 4.

Ice Cream Makers' Apparatus and Supplies, Catalog No. 302. N.p., n.d.

"Ice Cream Outcry." *Business Week,* June 13, 1942: 56–57.

"Ice-Cream Parlay." *Fortune* 48 (July 1953): 166.

"An Inventory of the Contents of the Governor's Palace Taken After the Death of Lord Botetourt," October 24, 1770. Botetourt Papers, O.A. Hawkins Collection of Virginians, Virginia State Library.

James W. Tufts, Patentee and Manufacturer of Arctic Soda Water Apparatus (catalog). N.p., 1887.

The King of All Confections: 1908 Automatic Parisian Ice Cream Cone Ovens (catalog). N.p., 1908.

Lansing, A. "Cold Licks and Hot Profits: Soft Ice Cream." *Collier's* 138 (August 3, 1956): 30+.

Leone, Steve. "Dixie War Lids." *The Ice Screamer* 66 (May 1995): 4–5.

Machine Ice Cream Freezers and Ice Breakers (catalog). N.p., n.d.

"Masser's Self-acting Patent Ice-cream Freezer and Beater." *Godey's Magazine and Lady's Book* 41 (July.1850): 124.

Match, Richard. "The World's Milkman." *Reader's Digest* 63 (September 1953): 82–86.

"Mechanical Refrigerators." *Consumers' Digest* 1, no. 1 (January 1937): 9–11.

"Mixing Ice Cream by Push Button." *Business Week,* July 23, 1960: 64, 67.

"Modern Ice Cream and the Philosophy of Its Manufacture." *Godey's Lady's Book* 60 (1860): 460–61.

Montgomery Ward and Company Catalogue No. 57, n.p., 1895; *No. 97,* n.p., 1922.

Morris, Charles E. "World's Largest Ice-Cream Plant." *Food Engineering* 61, no. 3 (1989): 85+.

Morrison, Joseph L. "The Soda Fountain." *American Heritage* 8, no. 5 (August 1962): 10–19.

National Archives. Patent File for Italo Marchiony. Record Group 241. File 746971.

National Archives. Patent and Patent Assignment Files for Nancy M. Johnson. Record Group 214. Liber R, 365.

O'Hagan, Anne."A Summer Evening in New York." *Munsey's Magazine* 21 (1899): 854.

The Original and Only Clad's Ice Cream Machinery Tools and Utensils (catalog). N.p., n.d.

Our Drummer (catalog). N.p., 1894.

"Phases of Ice Cream." *New York Daily Tribune,* July 13, 1902: II, 6.

"Poisoned by Ice Cream." *New York Daily Tribune,* July 7, 1884: 8.

Ranhofer, Charles. "Delmonico's Seen from the Kitchen." *Metropolitan,* December 1896: 351–56.

"Restaurant Patron Criticizes Ice Cream: From the St. Louis *Missouri Argus,* July 19, 1839." *Missouri Historical Review* 27, no. 4 (July 1933): 379–80.

Sears, Roebuck and Company Catalogue No. 104, 1897; *No. 110,* 1900; *No.111,* 1902; *Fall-Winter* 1928–29; *Spring-Summer* 1930; *Spring-Summer* 1934.

"Six Hundred Fifty Flavors Offer a Taste for Every Taste!" (press release). Baskin-Robbins Ice Cream, 1994.

Skow, John. "They All Scream for It." *Time* 118, no. 6 (August 10, 1981): 52–58.

Sloane, Eric. "Natural Ice." *American Heritage* 17, no. 5 (1966): 82–83.

Snow, Richard F. "King Cone." *Invention and Technology* 9, no. 2 (Fall 1993): 5.

"So You'll Eat Better." *American Mercury* 61, no. 260 (August 1945): 128.

"The Soda Fountain Business of St. Louis." *Pharmaceutical Era* 7 (June 1, 1892): 369-72.

"Soda Water in Chicago." *Pharmaceutical Era* 7 (June 15, 1892): 409–14.

Sokolov, Raymond. "Between Rock and a Soft Place." *Natural History* 102, no. 8 (1993): 68–71.

Stansbury, Frederick. "The Evolution of the Soda Water Industry in New York City." *Pharmaceutical Era* 7 (May 15, 1892): 329–36.

"A Steam Ice Cream Manufactory." *Scientific American* 71 (July 21, 1894): 40.

Stein, Bobbie. "Reuben Mattus Scooped the Competition with His Pricey and Nonsense-named Häagen-Dazs." *People Weekly* 16 (August 17, 1981): 85–87.

Taft, Mary A. "Woman and Her Spoons." *Harper's Bazaar* 34 (November 1901): 776–79.

"Thirty-one Flavors." *New Yorker* 47 (July 10, 1971): 19–20.

Tompson, Mary V. "Background Information for Dairying Program" (typed report). Mount Vernon Ladies' Association, Mount Vernon, Va.

"Twenty-eight Flavors Head West." *Life* 25 (September 6, 1948): 71–74.

United States Confectioners' Tool Works (catalog). N.p., n.d.

"U.S.S. Lexington: Carrier Upholds Our Fighting Tradition." *Yank: The Army Newspaper* 1, no. 2 (June 24, 1942): 4–5.

"Vanilla, Please." *Newsweek* 25, no. 10 (March 5, 1945): 72.

Volti, Rudi. "How We Got Frozen Food." *Invention and Technology* 9, no. 4 (Spring 1994): 47–56.

Walker, C. Lester. "Four Thousand Quarts Every Minute." *Nation's Business* 34 (August 1946): 53+.

Wharton, Don. "That Good Humor Man." *Reader's Digest* 60 (June 1952): 66–69.

White, E.F. "How to Run a Small Fountain Right." *Supply World* 13 (June 1900): 18.

Ziemba, John V. "Desk Top Computer Specializes in Mixes." *Food Engineering* 4, no. 8 (July-August 1974): S-13+.

Index

205